MASTERY

MASTERY

The Keys to Long-Term
Success and Fulfillment

George Leonard

A DUTTON BOOK

DUTTON
Published by the Penguin Group
Penguin Books USA Inc., 375 Hudson Street,
New York, New York 10014, U.S.A.
Penguin Books Ltd, 27 Wrights Lane, London W8 5TZ, England
Penguin Books Australia Ltd, Ringwood, Victoria, Australia
Penguin Books Canada Ltd, 2801 John Street,
Markham, Ontario, Canada L3R 1B4
Penguin Books (N.Z.) Ltd, 182–190 Wairau Road,
Auckland 10, New Zealand

Penguin Books Ltd, Registered Offices:
Harmondsworth, Middlesex, England

First published by Dutton, an imprint of New American Library,
a division of Penguin Books USA Inc.
Distributed in Canada by McClelland & Stewart Inc.

First Printing, February, 1991
10 9 8 7 6 5 4 3 2 1

REGISTERED TRADEMARK—MARCA REGISTRADA

Library of Congress Cataloging-in-Publication Data
Leonard, George Burr, 1923–
    Mastery : the keys to long-term success and fulfillment / George
Leonard.
        p.   cm.
      1. Success.   2. Self-realization.   I. Title.
    BF637.S8L445   1991
    158'.1—dc20   90–46343
                                                                CIP

Printed in the United States of America
Set in Garamond Light
Designed by Eve L. Kirch

For John and Julia Poppy

CONTENTS

ACKNOWLEDGMENTS

Heartfelt appreciation goes to *Esquire*'s editor emeritus Phillip Moffitt for his wise counsel and generous support, and for his empassioned and enduring advocacy of this book; he speaks with the authority of one who is himself on the path of mastery.

I owe a great deal to my aikido teachers, Frank Doran, Robert Nadeau, and Bill Witt, and especially to Nadeau, who introduced me to the idea of presenting exercises based on aikido principles to a wider, non–martial arts constituency. Richard Strozzi Heckler, Wendy Palmer, and I have been doing aikido together for eighteen years—first as students, then as teachers and co-owners of Aikido of Tamalpais: But we are more than fellow martial artists, for our lives touch in many ways; Richard and Wendy are part of this book. Annie Styron Leonard has once again been a loving critic and a perceptive editor.

Thanks to master tennis teacher Pat Blaskower for

her eloquence on the particulars of the mastery process, as presented in Chapter One, and to Joe Flower, who conducted interviews on the subject of mastery with leading sports figures. I'm grateful, as always, to Sterling Lord, an intrepid pathfinder for twenty-five years.

A special word of thanks goes to John and Julia Poppy, to whom this book is dedicated. John and I have been colleagues and friends for twenty-eight years—at *Look* magazine, at *Esquire*, and actually in all things. He has contributed immeasurably to each of the Ultimate Fitness features, bringing a rare intelligence, elegance, and clarity to the most difficult subjects. The light that is Julia Poppy, my sister, has illuminated my path for a lifetime, and her spirit has touched everything I've done. This book would not be possible without them both.

INTRODUCTION

In 1987, for the fourth straight year, the May issue of *Esquire* magazine featured a special section on what it called Ultimate Fitness. These special sections claimed a broader charter than is usual for such a subject. "Ultimately," I wrote in the first of the series, "fitness and health are related to everything we do, think and feel. Thus . . . what we are calling Ultimate Fitness has less to do with running a 2:30 marathon than with living a good life."

The previous Ultimate Fitness specials had enjoyed exceptionally high reader interest, but the May 1987 number was something else again. The subject this time was mastery, "the mysterious process during which what is at first difficult becomes progressively easier and more pleasurable through practice." The purpose of the feature was to describe the path that best led to mastery, not just in sports but in all of life, and to warn against the prevailing bottom-line mentality that puts quick, easy results ahead of long-term dedication to the journey itself.

The response was immediate and extravagant. Requests for extra copies, tearsheets, and reprints poured in. Management newsletters requested permission to reprint portions of the *Esquire* feature. Corporate CEOs gave photocopies to their officers. Training groups of a wide variety spent hours discussing the mastery principles. Letters to the editor were numerous and eloquent. A navy carrier pilot, for instance, wrote that he had been having trouble landing the F-14 Tomcat on an aircraft carrier. "I . . . was in the process of making a second and perhaps final attempt when I bought the May issue. Insights that I gained from Mr. Leonard's outline of the master's journey gave me the extra 10 percent of mental discipline that I needed to make the trek down this portion of my path a relatively easy one."

I knew a book was needed to provide a full understanding of how to get on and stay on the path of mastery, but at the time, I was working on a memoir of the 1960s. I thought interest in the subject might wane, but it hasn't. The many comments and inquiries that I continue to receive have convinced me more than ever that the quick-fix, fast-temporary-relief, bottom-line mentality doesn't work in the long run, and is eventually destructive to the individual and the society. If there is any sure route to success and fulfillment in life, it is to be found in the long-term, essentially goalless process of mastery. This is true, it appears, in personal as well as professional life, in economics as well as ice skating, in medicine as well as martial arts.

It was the martial arts, in fact, that gave me the original idea for the *Esquire* feature and for this book. I have practiced aikido since 1970, and have taught it regularly since 1976. With its sophisticated blending moves and full repertory of rolls and falls, aikido is generally known as the most difficult of the martial arts to master. On the training mat, every attempt at circumvention or overreaching is revealed; flaws are made manifest; the quick fix is impossible. At the same time, the pleasures of practice are intensified. The mat, I often tell my students, is the world, but it is the world under a magnifying glass.

An aikido school is therefore an ideal laboratory for studying the factors that work for and against long-term learning. As hundreds of students passed through our school, I began to recognize distinctive patterns in the way they approached the art. The types of learners I would later characterize as the dabbler, the obsessive, and the hacker (see Chapter Two) revealed themselves, in most cases, after only a few classes. I was surprised to discover that it wasn't necessarily the most talented who would persevere on the long road to black belt and beyond. I began to realize that although different people might take different paths to mastery, all of the paths led in the same general direction—one that could be clearly mapped.

But would my findings at the aikido school apply to other skills? Interviews conducted at the time of the *Esquire* special and since then, along with the extraordinary response to the magazine feature itself, have shown me that what is true for aikidoists is also true for learners in any nontrivial skill: managers, artists, pilots, schoolchildren, college students, carpenters, athletes, parents, religious devotees, and even entire cultures in the process of change.

Bottom-line thinking might now prevail, but the master's journey has deep roots. It also has deep resonance. One might say, in fact, that it's not so much an idea whose time has come as an idea that has always been with us—it's just that we need to be reminded. I'm pleased that so many people's lives have already been changed for the better through this reminder, and I hope the book will add to the number of those who are on the path.

PART ONE

THE MASTER'S JOURNEY

Introduction

Start with something simple. Try touching your forehead with your hand.

Ah, that's easy, automatic. Nothing to it. But there was a time when you were as far removed from the mastery of that simple skill as a nonpianist is from playing a Beethoven sonata.

First, you had to learn to control the movements of your hands (you were just a baby then) and somehow get them to move where you wanted them to. You had to develop some sort of kinesthetic "image" of your body so that you could know the relationship between your forehead and other parts of your body. You had to learn to match this image with the visual image of an adult's body. You had to learn how to mimic your mother's actions. Momentous stuff, make no mistake about it. And we haven't yet considered the matter of language—learning to decode sounds shaped as words and to match them to our own actions.

Only after all this could you play the learning game that parents everywhere play with their children: "Where's your nose? Where are your ears? Where's your forehead?" As with all significant learning, this learning was measured not in a straight line but in stages: brief spurts of progress separated by periods during which you seemed to be getting nowhere.

Still, you learned an essential skill. What's more important, you learned about learning. You started with something difficult and made it easy and pleasurable through instruction and practice. You took a master's journey. And if you could learn to touch your forehead, you can learn to play a Beethoven sonata or fly a jet plane, to be a better manager or improve your relationships. Our current society works in many ways to lead us astray, but the path of mastery is always there, waiting for us.

Chapter 1

What Is Mastery?

It resists definition yet can be instantly recognized. It comes in many varieties, yet follows certain unchanging laws. It brings rich rewards, yet is not really a goal or a destination but rather a process, a journey. We call this journey *mastery,* and tend to assume that it requires a special ticket available only to those born with exceptional abilities. But mastery isn't reserved for the supertalented or even for those who are fortunate enough to have gotten an early start. It's available to anyone who is willing to get on the path and stay on it—regardless of age, sex, or previous experience.

The trouble is that we have few, if any, maps to guide us on the journey or even to show us how to find the path. The modern world, in fact, can be viewed as a prodigious conspiracy against mastery. We're continually bombarded with promises of immediate gratification, instant success, and fast, temporary relief, all of which lead in exactly the wrong direction. Later, we'll take a look at the quick-fix, antimastery mentality that pervades our society, and see how it not only prevents us from developing our potential skills but threatens our health, education, career, relationships, and perhaps even our national economic viability. But first let's examine mastery itself.

The master's journey can begin whenever you decide to learn any new skill—how to touch-type, how to cook, how to become a lawyer or doctor or accountant. But it achieves a special poignancy, a quality akin to poetry or drama, in the field of sports, where muscles, mind, and spirit come together in graceful and purposive movements through time and space. Sports provide a good starting point for this exploration, in that results of training in the physical realm are rather quickly and clearly visible. So let's take a familiar sport, tennis, as a hypothetical case through which we can derive the principles underlying the mastery of all skills, physical or otherwise.

Say you're in fairly good physical shape but by no means a highly conditioned, skilled athlete. You've played around with movement sports such as volleyball and softball, which involve hand-eye coordination, and you've played a little tennis, but not much—which might be a good thing. If you're going to go for mastery, it's better to start with a clean slate rather than have to unlearn bad habits you picked up while hacking around. Now you've found a teacher, a pro with a reputation for grounding players in the fundamentals, and you've committed yourself to at least three visits a week to the tennis court. You're on the path to mastery.

It starts with baby steps. The teacher shows you how to hold the racket so that it will hit the ball at the correct moment in time. She has you bring the racket forward in a forehand swing until you find the position of maximum strength of the wrist. She stands in front of you on the same side of the net and tosses balls to your forehand, and after each hit, she asks you to tell her if you hit it early or late. She shows you how to move your shoulders and hips together with the motion of the arm, and to stride into the ball. She makes corrections, gives encouragement. You feel terribly clumsy and disjointed. You have to *think* to keep the parts of your body synchronized, and thinking gets in the way of graceful, spontaneous movement.

You find yourself becoming impatient. You were hoping to get exercise, but this practice doesn't give you enough even to break a sweat. You like to see the ball go across the net and into the dark green part of the court, but your teacher says you shouldn't even be thinking about that at this stage. You're the type of person who cares a lot about results, and you seem to be getting hardly any results at all. The practice just goes on and on: hold the racket correctly; know where the racket makes contact with the ball; move shoulders, hips, and arm together; stride into the ball—you seem to be getting exactly nowhere.

Then, after about five weeks of frustration, a light goes on. The various components of the tennis stroke begin to come together, almost as if your muscles *know* what they should do; you don't have to think about every little thing. In your conscious awareness, there's more room to see the ball, to meet it cleanly in a stroke that starts low and ends high. You feel the itch to hit the ball harder, to start playing competitively.

No chance. Until now your teacher has been feeding balls to you. You haven't had to move. But now you're going to have to learn to move side to side, back and forth, and on the diagonal, and then set up and swing. Again, you feel clumsy, disjointed. You're dismayed to find that you're losing some of what you'd gained. Just before you're ready to call it quits, you stop getting worse. But you're not getting any better, either. Days and weeks pass with no apparent progress. There you are on that damned plateau.

For most people brought up in this society, the plateau can be a form of purgatory. It triggers disowned emotions. It flushes out hidden motivations.

You realize you came to tennis not only to get exercise but also to look good, to play with your friends, to *beat* your friends. You decide to have a talk with your teacher. How long, you ask, will it take you to master this thing?

Your instructor responds, "Do you mean how long would it take for you to automatically get into position and hit a forehand effectively to a target?"

"Yes."

She pauses. It's a question she always dreads. "Well, for someone like you, who starts tennis as an adult, if you practice an hour three times a week, it would take, on average, five years."

Five years! Your heart sinks.

"Ideally, about half of that would be instruction. Of course, if you're particularly motivated, it could be less than that."

You decide to try another question. "How long will it be before I can play competitively?"

"Competitively? That's a loaded term."

"I mean playing to try to beat a friend."

"I would say you could probably start playing after about six months. But you shouldn't start playing with winning as a major consideration until you have reasonable control of forehand, backhand, and serve. And that would be about a year or a year and a half."

Another bitter dose of reality.

The teacher goes on to explain. The problem with

tennis isn't just that the ball moves and the racket moves, and you have to master all of that, but also that *you* have to move. In addition, unless you're hitting with a pro who can put the ball in the correct place, a lot of practice time on the court is spent picking up balls. Backboards are helpful. Ball machines are helpful. But playing for points, trying to beat a friend, really comes down to who gets the serve in the court and who misses the ball first. Points last only about three hits over the net. You don't get much practice. What you really need is to hit thousands of balls under fairly controlled circumstances at every step along the way: forehand, backhand, footwork, serve, spin, net play, placement, strategy. And the process is generally incremental. You can't skip stages. You can't really work on strategy, for example, until you've got placement pretty well under control. With the introduction of each new stage, you're going to have to start *thinking* again, which means things will temporarily fall apart.

The truth begins to sink in. Going for mastery in this sport isn't going to bring you the quick rewards you had hoped for. There's a seemingly endless road ahead of you with numerous setbacks along the way and—most important—plenty of time on the plateau, where long hours of diligent practice gain you no apparent progress at all. Not a happy situation for one who is highly goal-oriented.

You realize that you have a decision to make at some point along the journey, if not now. You're tempted to drop tennis and go out looking for another, easier sport. Or you might try twice as hard, insist on extra lessons, practice day and night. Or you could quit your lessons and take whatever you've learned out on the court; you could forget about improving your game and just have fun with friends who don't play much better than you. Of course, you could also do what your teachers suggests, and stay on the long road to mastery. What will you choose?

This question, this moment of choice, comes up countless times in each of our lives, not just about tennis or some other sport, but about everything that has to do with learning, development, change. Sometimes we choose after careful deliberation, but frequently the choice is careless—a barely conscious one. Seduced by the siren song of a consumerist, quick-fix society, we sometimes choose a course of action that brings only the illusion of accomplishment, the shadow of satisfaction. And sometimes, knowing little or nothing about the process that leads to mastery, we don't even realize a choice is being offered. Yet even our failures to choose consciously operate as choices, adding to or subtracting from the amount of our potential that we will eventually realize.

The evidence is clear: all of us who are born without serious genetic defects are born geniuses. Without an iota of formal instruction, we can master the overarching symbolic system of spoken language—and not just one language but several. We can decipher the complex code of facial expressions—a feat to paralyze the circuitry of even the most powerful computer. We can decode and in one way or another express the subtleties of emotional nuance. Even without formal schooling, we can make associations, create abstract categories, and construct meaningful hierarchies. What's more, we can invent things never before seen, ask questions never before asked, and seek answers from out beyond the stars. Unlike computers, we can fall in love.

What we call intelligence comes in many varieties. Howard Gardner of Harvard University and the Boston University School of Medicine has identified seven of them: linguistic, musical, logical/mathematical, spatial, bodily/kinesthetic, and two types of personal intelligences that might be described as intrapersonal and interpersonal. We vary in our giftedness in these seven at least. Still, each of us comes equipped with enough raw ability across the board to achieve that seemingly rare and mysterious state we call mastery in some mode of thought and expression, some interpersonal and entrepreneurial enterprise, some art or craft.

This is also true in the physical realm. It was once believed that our primitive ancestors were rather pitiable creatures compared with the other animals of the jungles and savannahs. Lacking the fangs, claws, and specialized physical abilities of the predators, our forefathers supposedly prevailed only because of their large brains and their ability to use tools. This supposition has downplayed the prodigious human ability to create complex, well-knit social groupings, a challenge which, more than toolmaking, accounts for the development of the large brain.

It also downplays the human body.

Much has been made of the blazing sprint-speed of the cheetah, the prodigious leaps of the kangaroo, the underwater skills of the dolphin, and the gymnastic prowess of the chimpanzee. But the fact of the matter is that no animal can match the human animal in all-around athletic ability. If we were to hold a mammal decathlon with events in sprinting, endurance running, long jumping, high jumping, swimming, deep diving, gymnastics, striking, kicking, and burrowing, other animals would win most of the individual events. But a well-trained human would come up with the best overall score. And in one event—endurance running—the human would outperform all other animals of comparable size, as well as some quite a bit larger. If we are born geniuses of thought and feeling, we are also geniuses *in potentia* of the body, and there is undoubtedly some sport, some physical pursuit in which each of us can excel.

But genius, no matter how bright, will come to naught or swiftly burn out if you don't choose the master's journey. This journey will take you along a path that is both arduous and exhilarating. It will bring you unexpected heartaches and unexpected rewards, and you will never reach a final destination. (It would be a paltry skill indeed that could be finally, completely mastered.) You'll probably end up learning as much about yourself as about the skill you're pursuing. And although you'll often be surprised at what and how you learn, your progress towards mastery will almost always take on a characteristic rhythm that looks something like this:

The Mastery Curve

There's really no way around it. Learning any new skill involves relatively brief spurts of progress, each of which is followed by a slight decline to a plateau somewhat higher in most cases than that which preceded it. The curve above is necessarily idealized. In the actual learning experience, progress is less regular; the upward spurts vary; the plateaus have their own dips and rises along the way. But the general progression is almost always the same. To take the master's journey, you have to practice diligently, striving to hone your skills, to attain new levels of competence. But while doing so—and this is the inexorable fact of the journey—you also have to be willing to spend most of your time on a plateau, to keep practicing even when you seem to be getting nowhere.

Why does learning take place in spurts? Why can't we make steady upward progress on our way toward mastery? As we saw in the case of tennis, we have to keep practicing an unfamiliar movement again and again until we "get it in the muscle memory" or "program it into the autopilot." The specific mechanism through which this takes place is not completely known, but it probably matches up fairly well with these informal descriptions. Karl Pribram, professor of neuroscience and a pioneering brain researcher at Stanford University, explains it in terms of hypothetical brain-body systems. He starts with a "habitual behavior system" that operates at a level deeper than conscious thought. This system involves the reflex circuit in the spinal cord as well as in various parts of the brain to which it is connected. This habitual system makes it possible for you to do things—return a scorching tennis serve, play a guitar chord, ask directions in a new language—without worrying just *how* you do them. When you start to learn a new skill, however, you do have to think about it, and you have to make an effort to replace old patterns of sensing, movement, and cognition with new.

This brings into play what might be called a cognitive system, associated with the habitual system, and an effort system, associated with the hippocampus (situated at the base of the brain). The cognitive and effort systems become subsets of the habitual system long enough to modify it, to teach it a new behavior. To put it another way, the cognitive and effort systems "click into" the habitual system and reprogram it. When the job is done, both systems withdraw. Then you don't have to stop and think about, say, the right grip every time you shift your racket.

In this light, you can see that those upward surges on the mastery curve are by no means the only time anything significant or exciting is happening. Learning generally occurs in stages. A stage ends when the habitual system has been programmed to the new task, and the cognitive and effort systems have withdrawn. This means you can perform the task without making a special effort to think of its separate parts. At this point, there's an apparent spurt of learning. *But this learning has been going on all along.*

Chapter 2

Meet the Dabbler, the Obsessive, and the Hacker

We all aspire to mastery, but the path is always long and sometimes rocky, and it promises no quick and easy payoffs. So we look for other paths, each of which attracts a certain type of person. Can you recognize yourself in any of the following three graphs?

The Dabbler

The Dabbler approaches each new sport, career opportunity, or relationship with enormous enthusiasm. He or she loves the rituals involved in getting started, the spiffy equipment, the lingo, the shine of *newness*.

When he makes his first spurt of progress in a new sport, for example, the Dabbler is overjoyed. He demonstrates his form to family, friends, and people he meets on the street. He can't wait for the next lesson. The falloff from his first peak comes as a shock. The plateau that follows is unacceptable if not incomprehensible. His enthusiasm quickly wanes. He starts missing lessons. His mind fills up with rationalizations. This really isn't the right sport for him. It's too competitive, noncompetitive, aggressive, nonaggressive, boring, dangerous, whatever. He tells everyone that it just doesn't fulfill his unique needs. Starting another sport gives the Dabbler a chance to replay the scenario of starting up. Maybe he'll make it to the second plateau this time, maybe not. Then it's on to something else.

The same thing applies to a career. The Dabbler loves new jobs, new offices, new colleagues. He sees opportunities at every turn. He salivates over projected earnings. He delights in signs of progress, each of which he reports to his family and friends. *Uh oh,* there's that plateau again. Maybe this job isn't right for him after all. It's time to start looking around. The Dabbler has a long resume.

In love relationships (perhaps an unexpected place to look for the signs of mastery, but a good one), the

Dabbler specializes in honeymoons. He revels in seduction and surrender, the telling of life stories, the display of love's tricks and trappings: the ego on parade. When the initial ardor starts to cool, he starts looking around. To stay on the path of mastery would mean changing himself. How much easier it is to jump into another bed and start the process all over again. The Dabbler might think of himself as an adventurer, a connoisseur of novelty, but he's probably closer to being what Carl Jung calls the *puer aeternus,* the eternal kid. Though partners change, he or she stays just the same.

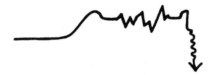

The Obsessive

The Obsessive is a bottom-line type of person, not one to settle for second best. He or she knows results are what count, and it doesn't matter how you get them, just so you get them fast. In fact, he wants to get the stroke just right during the very first lesson. He stays after class talking to the instructor. He asks what books and tapes he can buy to help him make progress faster. (He leans toward the listener when he talks. His energy is up front when he walks.)

The Obsessive starts out by making robust progress. His first spurt is just what he expected. But when he inevitably regresses and finds himself on a plateau, he simply won't accept it. He redoubles his effort. He pushes himself mercilessly. He refuses to accept his boss's and colleagues' counsel of moderation. He works all night at the office, he's tempted to take shortcuts for the sake of quick results.

American corporate managers by and large have joined the cult of the bottom line; their profile is often that of the Obsessive. They strive mightily to keep the profit curve angled upward, even if that means sacrificing research and development, long-term planning, patient product development, and plant investment.

In relationships, the Obsessive lives for the upward surge, the swelling background music, the trip to the stars. He's not like the Dabbler. When ardor cools, he doesn't look elsewhere. He tries to keep the starship going by every means at his command: extravagant gifts, erotic escalation, melodramatic rendezvous. He doesn't understand the necessity for periods of development on the plateau. The relationship becomes a rollercoaster ride, with stormy separations and passionate reconciliations. The inevitable breakup involves a great deal of pain for both partners, with very little in the way of learning or self-development to show for it.

Somehow, in whatever he is doing, the Obsessive manages for a while to keep making brief spurts of upward progress, followed by sharp declines—a jagged ride toward a sure fall. When the fall occurs, the Obsessive is likely to get hurt. And so are friends, colleagues, stockholders, and lovers.

The Hacker

The Hacker has a different attitude. After sort of getting the hang of a thing, he or she is willing to stay on the plateau indefinitely. He doesn't mind skipping stages essential to the development of mastery if he can just go out and hack around with fellow hackers. He's the physician or teacher who doesn't bother going to professional meetings, the tennis player who develops a solid forehand and figures he can make do with a ragged backhand. At work, he does only enough to get by, leaves on time or early, takes every break, talks instead of doing his job, and wonders why he doesn't get promoted.

The Hacker looks at marriage or living together not

as an opportunity for learning and development, but as a comfortable refuge from the uncertainties of the outside world. He or she is willing to settle for static monogamy, an arrangement in which both partners have clearly defined and unchanging roles, and in which marriage is primarily an economic and domestic institution. This traditional arrangement sometimes works well enough, but in today's world two partners are rarely willing to live indefinitely on an unchanging plateau. When your tennis partner starts improving his or her game and you don't, the game eventually breaks up. The same thing applies to relationships.

The categories are obviously not quite this neat. You can be a Dabbler in love and a master in art. You can be on the path of mastery on your job and a Hacker on the golf course—or vice versa. Even in the same field, you can be sometimes on the path of mastery, sometimes an Obsessive, and so on. But the basic patterns tend to prevail, both reflecting and shaping your performance, your character, your destiny.

At some of my lectures and workshop sessions, I describe the Master, the Dabbler, the Obsessive, and the Hacker. I then ask the people in the audience to indicate by a show of hands (leaving the Master out) which of the other three would best describe themselves. In almost every case, the response breaks down into nearly even thirds, and the discussion that follows shows how easily most people can identify with the three types who are the subject of this chapter.

These characters, then, have proven useful in helping us see why we're *not* on the path of mastery. But the real point is to get on that path and start moving. The first challenge we'll meet, as we'll see in the next chapter, is posed by our society.

Chapter 3

America's War Against Mastery

If you're planning to embark on a master's journey, you might find yourself bucking current trends in American life. Our hyped-up consumerist society is engaged, in fact, in an all-out war on mastery. We see this most plainly in our value system. Values were once inculcated through the extended family, tribal or village elders, sports and games, the apprenticeship system or traditional schooling, religious training and practice, and spiritual and secular ceremony. With the weakening or withering away of most of these agencies, value-giving in America has taken a strange new turn.

Our society is now organized around an economic system that seemingly demands a continuing high level of consumer spending. We are offered an unprecedented number of choices as to how we spend our money. We have to have food, clothing, housing, transportation, and medical care, but within certain limits we can choose among many alternatives. We are also enticed by a dazzling array of appealing nonnecessities—VCRs, vacation cruises, speedboats, microwave ovens. Every time we spend money, we make a statement about what we value; there's no clearer or more direct indication. Thus, all inducements to spend money—print advertisements, radio and television commercials, mailers, and the like—are primarily concerned with the inculcation of values. They have become, in fact, the chief value-givers of this age.

Try paying close attention to television commercials. What values do they espouse? Some appeal to fear (buy our travelers' checks because you're likely to be robbed on your next trip), some to logic, even to thrift (our car compares favorably to its chief competitors in the following ways, and is cheaper), some to snobbery (at an elegant country house, fashionably dressed people are drinking a certain brand of sparkling water), some to pure hedonism (on a miserable winter day in the city a young couple chances upon a travel agency; their eyes focus on a replica of a credit card on the window and they are instantly transported to a dreamy tropical paradise).

Keep watching, and an underlying pattern will emerge. About half of the commercials, whatever the subject matter, are based on a climactic moment: The cake has already been baked; the family and guests, their faces all aglow, are gathered around to watch an adorable three-year-old blow out the candles. The race is run and won; beautiful young people jump up and down in ecstasy as they reach for frosted cans of diet cola. Men are shown working at their jobs for all of a second and a half, then it's Miller time. Life at its best, these commercials teach, is an endless series of climactic moments.

And the sitcoms and soaps, the crime shows, and MTV all run on the same hyped-up schedule: (1) If you make smart-assed one-liners for a half hour, everything will work out fine in time for the closing commercials. (2) People are quite nasty, don't work hard, and get rich quickly. (3) No problem is so serious that it can't be resolved in the wink of an eye as soon as the gleaming barrel of a handgun appears. (4) The weirdest fantasy you can think of can be realized instantly and without effort.

In all of this, the specific content isn't nearly as destructive to mastery as is the *rhythm*. One epiphany follows another. One fantasy is crowded out by the next. Climax is piled upon climax. *There's no plateau.*

The Path of Endless Climax

Two generations of Americans have grown up in the television age, during which consumerism has achieved unprecedented dominance over our value system. It should come as no great surprise that many of us have the idea that our lives by all rights should consist of one climax after another. So what do we do when our own day-to-day existence doesn't match up? How do we keep those climactic moments coming without instruction or discipline or practice? It's easy. Take a drug.

Of course, it doesn't work. In the long run it destroys you. But who in the popular and commercial culture has much to say about the long run? Who would be willing to warn in their commercial messages that every attempt to achieve an endless series of climactic moments, whether drug-powered or not, ends like this?

The epidemic of gambling currently sweeping across the nation shows how explicit and blatant the campaign against any long-term effort has become. An ad for the Illinois lottery pictured a man scoffing at people buying savings bonds, and insisting that the only way an ordinary person could become a millionaire was by playing the lottery. The very first commercial seen during an ABC special on the crisis in our high schools showed a bull session among a group of attractive young people. The models for this commercial were probably over twenty-one, but could easily have passed for high schoolers. "I'm going for the Trans-Am," one of them said. Another informed her friends that she would take the Hawaiian vacation, and a third said he was going to win the cash prize of $50,000. While there seemed no doubt in these happy youths' minds that they were going to win the sweepstakes in question, they were statistically more likely to die by drowning in a cistern, cesspool, or well.

A radio commercial for another sweepstakes dramatized the story of a young man who was ashamed to be seen by his brother while cooking hamburgers in a fast food restaurant. He explains that he's working to buy tickets to a pro football game. The brother asks why he's doing that when he could try for the tickets in a sweepstakes. The young man is immediately convinced. He then burns the hamburger he's cooking and serves the french fries still frozen. "I don't care," he says happily. "I can win tickets. I don't need this job."

If you could impute some type of central intelligence to all of these commercial messages, you would have to conclude that the nation is bent on self-destruction. In any case, you might suspect that the disproportionate incidence of drug abuse in the United States, especially of drugs that give you a quick high, springs not so much from immoral or criminal impulses as from a perfectly understandable impulse to replicate the most visible, most compelling American vision of the good life—an endless series of climactic moments. This vision isn't just an invention of television. It resonates in the rhetoric about scoring ("I don't care how you win, just win"), about effortless learning, instant celebrities, instant millionaires, and the "number one" finger raised in the air when you score just once. It is the ruling entrepreneurial vision of America, even among young ghetto drug dealers. "Based on my experience," writes anthropologist Philippe Bourgois, who spent five years of living in and studying the culture of East Harlem, "I believe the assertion of the culture-of-poverty theorists that the poor have been badly socialized and do not share mainstream values is wrong. On the contrary, ambitious, energetic, inner-city youths are attracted to the underground economy precisely because they believe in the rags-to-riches American dream. Like many in the mainstream, they are frantically trying to get their piece of the pie as fast as possible."

The quick-fix, antimastery mentality touches almost everything in our lives. Look at modern medicine and pharmacology. "Fast, temporary relief" is the battle cry. Symptoms receive immediate attention; underlying causes remain in the shadows. More and more research studies show that most illnesses are caused by environmental factors or way of life. The typical twelve-minute office visit doesn't give the doctor time to get to know the patient's face, much less his or her way of life. It does give time for writing a prescription.

A pioneering study by Dr. Dean Ornish and his associates in San Francisco has proven conclusively that coronary artery disease, our number one cause of death, can be reversed by a long-term regimen of diet, moderate exercise, yoga, meditation, and group support. No drugs, no operations. This program has been criticized by some doctors as "too radical." If this is radical, then what do these doctors consider "conservative"? Is it a bypass operation that will split your chest wide open, that has a 5-percent chance of causing death, a 30-percent chance of causing neurological damage, a 50-percent chance of being unnecessary; an operation which might have to be repeated after a few years and which costs $30,000. But all that doesn't seem to matter. At least it's a quick fix.

Business and industry? Perhaps no other area of American life is more in need of the principles of mastery. "Gone is talk of balanced, long-term growth," writes Ralph E. Winter in a *Wall Street Journal* article on the current fad of streamlining. "Impatient shareholders and well-heeled corporate raiders have seen to that. Now anxious executives, fearing for their jobs or their companies, are focusing their efforts on trimming operations and shuffling assets to improve near-term profits, often at the expense of both balance and growth." The leveraged buyout sums it all up. There's an enormous climax. Certain people make a lot of money in a short time. Very little if any real value is added to the corporation, or to the national economy. And the corporate raider becomes a culture hero.

But today's hero can become tomorrow's pariah. Already there are signs of a massive and growing disillusionment with our instant billionaires, and also with crash diets, miracle drugs both legal and illegal, lotteries, sweepstakes, and all the flash and clutter that accrues from the worship of quick, effortless success and fulfillment. If we need a reminder of just how disastrous the war against mastery can be, we have the S&L crisis, which brought quick rewards to a few and is bringing prolonged hardship to many. Make no mistake; it's all connected. The same climate of thought that would lead some people to the promise that they can learn a new skill or lose weight without patient, long-term effort leads others to the promise of great riches without the production of value in return.

A War That Can't Be Won

I'm aware that this critique of certain American values comes at a moment of great triumph for America and the West. Throughout the world, even in nations whose leaders revile us, there's a rising desire for the American way of life. Totalitarian governments are standing on very shaky ground these days. The hunger for free democratic governance has never been stronger. Communism, with its centralized economic planning and control, is in full retreat. Freedom is doubtless the way to go. And throughout most of the world it's growing clear that nations need the system of feedback and individual incentive that obtains in a free market economy.

The victory is real and celebration is in order. But so is some cautious self-examination, for there's perhaps no more dangerous time for any society than its moment of greatest triumph. It would be truly foolish to let the decline of communism blind us to the long-term contradictions in a free market economy unrestrained by considerations of the environment and social justice, and driven by heedless consumerism, instant gratification, and the quick fix. Our dedication to growth at all costs puts us on a collision course with the environment. Our dedication to the illusion of endless climaxes puts us on a collision course with the human psyche.

Mastery applies to nations as well as to individuals. Our present national prosperity is built on a huge deficit and trillions of dollars worth of overdue expenditures on environmental cleanup, infrastructure repair, education, and social services—the quick-fix mentality. The failure to deal with the deficit goes along with easy credit and the continuing encouragement of individual consumption at the expense of saving and longer term gain. The celebration of results over process is reflected in shoddy workmanship and the ascendency of imported products. The urgent commercial appeals that paint life as a series of climactic moments are not unrelated to the current epidemics of drug abuse and gambling. Full shelves in the supermarkets and full lanes on the superhighways don't make up for the pitiful cries of crack babies, the breakdown of learning in and out of the schools, and the growing disparity between the rich and the poor.

America is still the most exciting of nations. Its freedom, its energy, its talent for innovation still inspire the world. But our time of grace might be running out. In the long run, the war against mastery, the path of patient, dedicated effort without attachment to immediate results, is a war that can't be won.

Chapter 4

Loving the Plateau

Early in life, we are urged to study hard, so that we'll get good grades. We are told to get good grades so that we'll graduate from high school and get into college. We are told to graduate from high school and get into college so that we'll get a good job. We are told to get a good job so that we can buy a house and a car. Again and again we are told to do one thing only so that we can get something else. We spend our lives stretched on an iron rack of contingencies.

Contingencies, no question about it, are important. The achievement of goals is important. But the real juice of life, whether it be sweet or bitter, is to be found not nearly so much in the products of our efforts as in the process of living itself, in how it feels to be alive. We are taught in countless ways to value the product, the prize, the climactic moment. But even after we've just caught the winning pass in the

39

Superbowl, there's always tomorrow and tomorrow and tomorrow. If our life is a good one, a life of mastery, most of it will be spent on the plateau. If not, a large part of it may well be spent in restless, distracted, ultimately self-destructive attempts to escape the plateau. The question remains: Where in our upbringing, our schooling, our career are we explicitly taught to value, to enjoy, even to love the plateau, the long stretch of diligent effort with no seeming progress?

I was fortunate in my middle years to have found aikido, a discipline so difficult and resistant to the quick fix that it showed me the plateau in sharp, bold relief. When I first started, I simply assumed that I would steadily improve. My first plateaus were relatively short and I could ignore them. After about a year and a half, however, I was forced to recognize that I was on a plateau of formidable proportions. This recognition brought a certain shock and disappointment, but somehow I persevered and finally experienced an apparent spurt of learning. The next time my outward progress stopped, I said to myself, "Oh damn. Another plateau." After a few more months there was another spurt of progress, and then, of course, the inevitable plateau. This time, something marvelous happened. I found myself thinking, "Oh boy. Another plateau. Good. I can just stay on it and keep practicing. Sooner or later, there'll be another spurt." It was one of the warmest moments on my journey.

The Joy of Regular Practice

At that time, the aikido school I attended was only eighteen months old, and there were no regular students above blue belt. Our teachers, the only black belts around, seemed to exist in an entirely different plane from the one on which we moved. I never even considered the possibility that I would rise to that rarefied plane. So there I was—an impatient, rather driven person who had always gone for the quickest, most direct route to a given goal—practicing regularly and hard for no particular goal at all, just for its own sake. Months would pass with no break in the steady rhythm of my practice. It was something new in my life, a revelation. The endless succession of classes was rewarding precisely because it was, in the Zen sense, "nothing special."

I went to class three or four times a week, from seven to nine P.M. When it was time to drive to the dojo (practice hall) in the city, the problems and distractions of the day began falling away. Just folding the quilted white cotton gi practice uniform softened my breathing and brought me a feeling of peace. The drive took about a half hour, across the bridge into the city, over a long hill that taxed my car's lowest gear, then finally down to a broad and noisy avenue noted for row upon row of car dealerships. Despite the noise outside, climbing the stairs to the second-story dojo was like entering a sanctuary, a place both alien to my customary existence and altogether familiar.

I loved everything about it, the ritual that was always the same yet always new: bowing upon entering, pulling my membership card from the rack on the front desk, changing to my gi in the dressing room. I loved the comforting smell of sweat, the subdued talk. I loved coming out of the dressing room and checking to see which other students were already warming up. I loved bowing again as I stepped on the mat, feeling the cool firm surface on the soles of my feet. I loved taking my place in the long row of aikidoists all sitting in seiza, the Japanese meditation position. I loved the entry of our teacher, the ritual bows, the warm-up techniques, and then my heart pounding, my breath rushing as the training increased in speed and power.

It wasn't always like that. Sometimes, when the moment came to go to class, I would be feeling particularly lazy. On those occasions I would be tempted to do almost anything rather than face myself once again on the mat. And sometimes I would give in to that inevitable human resistance against doing what's best for us, and waste an evening distracting myself.

I knew quite well, however, that when I did over-come my lethargy, I would be rewarded with a little miracle: I knew that, no matter how I felt on climbing the dojo stairs, two hours later—after hundreds of throws and falls—I would walk out tingling and fully alive, feeling so good, in fact, that the night itself would seem to sparkle and gleam.

This joy, I repeat, had little to do with progress or the achievement of goals. I was taken totally by surprise, in fact, when one of my teachers called a fellow student and me into his office after a weekend of marathon training and handed us brown belts, the rank next to black belt. One night about a year later, the four most advanced brown belts in the school happened to have a conversation during which we obliquely touched upon the possibility that we ourselves might someday achieve the rank of black belt. The idea was both exciting and troubling, and when I next came to class I was aware of something new: the worm of ambition was eating stealthily away at the center of my belly.

Maybe it was coincidence, but within three weeks of that conversation all four of us suffered serious injuries—a broken toe, torn ligaments in the elbow, a dislocated shoulder (mine), and an arm broken in three places. These injuries were effective teachers. After recovering, we settled back into steady, goalless practice. Another year and a half was to pass before the four of us made black belt.

This isn't to say that we didn't practice hard. The Hacker gets on a plateau and doesn't keep working. As I think back on that period, I realize that in spite of our many flaws we were definitely on the path of mastery. Unlike the Hacker, we were working hard, doing the best we could to improve our skills. But we had learned the perils of getting ahead of ourselves, and now were willing to stay on the plateau for as long as was necessary. Ambition still was there, but it was tamed. Once again we enjoyed our training. We loved the plateau. *And* we made progress.

This essential paradox becomes especially clear in a martial art that is exceptionally demanding, unforgiving, and rewarding. But it holds true, I think, in every human activity that involves significant learning—mental, physical, emotional, or spiritual. And despite our society's urgent and effective war against mastery, there are still millions of people who, while achieving great things in their work, are dedicated to the process as well as to the product—people who love the plateau. Life for these people is especially vivid and satisfying.

"It's my truest happiness," a writer friend told me. "It's the time when all the crap goes away. As soon as I walk into my study, I start getting cues of pleasure—my books on the shelves, the particular odor of the room. These cues begin to tie into what I've written and what I'm going to write. Even if I've stayed up all night, my fatigue disappears, just like that. There's a whole range of pleasure waiting for me, from making one sentence work to getting a new insight.''

"A lot of people go for things only because a teacher told them they should, or their parents," said Olympic gymnast Peter Vidmar. "People who get into something for the money, the fame, or the medal can't be effective. When you discover you own desire, you're not going to wait for other people to find solutions to your problems. You're going to find your own. I set goals for myself, but underlying all the goals and the work was the fact that I enjoyed it. I thought gymnastics was fun. And I had no idea that I might someday be an Olympian."

"The routine is important to me," said a successful painter who works in her studio for four hours five times a week. "When I get started, there's a wonderful sense of well-being. I like to feel myself plodding along. I specifically choose that word, *plod*. When it's going good, I feel 'this is the essential me.' It's the routine itself that feeds me. If I didn't do it, I'd be betraying the essential me."

When I was a boy, my father would let me go to his office with him on Saturday mornings. I don't think he had to go. He was simply drawn there; it was his place of practice. He was in the fire insurance business, and while he went through his mail, he would let me wander through the office, free to play with the marvelous mechanical contrivances of those days—the stately upright typewriters, the hand-operated adding machines, the staplers and paper punches, and the old dictaphone on which I could record a thin facsimile of my voice.

I loved the Saturday morning silence and the smells of glue and ink, rubber erasers and well-worn wood. I would play with the machines and make paper airplanes for a while but then, more likely than not, I would go into my father's office and just sit there watching him, fascinated by the depth of his concentration. He was in a world of his own, entirely relaxed and at the same time entirely focused as he opened the envelopes of various sizes and shapes, sorted the contents into piles, and made notes to his secretary. And all the time he worked, his lips were slightly parted, his breath steady and calm, his eyes soft, and his hands moving steadily, almost hypnotically. I remember wondering even then, when I was not more than ten years old, if I would ever have such a power of concentration or take such pleasure in my work. Certainly not at school, certainly not during my scattered, abortive attempts to do homework. I knew even then that he was an ambitious man with a burning desire for the extrinsic rewards of his work, including public recognition and even fame. But I also knew that he loved his work—the feel, the rhythm, the texture of it. My father's colleagues later told me that he was among the best in his field. Still, the public recognition he might have wished for never materialized, nor did the fame. But recognition is often unsatisfying and fame is like seawater for the thirsty. Love of your work, willingness to stay with it even in the absence of extrinsic reward, is good food and good drink.

The Face of Mastery

The look of deep concentration on my father's face as he did the work he loved is not unlike the expression that can be seen on the face of almost anyone on the path of mastery—even in the throes of physical exertion. Sports photography as we know it has been captured by the "thrill of victory/agony of defeat" school. Again and again we're shown climactic moments (prodigious exertion, faces contorted with pain or triumph), almost to the exclusion of anything else. But it seems to me that mastery's true face is relaxed and serene, sometimes faintly smiling. In fact, those we most admire in sports seem at times to enter another dimension. Besieged by opposing players, battered by the screams of the crowd, they make the difficult, even the supernatural, seem easy, and manage somehow to create harmony where chaos might otherwise prevail.

In preparing the *Esquire* special on mastery, I decided to see if I could find a series of pictures that would illustrate The Face of Mastery. I went through hundreds of prints and transparencies from the major photo agencies, and there, scattered among the "thrill of victory/agony of defeat" shots, was just what I was looking for: Steven Scott making the last turn in a mile race, his face serene, his body relaxed; Greg Louganis at the edge of the diving board, his face a study in calm concentration; Peter Vidmar doing floor exercises, his body in an impossibly strenuous position, his face reflective and composed; Kareem Abdul-Jabbar launching his "sky-hook" basketball shot over the hand of an opposing player, his face a revelation of inner delight. Abdul-Jabbar is not a man of small ego. I'm sure he loved the money, the fame, the privileges his career brought him. But he loved the sky-hook more.

Goals and contingencies, as I've said, are important. But they exist in the future and the past, beyond the pale of the sensory realm. Practice, the path of mastery, exists only in the present. You can see it, hear it, smell it, feel it. To love the plateau is to love the eternal now, to enjoy the inevitable spurts of progress and the fruits of accomplishment, then serenely to accept the new plateau that waits just beyond them. To love the plateau is to love what is most essential and enduring in your life.

PART TWO

THE FIVE
MASTER KEYS

Introduction

The human individual is equipped to learn and go on learning prodigiously from birth to death, and this is precisely what sets him or her apart from all other known forms of life. Man has at various times been defined as a building animal, a working animal, and a fighting animal, but all of these definitions are incomplete and finally false. Man is a learning animal, and the essence of the species is encoded in that simple term.

In this light, the mastery of skills that are not genetically programmed is the most characteristically human of all activities. The first and best of this learning involves no formal arrangements whatever; the world itself is school enough. We all participate in a master's journey in early childhood when we learn to talk or to walk. Every adult or older child around us is a teacher of language—the type of teacher who smiles at success, permits approximations, and isn't likely to indulge in lectures (i.e., the best type). We achieve an upright stance and bipedal locomotion with the help of the same encouraging, permissive instructors, along with the immediate and decisive assistance of gravity—a master teacher if ever there was one. Then, too, humans are genetically predisposed toward language and bipedal locomotion.

Later, however, we face the task of learning skills for which there's no cooperative surrounding environment, skills for which we aren't as genetically predisposed to develop. (Neither jet planes nor grand pianos were involved in the early evolution of homo sapiens.) More and more as we emerge into the teen and adult years, we must find our own doors to mastery. Chapters Five through Nine present five keys to opening those doors.

Chapter 5

Key 1: Instruction

There are some skills you can learn on your own, and some you can try to learn, but if you intend to take the journey of mastery, the best thing you can do is to arrange for first-rate instruction. The self-taught person is on a chancy path. There are advantages: you enjoy the license of not knowing what *can't* be done; you might wander into fertile territory previously ruled out by mainline explorers. Some of those who have taught themselves—Edison for one, Buckminster Fuller for another—have made it work. Most, however, have spent their lives reinventing the wheel, then refusing to concede that it's out of round. Even those who will some day overthrow conventional ways of thinking or doing need to know what it is they are overthrowing.

Instruction comes in many forms. For mastering most skills, there's nothing better than being in the hands of a master teacher, either one-to-one or in a small group. But there are also books, films, tapes, computer learning programs, computerized simulators (flight simulators, for example), group instruction, the classroom, knowledgeable friends, counselors, business associates, even "the street." Still, the individual teacher or coach can serve as a standard for all forms of instruction, the first and brightest beacon on the journey of mastery.

The search for good instruction starts with a look at credentials and lineage. Who was your teacher's teacher? Who was that teacher's teacher? And so on back to the timeless time when individual identity disappears in the myth of first beginnings. These are perhaps quaint questions in an age that has let the cord of lineage come almost completely unravelled, but good questions nonetheless. (Even tapes and books and computer learning programs have an ancestry.)

Respect for credentials, however, shouldn't blind you to other considerations. The instructor who advertises as an eighth-degree black belt in one martial art, ninth-degree in another, and light-middleweight champion of the world in both could be a lousy teacher. John McEnroe might turn up in later years as a superb tennis coach—but he might not. The teaching tactics of a Nobel laureate could turn out to be poison for the mind of a neophyte physicist. It's particularly challenging, in fact, for a top performer to become a first-rate teacher. Instruction demands a certain humility; at best, the teacher takes delight in being surpassed by his or her students. Gymnastics coach Bela Karole would have a very hard time performing the moves he has taught to both Nadia Comaneci of Romania and Mary Lou Retton of the USA.

To see the teacher clearly, look at the students. They are his work of art. If at all possible, attend an instructional session before choosing your teacher. Focus your attention on the students. Even more, on the *interaction*. Does the instructor proceed through praise or through damnation? There is the brand of teacher, often celebrated in myth if not in reality, who is famous for giving an absolute minimum of praise. When this teaching tactic works, it's through an economic principle, praise becoming so scarce a commodity that even a curt nod of grudging approval is taken to be highly rewarding. What doesn't work, despite a certain macho attitude to the contrary, is scorn, excoriation, humiliation—anything that destroys the student's confidence and self-esteem. Even the praise-stingy teacher must in some way show respect for the student in order to get long-term positive results. The best teacher generally strives to point out what the student is doing right at least as frequently as what she or he is doing wrong, which is just what UCLA coach John Wooden, perhaps the greatest basketball mentor of all time, managed to do all through his long, winning career. Wooden was observed to maintain approximately a fifty-fifty ratio between reinforcement and correction, with exceptional enthusiasm on both sides of the equation.

Look again at the students, the interaction. Do the more talented, more advanced students get all the goodies? How about the klutzes, the beginners? Maybe you're looking for the type of instructor who's comfortable only with the best, only with potential champions. There are such teachers, and they serve a useful function, but for me the essence of the instructor's art lies in the ability to work effectively and enthusiastically with beginners and to serve as a guide on the path of mastery for those who are neither as fast nor as talented as the norm. This service can be listed under altruism, but it's more than that. For to participate with a beginner in the first faltering mental and physical moves involved in learning a new skill is to penetrate the inner structure not only of that skill but also of the process of mastery itself. Knowledge, expertise, technical skill, and credentials are important, but without the patience and empathy that go with teaching beginners, these merits are as nothing.

The Best of Instructors, the Worst of Instructors

It was at the high-water mark of a war that had surged all the way around the globe that I first found myself in the instructor's role. The top six graduates of Class 44-C of the advanced flight school at Turner Field in Albany, Georgia—brand new second lieutenants with silver pilot's wings—were kept back and made flight instructors while the other 304 graduates were sent on to combat. Far from being pleased with our assignments, the six of us professed a burning desire for immediate combat duty, a sentiment that became maudlin after a few drinks at the officers club on our nights off. I was twenty years old. The other five new instructors were about the same age.

In March of 1944, despite our lack of experience, we were assigned students, and, without a word of advice, sent up to teach them to fly the B-25, a high-performance medium bomber of the time. The invasion of Fortress Europe was imminent. The Pacific campaign, it was predicted, would last for years. Pilots, like the planes they would fly, had to be produced by the tens of thousands, never mind such niceties as stringent safety procedures.

Flying conditions would have caused a major scandal in peacetime. Even on the darkest nights, with giant thunderstorms closing in, some hundred B-25s would jockey for position in the landing pattern at the end of each instructional period. There was nothing like a radar traffic control system; our lives hung on visual acuity, flying skill, and fast reflexes. During the summer of 1944, two spectacular midair collisions at Turner Field resulted in the destruction of four planes and the tragic loss of the instructors and cadets flying them. The crashes never made the newspapers. There was no time for sympathy or second chances. Student pilots who didn't measure up were washed out, discarded like defective components coming off a production line.

The six months I spent at Turner Field proved to be more challenging, and actually more dangerous, than the combat tour in the South Pacific that followed. After logging 600 hours as a flight instructor under the most demanding of conditions, I had gained a sure sense of the mastery of flight that has never left me.

And what about my students? Ah, that's another story.

Time provides no replays. But I am left, after all of these years, with crystalline memories of preternaturally white clouds soaring over deep green fields of cotton and corn, of the insistent engine sound that finally became no sound at all, of smoking engines and failed hydraulic systems, of illegal flights out over the Atlantic to play vertiginous games of follow-the-leader with other planes while our students held their breaths. But more than anything, I am left with a morality tale on the subject of instructing, in which I play the leading role. There's nothing I can do to change it. I was the best of instructors. I was the worst of instructors. The first does not justify the second.

Each of us was given four students to guide through the entire two months of advanced training. I quickly discovered that two of my students—cadets by the name of Stull and Thatcher—were quite talented. The other two—call them Brewster and Edmundson—were, at best, mediocre. This discrepancy suggested a plan: I would keep Stull and Thatcher together. I'd never let them fly with anyone else; they would be safe from contamination by lesser talents. This would allow me to initiate the two of them into a mode of flying a fellow instructor and I had developed while still cadets. We called it maximum performance, and it simply meant that we would fly as close as possible to perfection at all times, even when regulations didn't call for it, even when no one was watching.

And so, without mentioning the words maximum performance, I set standards for Stull and Thatcher approximately ten times more stringent than what was called for. Normally, while flying on instruments, pilots were given a leeway of 200 feet above or below the prescribed altitude, but I led Stull and

Thatcher to believe they had only a 20-foot margin of error. I insisted they hold their gyro compass heading right on the money at all times. I taught them, even when landing on a 10,000-foot runway, to touch down on the first hundred feet.

I gave Stull and Thatcher my very best, and they responded just as I had hoped they would. Even though I never let them fly with other cadets, they must have compared notes and figured out what I was up to. Sometimes, when I described a particularly unreasonable standard of performance with a straight face, they were unable to keep from smiling. After the first few weeks, I too couldn't keep a smile off my face. We were joined in a delicious conspiracy of excellence. On the days I was scheduled to fly with them, I awakened with a feeling of excitement and anticipation.

I can still see Stull and Thatcher with incredible clarity, one of them in the pilot's seat, the other standing in back and leaning down between the pilot's and copilot's seats to watch yet another perfect approach and landing. The pure, prophetic light of another time still pours in through the Plexiglas canopy—the towering clouds, the impossible blue of the sky—and the two cadets' faces still glow with the incomparable happiness that comes when you first embark on the journey of mastery.

Now for the hard part of the story.

After my first few flights with the cadets I'm calling Brewster and Edmundson, I simply lost interest. I was too young, too impatient, too arrogant in my espousal of maximum performance to endure their rather inept efforts at flying the B-25. Brewster was slim, patrician, and shy. Edmundson was heavy-set and confident, the squadron jokester. On one flight I thought he made a snide remark at my expense. I took the controls, climbed to 10,000 feet, and racked the plane around in maneuvers it was never meant to perform, leaving Edmundson and Brewster pale and shaken.

I went through the motions. Now and then I made an effort to bring them along, to discover what was blocking their progress, to develop their potential to its fullest extent. But my enthusiasms were short-lived. Some particularly blatant display of crudity on the controls by Edmundson or tentativeness on the part of Brewster would cause me to shake my head in despair and disgust, and either turn away and slump in my seat or take the controls and show them exactly how the maneuver should be done.

As it turned out, Brewster and Edmundson graduated along with Stull and Thatcher, but just barely. After the war, I happened to run into Brewster at a dance in Atlanta. He took the opportunity (the force of his resentment overcoming any shyness he might have felt) to let me know exactly what he thought about his experiences with me at Turner Field. I had no adequate reply. Long before that time, I had begun to feel guilty about the way I had handled my first assignment as an instructor. In fact, I never again segregated my students as I had done the first time. I graduated two more groups of pilots before leaving for combat, experiencing neither the exhilaration I had felt with Stull and Thatcher nor the despair I had felt with Brewster and Edmundson. I worked to control my impatience, to do the best I could with the slower students. Still, a continuing preoccupation with maximum performance, along with an extremity of youth, tended to frustrate my own performance as a teacher of the less talented.

The Magic of Teaching Beginners

Many years later, I found myself once again in the instructor's role, engaged this time in an art far more subtle and complex and difficult to learn than flying. I was forty-seven when a friend invited me to join the aikido class he was organizing. I had never heard of aikido, nor had I ever dreamed of becoming a martial artist. That was twenty years ago, and I can now say that practicing aikido has been the second most profound learning experience of my life. Teaching aikido has been the most profound.

Even before getting my first-degree black belt, I

was enlisted by my teacher as an assistant instructor. My job: teaching the basics of the art to beginners. Six years later, in October 1976, shortly after getting our black belts, two of my fellow aikidoists and I started our own dojo. From rather questionable beginnings fourteen years ago (it's not customary for first-degree black belts to start their own school), Aikido of Tamalpais has become a respected and happy dojo. We three founders have continued developing our skills, and have advanced to higher ranks. From the thousands of students who have practiced at our school for varying lengths of time have come twenty-eight black belts—not an insignificant number in a difficult art that offers no cheap degrees.

At this point, I'd like to be able to tell you that by now I've mastered the art of teaching slow students and beginners. But that wouldn't be true; I still have to work at it. I listen carefully when Wendy Palmer, one of my partners, tells me that teaching beginners and slow students is not only fascinating but pleasurable. The talented student, she believes, is likely to learn so fast that small stages in the learning process are glossed over, creating an opaque surface that hides the secrets of the art from view. With the slow student, though, the teacher is forced to deal with small, incremental steps that penetrate like X rays the very essence of the art, and clearly reveal the process through which the art becomes manifest in movement.

Gradually the mystery has unfolded. My experience as an instructor has shown me, for one thing, that the most talented students don't necessarily make the best martial artists. Sometimes, strangely enough, those with exceptional talent have trouble staying on the path of mastery. In 1987, my colleagues at *Esquire* and I conducted a series of interviews with athletes known as masters of their sports, which tended to confirm this paradoxical finding. Most of the athletes we interviewed stressed hard work and experience over raw talent. "I have seen so many baseball players with God-given ability who just didn't want to work," Rod Carew said. "They were soon gone. I've seen others with no ability to speak of who stayed in the big leagues for fourteen or fifteen years."

Good Horse, Bad Horse

In his book *Zen Mind, Beginner's Mind,* Zen master Shunryu Suzuki approaches the question of fast and slow learners in terms of horses. "In our scriptures, it is said that there are four kinds of horses: excellent ones, good ones, poor ones, and bad ones. The best horse will run slow and fast, right and left, at the driver's will, before it sees the shadow of the whip; the second best will run as well as the first one, just before the whip reaches its skin; the third one will run when it feels pain on its body; the fourth will run after the pain penetrates to the marrow of its bones. You can imagine how difficult it is for the fourth one to learn to run.

"When we hear this story, almost all of us want to be the best horse. If it is impossible to be the best one, we want to be the second best." But this is a mistake, Master Suzuki says. When you learn too easily, you're tempted not to work hard, not to penetrate to the marrow of a practice.

"If you study calligraphy, you will find that those who are not so clever usually become the best calligraphers. Those who are very clever with their hands often encounter great difficulty after they have reached a certain stage. This is also true in art, and in life." The best horse, according to Suzuki, may be the worst horse. And the worst horse can be the best, for if it perseveres, it will have learned whatever it is practicing all the way to the marrow of its bones.

Suzuki's parable of the four horses has haunted me ever since I first heard it. For one thing, it poses a clear challenge for the person with exceptional talent: to achieve his or her full potential, this person will have to work just as diligently as those with less innate ability. The parable has made me realize that if I'm the first or second horse as an instructor of fast learners, I'm the third or fourth horse as an instructor of slow learners. But there is hope. If I persevere and dedicate my efforts to bringing along every Brewster and Edmundson who shows up at our aikido school, I'll someday know this aspect of instructing all the way to the marrow of my bones.

So when you look for your instructor, in whatever skill or art, spend a moment celebrating it when you discover one who pursues maximum performance. But also make sure that he or she is paying exquisite attention to the slowest student on the mat.

Comparing Various Modes of Instruction

How about the other modes of instruction? In most cases, audio and video tapes have only limited effectiveness. Learning eventually involves interaction between the learner and the learning environment, and its effectiveness relates to the frequency, quality, variety, and intensity of the interaction. With tapes, there's no real interaction at all; information flows in one direction only. A videotape can show you an ideal golf swing to copy, and that's certainly better than nothing, but the tape has no way of observing your swing and telling you how well you're replicating the ideal. With remote control, the tape can be easily stopped, reversed, repeated, and in some cases played in slow motion—all of which makes it much better than instructional films or television programs, which march along at a steady rate, regardless of the learner's progress or understanding.

A book is also self-paced, and it's portable and handy. Like tape, its suffers from lack of feedback capability. Still, in spite of the marvels of the computer age, the book remains a major tool for learning especially in skills that are primarily cognitive. If a picture is sometimes worth a thousand words, then perhaps a moving picture is worth 10,000 words. But it's also true that one good paragraph sometimes has more power to change the individual and the world than any number of pictures.

The typical school or college classroom, unhappily, is not a very good place to learn. "Frontal teaching," with one instructor sitting or standing in front of twenty to thirty-five students who are sitting at fixed desks, is primarily an administrative expediency, a way of parceling out and keeping track of the flood of students in mass education. It's sad that over the past hundred years almost every aspect of our national life—industry, transportation, communication, computation, entertainment—has changed almost beyond recognition, while our schools remain essentially the same.

Take a look. There it is: one teacher giving out the same information at the same rate to a group of mostly passive students regardless of their individual abilities, cultural backgrounds, or learning styles. I've written at some length on this subject and on the type of reform that could remedy the situation through the self-pacing and individualizing capabilities of the computer and other new instructional modes. I believe that within ten or fifteen years at the most some sort of school reform along these lines is inevitable.

Meanwhile, there are still good teachers and bad teachers. Visits to hundreds of schools have convinced me that the teacher who can make the present system work is undoubtedly a master. He or she is not necessarily the one who gives the most polished lectures, but rather the one who has discovered *how to involve each student actively* in the process of learning. One award-winning mathematician at a major university was famous for intentionally making small mistakes when he wrote formulas on the chalkboard. Students sat on the edge of their chairs vying to be the first to catch the mistake and rush up to correct their professor—truly a master of the instructor's art.

Knowing When to Say Good-bye

Fortunate is the person who can find such a teacher, especially at the beginning of the learning process. Students at school up to and including college often don't have much choice. Even those of us who do have a choice sometimes make a bad one. If you should end up with a teacher who doesn't seem right for you, first look inside. You might well be expecting more than any teacher can give. But teachers as well as students can be lazy, excessively goal oriented, indifferent, psychologically seductive, or just plain inept. It's important to keep the proper psychological distance. If you're too far removed, there's no chance for the surrender that's part of the master's journey (see Chapter Seven); if you come too close, you lose all perspective and become a disciple rather than a student. The responsibility for good balance lies with student as well as teacher. When irreconcilable differences do occur, remember that the better part of wisdom is knowing when to say good-bye.

Bear in mind that on the path of mastery learning never ends. In the words of the great Japanese swordmaster Yamaoka Tesshu:

> *Do not think that*
> *This is all there is.*
> *More and more*
> *Wonderful teachings exist—*
> *The sword is unfathomable.*

Chapter 6

Key 2: Practice

It's an old joke that appears in many versions but always sends the same message. In one version, a couple of Texans in a Cadillac on their way to a concert are lost in New York's Lower East Side. They stop to question a bearded elder.

"How do you get to Carnegie Hall?" they ask.

"Practice!" he tells them.

That usage of the word—practice as a verb—is clear to all of us. You practice your trumpet, your dance routine, your multiplication tables, your combat mission. To practice in this sense implies something separate from the rest of your life. You practice in order to learn a skill, in order to improve yourself, in order to get ahead, achieve goals, make money. This way of thinking about practice is useful in our society; you obviously have to practice to get to Carnegie Hall.

For one who is on the master's journey, however, the word is best conceived of as a noun, not as something you *do,* but as something you *have,* something you *are.* In this sense, the word is akin to the Chinese word tao and the Japanese word do, both of which mean, literally, road or path. Practice is the path upon which you travel, just that.

A practice (as a noun) can be anything you practice on a regular basis as an integral part of your life—not in order to gain something else, but for its own sake. It might be a sport or a martial art. It might be gardening or bridge or yoga or meditation or community service. A doctor practices medicine and an attorney practices law, and each of them also *has* a practice. But if that practice is only a collection of patients or clients, a way of making a living, it isn't a *master's* practice. For a master, the rewards gained along the way are fine, but they are not the main reason for the journey. Ultimately, the master and the master's path are one. And if the traveler is fortunate—that is, if the path is complex and profound enough—the destination is two miles farther away for every mile he or she travels.

A woman in one of our workshops asked my wife, Annie, why she was still going to aikido classes. "I thought you'd already gotten your black belt," she said. It took Annie a few minutes to explain that a black belt is only one more step along an endless path, a license to go on learning for as long as you live.

In a nation obsessed with the achievement of goals ("It doesn't matter how you score; the score is all that counts." "Don't tell me how you are going to sell the ad, just sell it." "Winning isn't everything; it's the only thing."), devotion to the goalless journey might seem incomprehensible if not bizarre. But behind the slogans you read on the sports page and in the business section there's a deeper reality: the master goes along with the rhetoric about scoring and winning (in today's media climate, who would listen to anything else?), but secretly cherishes those games filled with delicious twists and turns of fortune, great plays, close calls, and magical finishes—regardless of who wins.

There's another secret: The people we know as masters don't devote themselves to their particular skill just to get better at it. The truth is, *they love to practice*—and because of this they do get better. And then, to complete the circle, the better they get the more they enjoy performing the basic moves over and over again.

Beginners at the basics classes at our aikido school will do a simple blending move about eight or ten times, then start looking around restlessly for something new to distract them. Black belts at the basics classes have the knowledge and experience—the *feel*—necessary to appreciate the subtleties and end-less possibilities contained within even the most ru-dimentary technique. I remember an aikido class years ago when I was a brown belt, the rank just below black belt. Our teacher started us doing a tech-nique called shiho-nage (four-way throw), then con-tinued with the same variation of the same technique for the entire two-hour class. After the first half hour, I began wondering what was coming next. (Our school rarely practiced the same technique for so long a time.) By the end of the first hour, however, I had settled into a steady, trancelike rhythm that obliterated all considerations of time or repetition. My perceptions expanded. The barely noticeable variations from one throw to the next became signif-icant and revealing. By the end of the second hour, I was hoping that the class would go on until mid-night, that it would never end.

Staying on the Mat

"The master," an old martial arts saying goes, "is the one who stays on the mat five minutes longer every day than anybody else." And not just in aikido. In August 1988, I visited the Seattle Seahawks' train-ing camp as a guest of the team's offensive coordi-nator. When the morning practice session was over, the players shambled off the field to the dressing room—all of the players except two, that is. One of the two kept running out, then wheeling suddenly to take a pass from the other. Again and again, he ran the same pattern, caught the same pass. The field was empty; the other players were inside taking their showers, getting dressed. The coaches, too, were gone and the spectators had drifted away. I remained there on the sidelines, fascinated. Who was this eager pass receiver? Surely, it was some brand new rookie, someone trying to get good enough to make the team. No, it was Steve Largent, not only the premier pass receiver of the Seattle Seahawks but the leading receiver in the history of the National Football League.

The master of any game is generally a master of practice. In his prime, Larry Bird of the Boston Celtics was perhaps the most complete basketball player of all time. Unable to jump as high or run as fast as many other players, he was named National Basketball Association Rookie of the Year for 1980, Most Valuable Player in two championship series, and the league MVP for three years in a row. Bird began developing his basketball practice at age four, and never stopped practicing. After the Celtics won the NBA championship in June 1986, reporters asked Bird what he planned to do next. "I've still got some things I want to work on," he was quoted as saying. "I'll start my off-season training next week. Two

hours a day, with at least a hundred free throws.''
Many professionals take some of the summer off, but
not Larry Bird. He runs for conditioning, up and
down the steepest hills he can find. On the blacktop
court with glass backboard at home in French Lick,
Indiana, he practices. During the season, in the Hel-
lenic College gym in Brookline, he practices. On road
trips, in arenas all around the country, before every
game, he practices.

During his years with the Celtics, Bird was known
for getting on the court an hour or two before everyone else to practice his shots—foul shots, fall-away
shots, three-pointers, shots from all sorts of angles.
Sometimes, just for fun, he would sit on the sideline
and pop them in, or find a seat in the first row and
float them in. No question, Bird likes to win. Still,
according to his agent Bob Woolf, that's not the main
reason he practices so diligently and plays so wholeheartedly. ''He does it just to enjoy himself. Not to
make money, to get acclaim, to gain stature. He just
loves to play basketball.''

Explicit skills such as those found in martial arts,
sports, dance, music, and the like provide explicit
examples of practice. But this second key to mastery
undergirds a wide variety of human endeavors. Good
business practice demands that managers keep the
mechanics of their operations current at all times, being especially diligent and disciplined in such basic

matters as budget, order fulfillment, and quality control. Families that stay together hold fast to certain rituals regardless of the haste and distractions of daily life; this might mean having one full, sit-down meal every day with every family member present. Nations also have their practice, as seen, for example, in the regular and heartfelt observance of national festivals and sacred days. This nation indulges in a questionable experiment in casually changing the dates of its holidays (''holy days'') for the sake of commerce and four-day weekends.

To practice regularly, even when you seem to be getting nowhere, might at first seem onerous. But the day eventually comes when practicing becomes a treasured part of your life. You settle into it as if into your favorite easy chair, unaware of time and the turbulence of the world. It will still be there for you tomorrow. It will never go away.

''How long will it take me to master aikido?'' a prospective student asks. ''How long do you expect to live?'' is the only respectable response. Ultimately, practice *is* the path of mastery. If you stay on it long enough, you'll find it to be a vivid place, with its ups and downs, its challenges and comforts, its surprises, disappointments, and unconditional joys. You'll take your share of bumps and bruises while traveling—bruises of the ego as well as of the body, mind, and spirit—but it might well turn out to be the most reliable thing in your life. Then, too, it might eventually make you a winner in your chosen field, if that's what you're looking for, and then people will refer to you as a master.

But that's not really the point. What is mastery? At the heart of it, mastery is practice. Mastery is staying on the path.

Chapter 7

Key 3: Surrender

The courage of a master is measured by his or her willingness to surrender. This means surrendering to your teacher and to the demands of your discipline. It also means surrendering your own hard-won proficiency from time to time in order to reach a higher or different level of proficiency.

The early stages of any significant new learning invoke the spirit of the fool (see the Epilogue). It's almost inevitable that you'll feel clumsy, that you'll take literal or figurative pratfalls. There's no way around it. The beginner who stands on his or her dignity becomes rigid, armored; the learning can't get through. This doesn't mean that you should surrender your own physical and moral center or passively accept teachings that would be bad for you. But you've already checked out your instructor (see Key 1). Now's the time for a certain suspension of disbelief. So your teacher asks you to begin by putting your finger on your nose and standing on one foot. Unless there's some compelling reason to the contrary, just surrender. Give it a try.

After all, learning almost any significant skill involves certain indignities. Your first few dives are likely to be belly flops—and they'll draw the attention of almost everyone at the pool. Are you willing to accept that? If not, forget diving. The face you draw in your first art class looks more like Mr. Potato Head than the Mona Lisa. Is that a good reason for giving up art? And how about those fluttering ankles the first few times you try ice skating? And the impact of the hard, cold ice on the part of the body normally reserved for spankings? Punishment of this sort isn't limited to beginners; it happens in the Olympics. If you want to get there, be prepared to take it.

And then there are the endless repetitions, the drudgery, the basic moves practiced over and over again. Who but a fool would embark on a musical career in the full knowledge that he or she might end up repeating all the major and minor scales perhaps a hundred thousand times each? To some people that prospect alone might seem to justify resisting any surrender. About halfway through my third aikido class, my teacher demonstrated tai no henko, the most basic blending movement in the art. Without a moment's thought, I heard myself saying, "We've already done that technique." That remark didn't even elicit a reply, just a faintly amused smile. My surrender was definitive: since then, I've practiced tai no henko at least 50,000 times.

Actually, the essence of boredom is to be found in the obsessive search for novelty. Satisfaction lies in mindful repetition, the discovery of endless richness in subtle variations on familiar themes.

Swordmaster Stories

The literature of the East is loaded with swordmaster-and-apprentice stories. All have the same general drift. A young man learns of a master of the sword who lives in a far province. After a long and difficult journey, he presents himself at the master's door and asks to become his student. The master closes the door in the young man's face. Every day thereafter, the young man comes to sit on the master's doorstep, simply waiting. A year passes, and the master grudgingly allows the young man to do chores around the house—chop wood, carry water. Months more go by, maybe years. One morning, without warning, the master attacks the young man from behind and whacks him on the shoulder with a bamboo sword, a shinai. The master has begun to teach alertness. At length, the master gives his apprentice his own shinai and continues teaching him the art of the sword, to which the student has been surrendering all along.

In a nation that has made a book entitled *Total Fitness in 12 Minutes a Week* into a national bestseller, such stories might tend to have little meaning. Still, the swordmaster myth has the power to penetrate our popular culture, if only in an Americanized version. The first, and best, *Karate Kid* movie condenses the years of the myth into a few months, having the apprentice painting the karate master's fence and waxing his car rather than chopping wood and carrying water.

Surrendering to your teacher and to the fundamentals of the art are only the beginning. There are times in almost every master's journey when it becomes necessary to give up some hard-won competence in order to advance to the next stage. This is especially true when you're stuck at a familiar and comfortable skill level. The parable of the cup and the quart applies here. There's a quart of milk on the table—within your reach. But you're holding a cup of milk in your hand and you're afraid to let go of the cup in order to get the quart.

Your fear isn't without foundation. If you've been shooting in the nineties for quite a while on the golf links and want to get your score down into the eighties or even the seventies, you might well have to give up the nineties for a while; you might have to take your game apart before putting it back together. This is true of almost any skill. For many years I had played jazz piano for my own amusement. I had developed a small repertory in a limited set of keys using rather unadventurous chording. Every time I wrote or spoke about the character I call the Hacker or looked at the curve describing the Hacker's progress, I thought about my own piano playing and said to myself, "That's me!"

About a year ago, egged on by my aikido partner, Wendy, a talented singer and guitarist, I found myself playing with a small jazz group, learning new songs in new keys, changing all of my chord voicing, and, in general, shooting for a level of play I had never dreamed of. At first everything started falling apart. Where was my comfortable old solo style? I had let go the cup and hadn't yet grasped the quart. I was floundering in the scary, slippery space between competencies.

Just then, we were given the opportunity of playing at a local jazz spot. Someone—could it have been me?—said, "Seize the day," and I found myself going straight from the land of the Hacker to the land of the Obsessive without even a side trip through the larger country of mastery, practicing so strenuously that I developed an inflamed tendon in my right little finger and had to ice my hand each time I played.

Somehow the performance passed without disaster, and now I'm groping my way toward the slow lane on the path of mastery in this skill.

A Tale of Two Experts

How do you respond when offered the chance of renouncing a present competency for a higher or different one? The story of two karate experts—call them Russell and Tony—trying to learn aikido might serve as a guide. Both of them were participants in an eight-week certification program that required aikido training five days a week. It was my job to teach the class.

Russell was small, wiry, intense, and scholarly—an exceptionally gracious person who went out of his way to be helpful to his fellow students. He held a doctorate, and was director of professional training in a large organization. In addition, he had a first-degree black belt in karate. Tony's schooling had been accomplished mostly on the streets of Jersey City. He had come to the martial arts early in life and now, at 31, he held a fourth-degree karate black belt and was owner of two karate schools.

From the moment Russell stepped on the training mat, he revealed that he was a trained martial artist. His individual warm-up routine included several karate moves. When called upon to deliver a punch during class, he resorted to the specialized style of his previous discipline. Once, on a two-hand grab attack, I noticed him moving purposefully to keep a maximum distance between his body and that of the person he was attacking. I suggested he stay closer and let himself flow with the attack. "Surely you jest," he said with a laugh. I told him that in order to learn the basic moves, it would be better just for now to forget defensive possibilities; we would learn to cover any openings later. I could see that Russell was finding it hard to let go of his expertise, and because of this failing to get the most out if his aikido training. After the first four weeks, he was falling behind some of those who had never done any martial art, and it was only at this point that he finally surrendered his prior competence and got on the path of mastery.

Tony's approach was different. From the beginning, he never made a move, not even a gesture, that might reveal he was an expert in another art. Without a hint of ostentation, he showed more respect than did any of the other students for his teachers—this in spite of his high rank. He carried himself with an air of calm sincerity and was unfailingly aware of everything going on around him. Along with this was a powerful presence that could be quickly recognized by any trained martial artist. Just by the way he sat, stood, and walked, Tony revealed himself as a fellow traveler on the path of mastery.

During a class at the end of the first four weeks, I had all the students sit at the edge of the mat, then asked Tony if he would show us one of his karate kata (predetermined sequence of movements). He bowed, walked to the center of the mat, and breathed deeply for a few moments. What followed brought a sharp intake of breath from almost all of us. Moving gracefully and faster than the eye could fully comprehend, Tony launched one swift and deadly strike and kick after another, leaping, spinning, emitting resounding kiai shouts as he dispatched imaginary foes at every point of the compass. When it was over, he once again bowed humbly and returned to the edge of the mat to take his place with the others—the most thoroughgoing beginner of them all.

Perhaps the best you can hope for on the master's journey—whether your art be management or marriage, badminton or ballet—is to cultivate the mind and heart of the beginning at every stage along the way. For the master, surrender means there are no experts. There are only learners.

Chapter 8

Key 4: Intentionality

It joins old words with new—character, willpower, attitude, imaging, the mental game—but what I'm calling intentionality, however you look at it, is an essential to take along on the master's journey.

The power of the mental game came to public awareness in the 1970s through the revelations of some of the nation's most notable sports figures. Golfer Jack Nicklaus, for example, let it be known that he never hit a shot without first clearly visualizing the ball's perfect flight and its triumphant destination, "sitting up there high and white and pretty on the green." A successful shot, Nicklaus told us, was 50 percent visualization, 40 percent setup, and only 10 percent swing. Premiere pro runningbacks described imaging each of their plays again and again the night before a game; they felt that their success on the field the next day was closely related to the vividness of their mental practice. Body builders and weightlifters testified to the value of intentionality. Arnold Schwarzenneger argued that pumping a weight one time with full consciousness was worth ten without mental awareness. He was joined by Frank Zane and others in vouching for the effect of the mind on such physical qualities as muscle and iron.

What had happened was that sports training and technique had reached an extremely high level of development—so high that further improvements along this line could come only in tiny increments. When Jack Nicklaus attributed only 10 percent of the success of a shot to the swing, it was perhaps because his swing was already nearly perfect. The realm of mind and spirit was the undiscovered land, the place where pioneers in sports performance could make the greatest gains.

To exploit this opportunity, a number of top-ranking teams and individuals have hired sports psychologists to teach relaxation, confidence, and the mental rehearsal of specific plays or moves. This has led to audiotapes and videotapes purported to hone the mental game for sports aspirants who can't afford their own psychologists. The messages on some of these tapes are less than sophisticated. Mind Communications, Inc., for example, puts out subliminal affirmations on audiotape. Beneath the sound of waves or "pink sound," certain words or phrases are spoken just below the level of ordinary awareness. The tape for football contains these phrases: "I know my plays. I am important. I can do it. I love to run. I relax. I use weights for strength. I get off the ball first. I avoid sugar, coffee, alcohol, tobacco. I love contact. I set a goal. I love exercise. I have good hands. I can beat my man. Drive, drive, drive. I breathe deeply and evenly. I am a winner." No research has yet been conducted to see if these messages make better football players.

Dr. Richard M. Suinn at Colorado State University has come up with a more sophisticated method called viseo-motor behavior rehearsal (VMBR), which combines exercises in deep relaxation with vivid mental imaging of the skill to be learned. In one study of VMBR, researchers at North Texas State University divided thirty-two students in a beginning karate class into four groups. They assigned each group a different practice to do at home during a six-week period in which they would meet twice a week for karate lessons. At the start, they gave each student baseline anxiety and skills tests, then launched them on their various types of practice: (1) deep muscle relaxation only; (2) imaging only—closing their eyes and doing karate moves in their mind's eye; (3) VMBR—relaxation exercises followed by imaging; and (4) no home practice. All the groups received traditional karate instruction.

At the end of the six weeks, the researchers again tested the students for anxiety, and the karate school gave its customary skill tests in basic moves and sparring. The VMBR and relaxation-only groups recorded lower levels of anxiety than the others. In sparring, the VMBR group clearly outscored the other three.

This test and others along the same line show results that are statistically significant but not spectacular. For one thing, the time period of most of these studies is relatively short; for another, the people used in the experiments are mostly beginners. These limitations make such studies less compelling than the numerous anecdotal reports of master athletes.

For me, the most compelling evidence of the power of imaging comes from direct experience on the aikido mat. Our particular lineage of the art employs many metaphors and images to go along with the mechanics of movement, and it is from the unsubstantial realm of mind or spirit that the most powerful physical results flow. For example, one version of nikkyo (a wrist lock) involves being grabbed at the wrist by an attacker, then holding the attacker's hand on your wrist while bringing your hand around and over his wrist and pressing downward at a certain angle. When performed properly, this subtle manuever can bring a much larger and stronger attacker to his or her knees.

A purely mechanical application of nikkyo might work, but only through the application of considerable muscular force. There are certain imaging strategies, however, that increase its effectiveness to a degree that isn't just "statistically significant," but truly startling. I ask my students to bring their hand, fingers extended, over the attacker's wrist as usual, then not to think of the wrist at all but rather "create" long extensions of these fingers to go right through the attacker's face like laser beams and touch the base of the skull. From this point, they simple stroke gently downward on the attacker's spine with their imaged finger extensions. All other things being equal, the effectiveness of the technique depends on the vividness of the image. In my own aikido practice, the imaged technique seems considerably more effective than muscular force alone; sometimes, an attacker goes down like a shot with a startled look on his face while I am unaware of using any muscular force at all.

What Is Really Real?

How do we explain the discrepancy between the mechanical and the imaged application? Are the magically extended fingers mere figments of the imagination or are they in some way "real"? The easiest explanation derives from mechanics alone: Perhaps the image of extended fingers stroking down the attacker's spine simply provides guidance for bringing the aikidoist into the proper alignment for the application of nikkyo. It certainly does that. But many years of experience have convinced me that more than alignment is involved. My logical mind tells me I don't really have fingers three feet long that can penetrate through another person's body to his or her spine. Still, the truly effortless, seemingly miraculous applications of the technique occur only when the mental image is vividly clear and when I can somehow "feel" my fingers moving down the attacker's spine.

Which brings us to the question of what is really "real." Is consciousness a mere epiphenomenon, as behaviorist B. F. Skinner would have it? Or is the poet William Blake right in suggesting that mental things alone are real? Or, if mental constructs and the stuff of the objective world are both real, though occupying different classes of reality, then what is the nature of the interaction between the two classes? These are large questions for a short book—even for a long one. Still, it's possible to say rather briefly (and obviously) that thought, images, feelings, and the like are quite real and that they do have a great influence on the world of matter and energy. Indeed, it's possible to argue that pure information is more persistent than what we class as substantial—or perhaps that both are at essence the same thing. "More and more, the universe looks like a great thought rather than a great machine," says astronomer Sir James Jeans.

Solomon's temple, for example, no longer exists in the form of wood, stone, and gold; you can't find it anywhere. Yet it bursts into graphic, detailed existence in your mind's eye when you read First Kings 6 and 7 of the Bible. Neither Scarlett O'Hara nor Anna Karenina were ever made flesh, yet it might be the case that you know them better than your next-door neighbor. Your portable transistor radio is certainly real; you can feel it in your hands. But so is the wiring diagram for that radio, and so is that diagram as it evolved in the mind of the inventor. Which is *more* real? It's hard to say. While the underlying structure, the abstract relationship among the parts, is the same in all three forms, it can be argued that what is most abstract is most fundamental and often most persistent over time. The diagram or the mental picture will probably outlast the radio you hold in your hands. And these insubstantial forms have an additional advantage: if you want to make changes in the relationships of the parts, it's easier to do so in the diagram or the mind than in the three-dimensional radio.

What's the role of intentionality here? It's certainly involved in the creation of the structure-as-idea. It's also involved in the transformation of that structure from one of its forms to another. This sort of transformation, in fact, is what the process of mastery is all about. Sometimes I have my students hold the vision or the feeling of a certain throw in their mind, and then practice it over and over for an hour or more until they are drenched with sweat and wiped clean of their previous thoughts or feelings about the throw. This use of intentionality often produces favorable results in the palpable, three-dimensional world of the martial arts.

Thoughts, images, and feelings are indeed quite real. Einstein's thought that energy is equal to mass times the speed of light squared ($E = MC^2$) eventually unleashed awesome power. The transformation of that thought into heat and percussion was a long and arduous process. Still, the thought, the vision, the intentionality, was primary.

"All I know," said Arnold Schwarzenneger, "is that the first step is to create the vision, because when you see the vision there—the beautiful vision—that creates the 'want power.' For example, my wanting to be Mr. Universe came about because I saw myself so clearly, being up there on the stage and winning."

Intentionalty fuels the master's journey. Every master is a master of vision.

𝓩 Chapter 9

Key 5: The Edge

Now we come, as come we must in anything of real consequence, to a seeming contradiction, a paradox. Almost without exception, those we know as masters are dedicated to the fundamentals of their calling. They are zealots of practice, connoisseurs of the small, incremental step. At the same time—and here's the paradox—these people, these masters, are precisely the ones who are likely to challenge previous limits, to take risks for the sake of higher performance, and even to become obsessive at times in that pursuit. Clearly, for them the key is not either/or, it's both/and.

Chuck Yeager, the hero of Tom Wolfe's book *The Right Stuff,* is considered by many to be the best pilot who ever lived. Near the end of his autobiography, *Yeager,* he sums up what it means to be a great pilot, to have the "right stuff." In the first two pages of this summary, he cites "experience" three times. "If there is such a thing as the 'right stuff' in piloting," Yeager tells us, "then it is experience."

And yet, this proponent of the plateau, this traveler on the endless path, is also a man who speaks with wicked delight about "exploring the edges of the envelope." The night before he was scheduled to make a faster-than-sound flight for the first time in history, Yeager fell off a horse during a wild twilight ride and seriously sprained his shoulder. This injury would make it impossible for him to close the hatch on the X-1 rocket plane in the normal manner after he was loaded into it from the mother ship at 20,000 feet. Undaunted, he took along a broom handle so that he could close the door with his other hand—then went on to push through the sound barrier despite his injury.

The trick here is not only to test the edges of the envelope, but also to walk the fine line between endless, goalless practice and those alluring goals that appear along the way. At our dojo, we present aikido, first of all, as an endless path. But we also have periodic examinations that are rigorous, challenging, and sometimes quite dramatic. The exam for first-degree black belt is, in particular, a rite of passage. The candidate faces a three- to six-months-long period leading up to the exam, which becomes not only an intensive cram course in advanced techniques but also a physical and psychological trial by fire. During this ordeal, no personal flaw, no secret idiosyncracy, is likely to remain hidden. If all goes well, the exam itself becomes an expression not of ego but of essence, a climactic and transcendent moment in a long journey. But the journey is what counts. In the words of the ancient Eastern adage: "Before enlightenment, chop wood and carry water. After enlightenment, chop wood and carry water." The new black belt is expected to be on the mat the next day, ready to take the first fall.

Playing the edge is a balancing act. It demands the awareness to know when you're pushing yourself beyond safe limits. In this awareness, the man or woman on the path of mastery sometimes makes a conscious decision to do just that. We see this clearly in running, a sport so pure, so explicit that everything is likely to come quickly into full view. Running fast and hard almost always demands playing the edge, and it can't be denied that runners and would-be runners should be offered safe and sensible programs and warned against the dangers and pitfalls of their practice. Those who wish to run for specific, practical benefits—weight control, stress reduction, a healthy heart—must be given their due, but to limit the dialogue to such practical considerations is to demean the human spirit. Many people run not to lose weight but to loosen the chains of a mechanized culture, not to postpone death but to savor life. For those runners, the admonitions of critics who warn against the dangers of the sport are moot; they run quite consciously, as informed, consenting adults, to exceed their previous limits and to press the edges of the possible, whether this means completing their first circuit of a four-hundred-meter track without walking, or fighting for victory in a triathlon, as in an episode recounted in *American Medical News.*

> Few moments in sports history have so poignantly captured the agony of defeat as when twenty-three-year-old Julie Moss was leading the women's division of the twenty-six-mile marathon on Hawaii's Ironman Triathlon World Championship.
>
> With only one hundred yards left between her and the finish, Moss fell to her knees. She then rose, ran a few more yards, and collapsed again. As TV cameras rolled, she lost control of her bodily functions. She got up again, ran, fell, and then started crawling. Passed by the second-place runner, she crawled across the finish line, stretched out her arm, and passed out.
>
> Jim McKay of ABC Sports called it "heroic . . . one of the greatest moments in the history of televised sport." Gilbert Lang, M.D., an orthopedic surgeon at Roseville (California) Commu-

nity Hospital and a longtime endurance runner, calls it "stupid—very nearly fatal."

Both Lang and McKay are right: it was stupid and heroic. Surely no runner should be encouraged to go so near the edge of death. But what type of world would it be, how meager and pale, without such heroics? Perhaps there would be no human world at all, for there must have been countless times before the dawn of history when primitive hunters in pursuit of prey gave all of themselves in this way so that members of their bands, our distant ancestors, could live. People such as Julie Moss run for all of us, reaffirming our humanity, our very existence. And there is reason to believe that most of the people we know as masters share her stupid, heroic desire to use herself to the limit, to finish at all cost, to attain the unattainable.

But before you can even consider playing this edge, there must be many years of instruction, practice, surrender, and intentionality. And afterwards? More training, more time on the plateau: the never-ending path again.

PART THREE

TOOLS FOR MASTERY

Introduction

As the moment of departure draws near, it's time to get down to some specifics. How can you avoid backsliding? Where will you get the energy for your journey? What pitfalls will you encounter along the path? How can you apply mastery to the commonplace things of life? What should you pack for the journey?

Here are some travelers' tips, some parting gifts, and then—bon voyage!

Chapter 10

Why Resolutions Fail—and What to Do About It

You resolve to make a change for the better in your life. It could be any significant change, but let's say it involves getting on the path of mastery, developing a regular practice. You tell your friends about it. You put your resolution in writing. You actually make the change. It works. It feels good. You're happy about it. Your friends are happy about it. *Your life is better.* Then you backslide.

Why? Are you some kind of slob who has no willpower? Not necessarily. Backsliding is a universal experience. Every one of us resists significant change, no matter whether it's for the worse or for the better. Our body, brain, and behavior have a built-in tendency to stay the same within rather narrow limits, and to snap back when changed—and it's a very good thing they do.

Just think about it: if your body temperature

moved up or down by 10 percent, you'd be in big trouble. The same thing applies to your blood-sugar level and to any number of other functions of your body. This condition of equilibrium, this resistance to change, is called homeostasis. It characterizes all self-regulating systems, from a bacterium to a frog to a human individual to a family to an organization to an entire culture—and it applies to psychological states and behavior as well as to physical functioning.

The simplest example of homeostasis can be found in your home heating system. The thermostat on the wall senses the room temperature; when the temperature on a winter's day drops below the level you've set, the thermostat sends an electrical signal that turns the heater on. The heater completes the loop by sending heat to the room in which the thermostat is located. When the room temperature reaches the level you've set, the thermostat sends an electrical signal back to the heater, turning it off, thus maintaining homeostasis.

Keeping a room at the right temperature takes only one feedback loop. Keeping even the simplest single-celled organism alive and well takes thousands. And maintaining a human being in a state of homeostasis takes billions of interweaving electrochemical signals pulsing in the brain, rushing along nerve fibers, coursing through the bloodstream.

One example: each of us has about 150,000 tiny

thermostats in the form of nerve endings close to the surface of the skin that are sensitive to the loss of heat from our bodies, and another sixteen thousand or so a little deeper in the skin that alert us to the entry of heat from without. An even more sensitive thermostat resides in the hypothalamus at the base of the brain, close to branches of the main artery that brings blood from the heart to the head. This thermostat can pick up even the tiniest change of temperature in the blood. When you start getting cold, these thermostats signal the sweat glands, pores, and small blood vessels near the surface of the body to close down. Glandular activity and muscle tension cause you to shiver in order to produce more heat, and your senses send a very clear message to your brain, leading you to keep moving, to put on more clothes, to cuddle closer to someone, to seek shelter, or to build a fire.

Homeostasis in social groups brings additional feedback loops into play. Families stay stable by means of instruction, exhortation, punishment, privileges, gifts, favors, signs of approval and affection, and even by means of extremely subtle body language and facial expressions. Social groups larger than the family add various types of feedback systems. A national culture, for example, is held together by the legislative process, law enforcement, education, the popular arts, sports and games, economic rewards that favor certain types of activity, and by a complex web of mores, prestige markers, celebrity role modeling, and style that relies largely on the media as a national nervous system. Although we might think that our culture is mad for the new, the predominant function of all this—as with the feedback loops in your body—is the survival of things as they are.

The problem is, homeostasis works to keep things as they are even if they aren't very good. Let's say, for instance, that for the last twenty years—ever since high school, in fact—you've been almost entirely sedentary. Now most of your friends are working out, and you figure that if you can't beat the fitness revolution, you'll join it. Buying the tights and running shoes is fun, and so are the first few steps as you start jogging on the high school track near your house. Then, about a third of the way around the first lap, something terrible happens. Maybe you're suddenly sick to your stomach. Maybe you're dizzy. Maybe there's a strange, panicky feeling in your chest. Maybe you're going to die.

No, you're going to die. What's more, the particular sensations you're feeling probably aren't significant in themselves. What you're really getting is a homeostatic alarm signal—bells clanging, lights flashing. *Warning! Warning! Significant changes in res-*

piration, heart rate, metabolism. Whatever you're doing, stop doing it immediately.

Homeostasis, remember, doesn't distinguish between what you would call change for the better and change for the worse. It resists *all* change. After twenty years without exercise, your body regards a sedentary style of life as "normal"; the beginning of a change for the better is interpreted as a threat. So you walk slowly back to your car, figuring you'll look around for some other revolution to join.

Take another case, involving a family of five. The father happens to be an alcoholic who goes on a binge every six to eight weeks. During the time he's drinking, and for several days afterward, the family is in an uproar. It's nothing new. These periodic uproars have become, in fact, the normal state of things. Then, for one reason or another, the father stops drinking. You'd think that everyone in the family would be happy, and they are—for a while. But homeostasis has strange and sneaky ways of striking back. There's a pretty good chance that within a very few months some other family member (say, a teenage son) will do something (say, get caught dealing drugs) to create just the type of uproar the father's binges previously triggered. Without wise professional counsel, the members of this family won't realize that the son, unknowingly, has simply taken the father's place to keep the family system in the condition that has become stable and "normal."

No need here to count the ways that organizations and cultures resist change and backslide when change does occur. Just let it be said that the resistance here (as in other cases) is proportionate to the size and speed of the change, not to whether the change is a favorable or unfavorable one. If an organizational or cultural reform meets tremendous resistance, it is because it's either a tremendously bad idea or a tremendously good idea. Trivial change, bureaucratic meddling, is much easier to accept, and that's one reason why you see so much of it. In the same way, the talkier forms of psychotherapy are acceptable, at least to some degree, perhaps because they sometimes change nothing very much except the patient's ability to talk about his or her problems. But none of this is meant to condemn homeostasis. We want our minds and bodies and organizations to hold together. We want that paycheck to arrive on schedule. In order to survive, we need stability.

Still, change does occur. Individuals change. Families change. Organizations and entire cultures change. Homeostats are reset, even though the process might cause a certain amount of anxiety, pain, and upset. The questions are: How do you deal with homeostasis? How do you make change for the better easier? How do you make it last?

These questions rise to great importance when you embark on the path of mastery. Say that after years of hacking around in your career, you decide to approach it in terms of the principles of mastery. Your whole life obviously will change, and thus you'll have to deal with homeostasis. But even if you should begin applying mastery to pursuits such as gardening or tennis, which might seem less than central to your existence, the effects of the change might ripple out to touch almost everything you do. Realizing significantly more of your potential in almost anything can change you in many ways. And however much you enjoy and profit from the change, you'll probably meet with homeostasis sooner or later. You might experience homeostatic alarm signals in the form of physical or psychological symptoms. You might unknowingly sabotage your own best efforts. You might get resistance from family, friends, and co-workers. And you can consider yourself fortunate indeed if you don't find yourself on that old, familiar slide back to the ways of the Dabbler, or the Obsessive, or the Hacker.

Ultimately, you'll have to decide if you really do want to spend the time and effort it takes to get on and stay on the path. If you do, here are five guidelines that might help. While these guidelines are focused on mastery, they could also be applied to any change in your life.

1. Be aware of the way homeostasis works. This might be the most important guideline of all. Expect resistance and backlash. Realize that when the alarm bells start ringing, it doesn't necessarily mean you're sick or crazy or lazy or that you've made a bad decision in embarking on the journey of mastery. In fact, you might take these signals as an indication that your life is definitely changing—just what you've wanted. Of course, it might be that you *have* started something that's not right for you; only you can decide. But in any case, don't panic and give up at the first sign of trouble.

You might also expect resistance from friends and family and co-workers. (Homeostasis, as we've seen, applies to social systems as well as individuals.) Say you used to struggle out of bed at 7:30 and barely drag yourself to work at 9:00. Now that you're on a path of mastery, you're up at 6:00 for a three-mile run, and in the office, charged with energy, at 8:30. You might figure that your co-workers would be overjoyed, but don't be too sure. And when you get home, still raring to go, do you think that your family will welcome the change? Maybe. Bear in mind that an entire system has to change when any part of it changes. So don't be surprised if some of the people you love start covertly or overtly undermining your self-improvement. It's not that they wish you harm, it's just homeostasis at work.

2. Be willing to negotiate with your resistance to change. So what should you do when you run into resistance, when the red lights flash and the alarm bells ring? Well, you don't back off, and you don't bull your way through. Negotiation is the ticket to successful long-term change in everything from increasing your running speed to transforming your organization. The long-distance runner working for a faster time on a measured course negotiates with homeostasis by using pain not as an adversary but as the best possible guide to performance. The change-oriented manager keeps his or her eyes and ears open for signs of dissatisfaction or dislocation, then plays the edge of discontent, the inevitable escort of transformation.

The fine art of playing the edge in this case involves a willingness to take one step back for every two forward, sometimes vice versa. It also demands a determination to keep pushing, but not without awareness. Simply turning off your awareness to the warnings deprives you of guidance and risks damaging the system. Simply pushing your way through despite the warning signals increases the possibility of backsliding.

You can never be sure exactly where the resistance

will pop up. A feeling of anxiety? Psychosomatic complaints? A tendency toward self-sabotage? Squabbles with family, friends, or fellow workers? None of the above? Stay alert. Be prepared for serious negotiations.

3. Develop a support system. You can do it alone, but it helps a great deal to have other people with whom you can share the joys and perils of the change you're making. The best support system would involve people who have gone through or are going through a similar process, people who can tell their own stories of change and listen to yours, people who will brace you up when you start to backslide and encourage you when you don't. The path of mastery, fortunately, almost always fosters social groupings. In his seminal book *Homo Ludens: A Study of the Play Element in Culture,* Johan Huizinga comments upon the tendency of sports and games to bring people together. The play community, he points out, is likely to continue even after the game is over, inspired by "the feeling of being 'apart together' in an exceptional situation, of sharing something important, of mutually withdrawing from the rest of the world and rejecting the usual norms." The same can be said about many other pursuits, whether or not they are formally known as sports—arts and crafts, hunting, fishing, yoga, Zen, the professions, "the office."

And what if your quest for mastery is a lonely one? What if you can find no fellow voyagers on that particular path? At the least, you can let the people close to you know what you're doing, and ask for their support.

4. Follow a regular practice. People embarking on any type of change can gain stability and comfort through practicing some worthwhile activity on a more or less regular basis, not so much for the sake of achieving an external goal as simply for its own sake. A traveler on the path of mastery is again fortunate, for practice in this sense (as I've said more than once) is the foundation of the path itself. The circumstances are particularly happy in case you've already established a regular practice in something else before facing the challenge and change of beginning a new one. It's easier to start applying the principles of mastery to your profession or your primary relationship if you've already established a regular morning exercise program. Practice is a habit, and any regular practice provides a sort of underlying homeostasis, a stable base during the instability of change.

5. Dedicate yourself to lifelong learning. We tend to forget that learning is much more than book learning. To learn is to change. Education, whether it involves books, body, or behavior, is a process that changes the learner. It doesn't have to end at college graduation or at age forty or sixty or eighty, and the best learning of all involves learning how to learn—that is, to change. The lifelong learner is essentially one who has learned to deal with homeostasis, simply because he or she is doing it all the time. The Dabbler, Obsessive, and Hacker are all learners in their own fashion, but lifelong learning is the special province of those who travel the path of mastery, the path that never ends.

Chapter 11

Getting Energy for Mastery

If you think you simply don't have the time or the energy to dedicate yourself to mastery, consider the old adage that if you want to get something done, ask a busy person to do it. Most of us know at least one of those prodigies of energy who get far more than their share of the world's work and play accomplished. When we stop to think about it, in fact, almost all of us can bring to mind periods when we, too, were bursting with energy; when no mountain seemed too high for us; when the boundaries between work and play blurred and finally disappeared. Remember when you could barely keep your eyes open in class, yet were totally awake and alert during hours of tough after-school sports practice? And how about that rush of energy at the beginning of a love affair, or during a challenging job situation, or at the approach of danger?

A human being is the kind of machine that wears out from *lack* of use. There are limits, of course, and we do need healthful rest and relaxation, but for the most part we gain energy by using energy. Often the best remedy for physical weariness is thirty minutes of aerobic exercise. In the same way, mental and spiritual lassitude is often cured by decisive action or the clear intention to act. We learn in high school physics that kinetic energy is measured in terms of motion. The same thing is true of human energy: it comes into existence through use. You can't hoard it. As Frederich S. (Fritz) Perls, founder of Gestalt therapy, used to say, "I don't want to be saved, I want to be *spent.*" It might well be that all of us possess enormous stores of potential energy, more than we could ever hope to use.

If this is so, then why do we so often feel drained, unable to drag ourselves to the simplest task? Why do we leave those letters unanswered, that leaky faucet unrepaired? Why do we resist our own most constructive and creative impulses and squander our best energy on busywork? Why do we sit for hours in the babbling bath of television while life's abundant opportunities drift past unseen?

It starts in earliest childhood. Watch an unfettered eighteen-month-old for a couple of hours. This miniature prodigy of energy has an important job (call it raw, unadulterated learning), and he ruthlessly exploits everything in his environment, that he can see, hear, taste, smell, and feel to get that job done. Some restraints must be imposed, but we tend to impose far more than safety requires. After all, we adults have already forfeited much of our energy and are easily exhausted. So we might say, "Why can't you be still?" or "I can't stand that yammering for one more second." We might try angry commands, physical restraint, or—God help us—physical punishment. More likely, we'll put the learning process on hold by parking the learner in front of the television set, no matter what's on. There! That's better! Now the kid's as lethargic as we are.

In school the child gets even worse news: learning is dull. There's only one right answer to every question, and you'd better learn that answer by sitting still and listening passively, not *doing* anything. The conventional classroom setup, with twenty to thirty-five kids forced to do the same thing at the same time, makes individual initiative and exploration nearly impossible. There's certainly little space for the playful exuberance that accompanies high energy. Six-year-old Johnny wants to sing a song to the class. "Not now, Johnny. We have work to do." Or worse: "Don't be *silly,* Johnny." That teacher's voice still resonates in forty-year-old Johnny's subconscious whenever he's tempted to be spontaneous.

With   maddening   inefficiency,   conventional

schooling finally manages to teach reading and writing and figuring and a smattering of facts, but the operative words are too often *don't, no,* and *wrong.* The fundamental learning is negative. "It is in fact nothing short of a miracle," Albert Einstein wrote, "that the modern methods of instruction have not yet entirely strangled the holy curiosity of inquiry. . . . It is a very grave mistake to think that the enjoyment of seeing and searching can be promoted by means of coercion and sense of duty."

But it isn't just school. Peer groups at every stage of life exert a leveling influence. Conformity is valued. High energy is feared as a threat to conformity. And, of course, it often is. There's something frightening about the unbridled release of human energy. The psychopath, for example, is one who has failed to internalize society's restraints. Sometimes possessing unusual charm and persuasiveness, always lacking conscience and remorse, he is able to direct seemingly superhuman amounts of energy to his goals, which tend to the short-term and self-serving.

This dark energy both dismays and fascinates us. We find ourselves strangely attracted to the man in the black hat, to villains and rogues of all types, precisely because they so blatantly express what we won't even acknowledge in ourselves. And look at the daily news, at the rapacious preachers, the phony gurus, the larcenous financiers, the organizers of shadowy armies and arms deals—all of them short on scruples and long on passionate intensity. We have reason to be wary of the driven personality, the zealot. No wonder society wants to "socialize" us, to squash our energy.

That's the downside, but there's also that legion of thoughtful and responsible people who have somehow retained their native energy and know how to put it to work for their benefit and ours. The energy they manifest is to a large extent available to all of us. If we could tap as little as an added 10 percent of this vast resource, our lives would be significantly altered. Here's how to get started:

1. Maintain physical fitness. We all know physically fit people who sit around shuffling papers all day. And we also know those energy demons who still maintain that when the urge to exercise comes over them, they simply lie down until it passes. But, all things being equal, physical fitness contributes enormously to energy in every aspect of our lives. We might also suspect that, all things again being equal, those people who feel good about themselves, who are in touch with nature and their own bodies, are more likely to use their energy for the good of this planet and its people than those who live sedentary, unhealthy lives.

2. Acknowledge the negative and accentuate the positive. The power of positive thinking informs everything from pop-preacher Norman Vincent Peale's book of the same name to Skinnerian psychology to the newest management-training seminars. Optimism gets regularly trashed by intellectuals as well as by self-proclaimed ''tough-minded'' journalists and commentators, but numerous studies show that people with a positive outlook on life suffer far less sickness than those who see the world in negative terms.

They also have more energy.

Tom Peters, author of *In Search of Excellence,* and perhaps the nation's top management consultant, speaks of ''an almost spooky similarity of language'' among the managers of America's most successful companies. To a man and a woman, they stress the value of a positive attitude and the effectiveness of praise and other forms of positive feedback. ''The most successful managers,'' Peters told me, ''are those who are unwilling to tolerate the negative stuff.'' Peters cites one study's findings that very successful people had had ''an obnoxiously high level of praise piled on them in childhood—praise to the point of embarrassment. It seems you can hardly overdo it.''

Is it possible to be *too* positive? Only if you deny the existence of negative factors, of situations in your life and in the world at large that need correcting.

Some Eastern philosophies as well as certain Western religions and quasi-religions do just that. Their insistence that evils and ills are nothing more than illusion comforts the converted but often leads to a harmful denial of personal reality and a callousness toward the injustices in the world. Generally, denial inhibits energy, while realistic acknowledgment of the truth releases it.

Even serious blows in life can give you extra energy by knocking you off dead center, shaking you out of your lethargy—*but not if you deny the blows are real.* Acknowledging the negative doesn't mean sniveling; it means facing the truth and then moving on. Simply describing what's wrong with your life to a good friend is likely to make you feel better and more energetic.

Once you've dealt with the negative, you're free to concentrate on the best in yourself. Whenever possible, avoid teachers and supervisors who are highly critical in a negative sense. Telling people what they're doing wrong while ignoring what they're doing right reduces their energy. When it's your turn to teach or supervise or give advice, you might try the following approach: "Here's what I like about what you're doing, and here's how you might improve it."

3. Try telling the truth. "There's nothing more energizing to a corporation than for people to start telling one another truth," says Dr. Will Schutz, who popularized truth-telling encounter groups in the 1960s and is now a corporate consultant. "One of the first results we got after our sessions with corporate executives was that their meetings were shorter than before. One company reported that hour-and-a-half meetings now take twenty minutes. 'We just say what we want to say. We don't have to spend a lot of time and energy *not* saying something.' Lies and secrets are poison in organizations—people's energy is devoted to deceiving and hiding and remembering who it is you don't want to tell what to. When people start telling the truth, you see almost immediate reductions in mistakes and increases in productivity."

Truth-telling works best when it involves revealing your own feelings, not when used to insult others and to get your own way. All in all, it has a lot going for it—risk, challenge, excitement, and the release of all of that energy.

4. Honor but don't indulge your own dark side. God knows how much energy we have locked up in the submerged part of our personality, in what Carl Jung calls the shadow. Poet and storyteller Robert Bly gives a modern setting to Jung's ideas in his book *A Little Book on the Human Shadow.* The young child, Bly tells us, can be visualized as a lively ball of energy that radiates in all directions. But the parents don't like certain parts of the ball. In order to keep the parents' love, the child puts the parts of him that they don't like in an invisible bag that he drags behind him. "By the time we go to school," Bly writes, "the bag is quite large. Then our teachers have their say: 'Good children don't get angry over such little things.' So we take our anger and put it in the bag." By age twenty, he maintains, only a thin slice of our original energy is left.

But the energy we've hidden away can still be available to us. And putting those forbidden parts of our personality to work doesn't involve indulging ourselves and literally acting out the submerged part. Anger, for instance, contains a great deal of energy. If we've repressed that emotion so effectively that we can't even feel it, we obviously can't use the energy that goes along with it in any conscious, constructive way. But if we take our anger out of the bag simply to indulge it, if we let anger become a knee-jerk response, we dissipate its considerable power. There are times when it's appropriate to express anger, but there's also the possibility of taking the fervid energy of indignation, even of rage, and putting it to work for positive purposes. In other words, when you feel your anger rising, you can choose to go and work furiously on a favorite project, or to transmute the energy beneath your anger to fuel that you can use on your journey of mastery.

We'll enjoy a much more energetic world when society stops forcing us to put so much of ourselves into that invisible bag. Until then, we can note that the prodigies of energy whom we admire are precisely those people who know how to utilize the blazing energy that flows from that which has been called dark.

5. *Set your priorities.* Before you can use your potential energy, you have to decide what you're going to do with it. And in making any choice, you face a monstrous fact: to move in one direction, you must forgo all others. To choose one goal is to forsake a very large number of other possible goals. A friend of mine, twenty-nine and still looking for a cause, a purpose in life, said, "Our generation has been raised on the idea of keeping your options open. But if you keep all your options open, you can't do a damned thing." It's a problem: How can any one option, any one goal, match up to the possibilities contained in all others?

This troubling equation applies to everything from lifetime goals to what you're going to do in the next ten minutes. Should you clean out that messy closet or start reading that new book or write that letter? An affluent, consumer-oriented way of life multiplies the choices that face you. Television makes it even more complicated. By offering endless possibilities, it tempts you to choose none, to sit staring in endless wonder, to become comatose. Indecision leads to inaction, which leads to low energy, depression, despair.

Ultimately, liberation comes through the acceptance of limits. You can't do everything, but you can do one thing, and then another and another. In terms of energy, it's better to make a wrong choice than none at all. You might begin by listing your priorities—for the day, for the week, for the month, for a lifetime. Start modestly. List everything you want to do today or tomorrow. Set priorities by dividing the items into A, B, and C categories. At the least, accomplish the A items. Try the same thing with long-term goals. Priorities do shift, and you can change them at any time, but simply getting them down in black and white adds clarity to your life, and clarity creates energy.

6. *Make commitments. Take action.* The journey of mastery is ultimately goalless; you take the journey for the sake of the journey itself. But, as I've pointed out, there are interim goals along the way, the first of which is simply starting the journey. And there's nothing quite so immediately energizing on any journey as the intermediate goal of a tough, firm

deadline—as is well known to anyone who has faced an opening-night curtain, a business-deal closing date, or a definite press time for an article or book. At our aikido school, a notice is placed on the bulletin board four times a year asking qualified students to sign up for ranking exams. Some students sign immediately, while others wait until a few days before the exam. It's instructive to watch the immediate surge of clarity and energy during training that comes from the simplest act of writing one's name on a notice. Those who sign late suffer from having less time in which to enjoy the energy that flows from commitment.

The gift of an externally imposed deadline isn't always available. Sometimes you need to set your own. But you have to take it seriously. One way to do this is to make it public. Tell people who are important in your life. The firmer the deadline, the harder it is to break, and the more energy it confers. Above all else, move and keep moving. Don't go off half cocked. Take time for wise planning, but don't take forever. "Whatever you can do, or dream you can— begin it," Goethe wrote. "Boldness has genius, power, and magic in it."

7. *Get on the path of mastery and stay on it.* Over the long haul, there's nothing like the path of mastery to lead you to an energetic life. A regular practice not only elicits energy but tames it. Without the

firm underpinnings of a practice, deadlines can produce violent swings between frantic activity and collapse. On the master's journey, you can learn to put things in perspective, to keep the flow of energy going during low moments as well as high. You also learn that you can't hoard energy; you can't build it up by not using it. Adequate rest is, of course, a part of the master's journey, but, unaccompanied by positive action, rest may only depress you.

It might well be, in fact, that much of the world's depression and discontent, and perhaps even a good share of the pervasive malaise that leads to crime and war, can ultimately be traced to our unused energy, our untapped potential. People whose energy is flowing don't need to take a drug, commit a crime, or go to war in order to feel fully awake and alive. There's enough constructive, creative work for everybody, with plenty left over. All of us can increase our energy, starting now.

Chapter 12

Pitfalls Along the Path

It's easy to get on the path of mastery. The real challenge lies in staying on it. The most dedicated traveler will find pitfalls as well as rewards along the way. You probably can't avoid them all, but it helps to know they're there. Here are thirteen you might run into on your journey.

1. Conflicting way of life. The path of mastery doesn't exist in a vacuum. It wends its way through a landscape of other obligations, pleasures, relationships. The traveler whose main path of mastery coincides with career and livelihood is fortunate; others must find space and time outside regular working hours for a preferred practice that brings mastery but not a living wage. The trick here is to be realistic: will you actually be able to balance job and path? But don't despair, we all possess great stores of unused energy (see Chapter Eleven). And as for time, how about those seven hours a day (the national average) spent watching television. There's also the matter of family and friends. Do you have their support for what you're doing? Especially, do you have your spouse's support? "Never marry a person," psychologist Nathaniel Brandon tells his clients, "who is not a friend of your excitement." The point is, when things aren't going well on your path of mastery, don't forget to check out the rest of your life. Then consider the possibility that the rest of your life can be lived in terms of mastery principles.

2. Obsessive goal orientation. As pointed out numerous times in this book, the desire of most people today for quick, sure, and highly visible results is perhaps the deadliest enemy of mastery. It's fine to have ambitious goals, but the best way of reaching them is to cultivate modest expectations at every step along the way. When you're climbing a mountain, in other words, be aware that the peak is ahead, but don't keep looking up at it. Keep your eyes on the path. And when you reach the top of the mountain, as the Zen saying goes, keep on climbing.

3. Poor instruction. You've already read about the importance of good instruction and how to recognize bad instruction (see Chapter Five). To repeat a couple of points: surrender to your teacher, but only as a teacher, not as a guru. Don't bounce from one teacher to another, but don't stick with a situation that's not working, just out of inertia. And remember: the ultimate responsibility for your getting good instruction lies not with your teacher but with you.

4. Lack of competitiveness. Competition provides spice in life as well as in sports; it's only when the spice becomes the entire diet that the player gets sick. Competition can provide motivation. It can also help hold games and other enterprises together; to compete with someone, you have to agree to run on the same track. Take competition as an opportunity to hone your hard-won skills to a fine edge. Failing to play wholeheartedly with a will to win degrades the game and insults the opponent. Winning is an essential element in the journey, but it isn't the only thing. Winning graciously and losing with equal grace are the marks of a master.

5. Overcompetitiveness. The would-be master who thinks about nothing but winning is sure to lose in the long run. The statement "Winning isn't everything, it's the only thing" is one of the greatest of hoaxes. Think about it: if winning is the *only* thing, then practice, discipline, conditioning, and character are *nothing.* It's said that winning is a habit—but so is losing. The "number one" criterion, with its attendant overcompetitiveness, creates far more losers than winners. Who knows how many potential Olympic medalists have turned away from sports because of youth-league coaches who preach that the purpose of life lies in beating the school on the other side of town, and that it doesn't matter how you play the game, just so you win.

6. Laziness. Laziness can be analyzed in psychiatric terms—such as resistance and dependence—but it might be more useful just to get right down to the word itself, which is defined as "Disinclined to action or exertion; averse to labor, indolent; idle; slothful." The bad news is that laziness will knock you off the path. The good news is that the path is the best possible cure for laziness. Courage.

7. Injuries. If your path is a physical one, and if you're like most of us, you'll probably encounter injuries somewhere along the way. Minor ones come with the territory. There are also serious injuries, which can take you off the path temporarily or even permanently. Except in heavy-contact sports, most of these serious injuries are probably avoidable. People get hurt because of obsessive goal orientation, because they get ahead of themselves, because they lose consciousness of what's going on in their own bodies, in the here and now. The best way of achieving a goal is to be fully present. Surpassing previous limits involves negotiating with your body, not ignoring or overriding its messages. Negotiation involves awareness. Avoiding serious injury is less a matter of being cautious than of being conscious. All of this is also true to some extent of mental and emotional as well as physical injuries.

8. Drugs. Drugs can give you the illusion of getting the immediate success this culture is always promising you. Travelers on the fast track can use drugs to experience climactic upward surges without spending any time on the plateau. At first, it might seem to work, but regular use leads inevitably to disaster. If you're on drugs, you're not on the path.

9. Prizes and medals. Excessive use of external motivation can slow and even stop your journey to mastery. Studies show that rewarding schoolchildren by giving them gold stars initially speeds up their learning, but their progress soon levels off, even if you increase the number of stars. When you stop giving stars, their progress falls to a level lower than that of matched groups of children who got no stars in the first place. A report on the physiological limits of running speed shows that the major factor stopping the improvement of a champion runner's speed is setting a record or winning an important medal. "The champions stop not at a given speed but when they set a record," authors Henry W. Ryder, Harry Jay Carr, and Paul Herget wrote in the June 1976 *Scientific American.* "Succeeding champions do the same. They telescope in their relatively short racing lives all the achievements of the great runners of the past and then stop with a gold medal just as their predecessors did. Since it is the medal and not the speed that stops them, the speeds they reach cannot be considered in any way the ultimate physiological limit." Perhaps we'll never know how far the path can go, how much a human being can truly achieve, until we realize that the ultimate reward is not a gold medal but the path itself.

10. Vanity. It's possible that one of the reasons you got on the path of mastery was to look good. But to learn something new of any significance, you have to be willing to look foolish. Even after years of practice, you still take pratfalls. When a Most Valuable Player candidate misjudges a ball and falls on his duff, he does it in the sight of millions. You should be willing to do it before your teacher and a few friends or fellow students. If you're always thinking about appearances, you can never attain the state of concentration that's necessary for effective learning and top performance.

11. Dead seriousness. Without laughter, the rough and rocky places on the path might be too painful to bear. Humor not only lightens your load, it also broadens your perspective. To be deadly serious is to suffer tunnel vision. To be able to laugh at yourself clears the vision. When choosing fellow voyagers, beware of grimness, self-importance, and the solemn eye.

12. Inconsistency. Consistency of practice is the mark of the master. Continuity of time and place (where this is feasible) can establish a rhythm that buoys you up, carries you along. There is even value in repeating favorite rituals before, during, and after practice. Psychologist Mihaly Csikszentmihalyi, who has studied a state of happy concentration called ''flow,'' points out that some surgeons wash their hands and put on their gowns in precisely the same way before each operation, thus stripping their minds of outside concerns and focusing their attention fully on the task at hand. Inconsistency not only loses you practice time, but makes everything more difficult when you do get around to practicing. But if you should happen to miss a few sessions, don't use that as an excuse to quit entirely. The path of mastery takes many twists and turns and calls for a certain flexibility of strategy and action. Consistency is of the essence, but a foolish consistency, as Ralph Waldo Emerson tells us, "is the hobgoblin of little minds."

13. Perfectionism. In a way, it's a pity that technology has brought so many masterful performances into our homes. "Twenty-four hours of world-class orchestras" is what the local classical music station promises me. And these performances are not only meticulously rehearsed, but recorded repeatedly, with the very best passages spliced together, and the entire recording electronically enhanced. Traveling exhibits bring the works of Van Gogh, Degas, Gauguin, and Manet to our local art museums. And on television we can watch top athletes, dancers, ice skaters, singers, actors, comics, and pundits, all giving us their best. Compared to this, how can we even talk about mastery? Then there are those of us who are simply self-critical. Even without comparing ourselves to the world's greatest, we set such high standards for ourselves that neither we nor anyone else could ever meet them—and nothing is more destructive to creativity than this. We fail to realize that mastery is not about perfection. It's about a process, a journey. The master is the one who stays on the path day after day, year after year. The master is the one who is willing to try, and fail, and try again, for as long as he or she lives.

Chapter 13

Mastering the Commonplace

Our preoccupation with goals, results, and the quick fix has separated us from our own experiences. To put it more starkly, it has robbed us of countless hours of the time of our lives. We awaken in the morning and hurry to get dressed. (Getting dressed doesn't count.) We hurry to eat breakfast so that we can leave for work. (Eating breakfast doesn't count.) We hurry to get to work. (Getting to work doesn't count.) Maybe work will be interesting and satisfying and we won't have to simply endure it while waiting for lunchtime to come. And maybe lunch will bring a warm, intimate meeting, with fascinating conversation. But maybe not.

In any case, there are all of those chores that most of us can't avoid: cleaning, straightening, raking leaves, shopping for groceries, driving the children to various activities, preparing food, washing dishes, washing the car, commuting, performing the routine, repetitive aspects of our jobs. This is the "in-between time," the stuff we have to take care of before getting on to the things that count. But if you stop to think about it, most of life is "in between." When goal orientation comes to dominate our thoughts, little that seems to really count is left. During the usual nonplayoff year, the actual playing time for a National Football League team is sixteen hours. For the players, does this mean that the other 8,744 hours of the year are "in between"? Does all time take its significance only in terms of the product, the bottom line? And if winning, as the saying goes, is the *only* thing, does that mean that even the climactic hours achieve their worth merely through victory?

There's another way of thinking about it. Zen practice is ostensibly organized around periods of sitting in meditation and chanting. Yet every Zen master will tell you that building a stone wall or washing dishes is essentially no different from formal meditation. The quality of a Zen student's practice is defined just as much by how he or she sweeps the courtyard as by how he or she sits in meditation. Could we apply this way of thinking to less esoteric situations? Could all of us reclaim the lost hours of our lives by making everything—the commonplace along with the extraordinary—a part of our practice?

Driving as High Art

Take driving, for instance. Say you need to drive ten miles to visit a friend. You might consider the trip itself as in-between time, something to get over with. Or you could take it as an opportunity for the practice of mastery. In that case, you would approach your car in a state of full awareness, conscious of the time of day, the temperature, the wind speed and direction, the angle of the sun, or the presence of rain, snow, or sleet. Let this awareness extend to your own mental, physical, and emotional condition. Take a moment to walk around the car and check its external condition, especially that of the tires. Make sure the windshield and windows are clean enough to provide good visibility. Check the oil and other fluid levels if it's time to do so.

Open the door and get in the driver's seat, performing the next series of actions as a ritual: fastening the seat belt, adjusting the seat and the rearview mirrors, checking the pressure on the brake pedal and the play of the steering wheel. Then, before starting the engine, relax and take a deep breath. Pay special attention to releasing any tension in your neck, shoulders, and abdomen. Lean back so that your back makes firm contact with the seat back, as if you're sinking *into* it. Become aware of the pressure of your buttocks and legs on the seat itself; feel yourself merging with the seat, becoming one with the entire car.

Start the engine and attend carefully to its sounds and vibrations. Check all of the gauges; make sure there's plenty of fuel. Bring to mind any problems you've been having with the car lately and consider how this might affect your trip. As you begin moving, make a silent affirmation that you'll take responsibility for the space all around your vehicle at all times—the back and sides as well as the front—and that, insofar as possible, you'll drive in such a way as to avoid an accident, no matter what other cars might do.

Taking this short trip will afford you many opportunities for practicing mastery. We tend to downgrade driving as a skill simply because it's so common. Actually, maneuvering a car through varying conditions of weather, traffic, and road surface calls for an extremely high level of perception, concentration, coordination, and judgment. In the 1960s, UCLA brain researchers measured the brainwave activity of astronaut candidates practicing a moon landing in a simulator and also driving on a Los Angeles freeway. As it turned out, driving on the freeway occasioned more brain activity.

These are a few of the particularly exquisite skills offered every driver: anticipating the possible moves of all the cars in your field of action; entering a curve at the correct speed and accelerating slightly during the turn; braking smoothly and with a feeling of continuity rather than rushing up behind another car and slamming on the brakes; engaging the clutch on a stick shift with perfect synchrony; changing lanes on a busy freeway without discomforting other drivers; dealing gracefully with the unexpected.

Driving can be high art, finely balanced between long periods of seeming routine and brief moments of terrifying challenge, with the possibility of injury or death always waiting around the next corner. These considerations lend added weight to the need for mastery in driving. But your practice of far humbler skills can also gain from an application of mastery principles.

Household Rhythm

Take dishwashing, for example. You can perform that chore in a hurried and haphazard way, with your main goal being to get it behind you as quickly as possible. Or you can do it as a meditation, a dance. If you choose this option, take a moment to compose yourself before beginning. Briefly balance and center yourself (see Chapter Fourteen). Decide on the general sequence of your work, then begin. Maintain full awareness of each of your movements. Even though your hands are most directly involved, pay attention to the rest of your body, especially the feet, abdomen, shoulders, and back. Imagine that all of your movements are emanating from your physical center of mass, a point about an inch below your navel. Go for efficiency, elegance, and grace in your motions; avoid hasty shortcuts. Rather than thinking about getting the job finished and going on to something else, stay wholly focused on the moment, on the task at hand. Above all, don't hurry. You might discover that by not hurrying you'll finish the dishes sooner than would ordinarily be the case. The odds are good that you'll feel better at the end.

Life is filled with opportunities for practicing the inexorable, unhurried rhythm of mastery, which focuses on process rather than product, yet which, paradoxically, often ends up creating more and better products in a shorter time than does the hurried, excessively goal-oriented rhythm that has become standard in our society. Making this rhythm habitual takes practice. The canister vacuum cleaner is a particularly fiendish teacher in the quest for mastery of the commonplace. The snakelike vacuum tube and long power cord seem specifically designed to snag on every available object in the room. The canister seems obstinately determined either to bump into or get hung up on every piece of furniture. The attachment connected to the vacuum tube invariably seems the wrong one for the next task at hand. The power cord reaches its limit and has to be replugged at the most inconvenient moments.

Those of you who have managed to avoid vacuuming don't know what you're missing: an onerous chore, yes, but also a fine opportunity—no less taxing than balancing your books or getting the footnotes straight on your dissertation or working out a kink in your golf swing—for practicing some of the skills you'll need on the path. The person who can vacuum an entire house without once losing his or her composure, staying balanced, centered, and focused on the process rather than pressing impatiently for completion, is a person who knows something about mastery.

The Challenge of Relationships

On the level of personal experience, all of life is seamless, despite society's untiring efforts to break it up into compartments. The way we walk, talk to our children, and make love bears a significant relationship to the way we ski, study for a profession, or do our jobs. It's truly bizarre, when you stop to think about it, that we are sometimes quite willing to give full attention to developing our tennis game while leaving such "commonplace" things as relationships largely to chance.

The truth of the matter is that if you have to work

at a sport to achieve mastery, you also have to work, and generally work even more diligently, to achieve mastery in relationships. In both, there will be ups and downs and long periods on the plateau. And you'll eventually discover, in every significant area of your life, that the most important learning and development takes place during your time on the plateau. The same principles apply here as elsewhere. Note in the following paragraphs, for example, how the five keys to mastery can be applied to relationships.

Instruction. Some people sneer at the notion of counseling for couples, or books and tapes about better relationships. It's true that some of the counseling is vapid, and the language in some of the books and tapes can make you gag, but an intimate relationship can become insular before either partner knows it, and it's hard to solve every problem alone. If you're on the path of mastery, whether in sports or relationships or anything else, you'll invariably seek the best guidance available, whether it's a counselor, a book, or a sympathetic, unbiased friend. But shop around, choose carefully, get recommendations.

Practice. The sportsperson is willing to devote several concentrated sessions a week to a sport. Couples on the path of mastery might do at least that much, setting aside specific times just for the relationship, apart from children, friends, work, and the usual entertainments. But practice, as we've seen, goes beyond that, involving a certain steadfastness, an ability to take pleasure in the endless repetition of ordinary acts.

Surrender. The ability to surrender to your art is a mark of the master, whether the art is martial or marital. Can you let go of an outworn behavior pattern without knowing exactly what will replace it? Are you willing at times to yield totally on some long-standing dispute for the sake of growth and change in your relationship? The tricky part is learning to lose your ego without losing your balance. The stronger you are the more you can give of yourself. The more you give of yourself, the stronger you can be.

Intentionality. To cultivate a positive attitude is to take a large step on the path of mastery in relationships. In addition, mental toughness (the ability to focus on a problem or a long-term goal) combined with openness and imagination (the ability to see options and visualize desired states) can be applied to relationships as well as to sports, or anything else.

The Edge. The path of mastery is built on unrelenting practice, but it's also a place of adventure. A couple on the path stays open to experience and is willing to play new games, dance new dances together. Perhaps the greatest adventure of all is intimacy: the willingness to strip away one layer of reticence after another, and on certain occasions to live entirely in the moment, revealing everything and expecting nothing in return.

The point of this chapter is that the principles of mastery can guide you, whatever skill you seek to develop, whatever path you choose to walk. In the words of Chinese Zen master Layman P'ang (c. 740–808 A.D.):

> *My daily affairs are quite ordinary;*
> *but I'm in total harmony with them.*
> *I don't hold on to anything, don't reject anything;*
> *nowhere an obstacle or conflict.*
> *Who cares about wealth and honor?*
> *Even the poorest thing shines.*
> *My miraculous power and spiritual activity:*
> *drawing water and carrying wood.*

Ultimately, nothing in this life is "commonplace," nothing is "in between." The threads that join your every act, your every thought, are infinite. All paths of mastery eventually merge.

Chapter 14

Packing for the Journey

Enough delay. It's time to get packed and get on the path. Maybe you're starting something new, a journey into an unfamiliar realm of mastery. Maybe you've decided to get on the path, at long last, in some old skill you've been dabbling in, obsessing over, or hacking at for months or years. Or maybe you've vowed to treat your entire life, to the best of your ability, as a process of mastery.

In any case, here's a checklist of what you'll be taking along from this guidebook, followed by a few parting gifts for your knapsack to make your journey more pleasant and to use on those inevitable occasions when the path seems steep and rocky and hard to bear. Start with the checklist. Take a look at these items as you put them in your traveling bag and refer back to them at any time during your trip.

Now for a few parting gifts. The following mind-body exercises are taken from Leonard Energy Training (LET), a discipline inspired by my practice of aikido. This work has been introduced, since 1973, to around 50,000 people, ranging from athletes to corporate executives to couples interested in improving their relationships. LET uses the body as a metaphor for the way you deal with the problems of daily life, and as a learning facility for changing the way you deal with those problems, whether the problems are physical, mental, or emotional. It can be especially useful for those embarked on the journey of mastery.

Balancing and centering. To be balanced means that the weight of your body is distributed evenly, right and left, forward and back, all the way from the head to the toes. To be centered means that bodily awareness is concentrated in the center of the abdomen rather than, say, the head or shoulders, and that movement is initiated from this center. The important point to bear in mind here is that to be psychologically balanced and centered depends to a great extent on being physically balanced and centered.

For most of us top-heavy, forward-pushing Westerners, something as simple as focusing our attention on the abdomen can sometimes bring extraordinary results. During a moment of crisis, for example, just touching yourself lightly at the physical center (a point in the abdomen an inch or two below the navel) can significantly alter your attitude and your ability to deal with whatever situation you face. Try this: stand normally and draw your attention to the top of your body by tapping yourself a couple of times on the forehead. Then have a partner push you from behind at the shoulder blades just hard enough to make you lose your balance and take a step forward. Next, stand exactly the same way and draw your attention to your center by tapping yourself a couple of times about an inch or two below the navel. Then have your partner push you exactly the same way with exactly the same force as before. Most people find they are more stable with their attention on their centers.

You'll need someone to read these instructions

while one or more people go through the full balancing and centering procedure. Read slowly and clearly, pausing for a while wherever there are ellipses.

"Please stand with your feet slightly farther apart than your shoulders, eyes open, knees not locked and not bent, trunk upright, arms relaxed by your sides. . . . Now take the fingers of your right hand and touch them to a spot an inch or two below your navel. Press in firmly toward the center of your abdomen. . . . Now drop your right hand to your side. . . . Breathe normally. Let the breath move downward through your body as if it were going directly to your center. Let your abdomen expand with the incoming breath, from the center outward to the front, to the rear, to the sides of the pelvis, and to the floor of the pelvis. . . .

"As your breathing continues in a relaxed manner, lift your arms in front of you, with the wrists entirely limp. Shake your hands so hard that your entire body vibrates. . . . Now lower your arms slowly to your sides. As soon as they touch your legs, let them start rising very slowly, directly in front of you, just as if you were standing up to your neck in warm salt water and as if your arms were floating up to the surface. As the arms rise, lower your body by bending the knees slightly. Let your hands hang loosely, palms down, just as they would if floating in salt water. Keep the trunk upright. When your arms reach the horizontal, put the palms forward into the position you would use if gently pushing a beach ball on the surface of the water—shoulders relaxed. Now sweep your arms from left to right and right to left as if you could sense or 'see' things around you through your open palms. . . .

"Shake out your hands and repeat the process. Lower your arms to your sides and let them float up again. As the arms rise, the body lowers slightly. Knees bent, trunk upright. Now put the palms forward and sweep your arms from side to side as if sensing the world through your palms. . . .

"All right. Drop your hands, and this time leave them hanging by your sides naturally, in a totally relaxed manner. . . . Close your eyes. Knees not locked and not bent. Now check to see if your weight is distributed evenly between your right and left foot. Shift your weight very slightly from side to side, fine-tuning your balance. . . . Now check to see that your weight is balanced evenly between the heels and balls of your feet. . . . Knees not locked and not bent. . . . Please leave your eyes closed and shift to a more comfortable position any time you wish. . . . Now move your head forward and backward to find the point at which it can be balanced upright on your spine with the least muscular effort. Be sensitive, as if you were fine-tuning a distant station on your radio. . . .

"Take a moment to relax your jaw . . . your tongue . . . the muscles around your eyes . . . your forehead, temples, scalp . . . the back of your neck. . . .

"Now, with a sharp inhalation of breath, raise and tighten your shoulders. . . . As you exhale, let your shoulders drop. They aren't slumping forward, but melting straight downward, like soft, warm chocolate. With each outgoing breath, let them melt a little farther. . . . Let that same melting sensation move down your arms, down to your hands. Feel your hands become heavy and warm. . . . Let the feeling of melting move down your shoulder blades . . . your rib cage, front, back, and sides . . . down to your diaphragm. . . . Let all of your internal organs rest, relax, soften. . . . And now the lower pelvic region; let that relax also. Release all tension. With each outgoing breath, let go a bit more. . . . Let the melting, relaxing sensation move down your legs to your feet. . . . Feel your feet warming the floor and the floor warming your feet. Sense the secure embrace of gravity that holds you to the earth and holds the earth to you. . . .

"Now consider the back half of your body. What if you could sense what is behind you? What would that be like? What if you had sensors, or 'eyes,' in the small of your back? . . . At the back of your neck?

. . . At the back of your knees? . . . At the back of your heels? . . . With your eyes closed, can you get the general *feel* of what is behind you? . . .

"Now send a beam of awareness throughout your entire body, seeking out any area that might be tense or rigid or numb. Just illuminate that area; focus on it. Sometimes awareness alone takes care of these problems. . . .

"Once more, concentrate on your breathing. . . . Be aware of the rhythm. . . . Now, in synchrony with an incoming breath, let your eyes open. Don't look at any one thing in particular. Just let the world come in. . . . With eyes soft and relaxed, walk around slowly, maintaining the relaxed and balanced state you've achieved. . . . Let your physical center be a center of awareness. . . . Ask yourself if things look and feel different to you after this exercise."

Once you've gone through the balancing and centering procedure a few times, you'll find that you can recreate it rather quickly—in as little as a few seconds, in fact. To repeat the most important point: the body can be considered a metaphor for everything else. Your relationships, your work, your chores, your entire life can be centered and balanced.

Returning to center. There will be moments on the path, no matter how skillful and well-balanced you might be, when you'll be knocked off center. But don't despair; you can practice for this eventuality. And if you stay aware, it's possible to return to the balanced and centered state at an even deeper level. Here are two ways to practice regaining your center.

1. Stand with eyes closed; balance and center yourself. Then, with knees bent, lean over from the waist. Let your arms hang down toward the floor. When you've become accustomed to this position, straighten up rather suddenly and immediately open your eyes. Fully experience your sense of disorientation; don't struggle forcibly to regain your composure. Rather than that, touch your center with one hand and settle down into a balanced and centered state. Be aware of what happens during the process. Does the condition of being centered and balanced seem somehow deeper and more powerful after having been momentarily lost?

2. Go through your balancing and centering procedure while standing with eyes open. Leaving the eyes open, spin several times to the left, then to the right—just enough to become slightly dizzy. Don't overdo it. Then stop spinning, touch your center, and return to the balanced and centered state with increased awareness of the soles of your feet. Again, be aware of what goes on during the process of regaining center.

Remember the feeling of these two exercises when

you're knocked off center either physically or psychologically.

Gaining energy from unexpected blows. No matter how well we plan it, life is bound to include sudden shocks—physical or psychological misfortunes that come when we least expect them. The unexpected blow can range from the loss of a favorite piece of jewelry to the loss of a loved one, from being fired to having your mate leave you. Sometimes we struggle blindly against such misfortunes, which only gives them additional power over our lives. Sometimes we steel ourselves and deny the pain and shock, which tends to block *all* of our feelings and makes it impossible to gain anything positive from the experience. Sometimes we waste our time by doing nothing but bemoaning our ill fortune. Here's a different approach, a way to gain energy from even a serious blow. You might call it taking the hit as a gift.

Have someone stand silently behind you. With eyes open, balance and center yourself. When you're ready, hold your arms out to the sides at forty-five degree angles. This is the signal for the person behind you to quietly walk up and grab one of your wrists with just enough impact to startle you; that is, to simulate an unexpected blow. Don't struggle against the grab or try to pretend you weren't upset. Instead, become fully aware of just how the grab affected you. Describe it aloud, as specifically as possible. (For example, "My heart seemed to jump up into my throat" or "My eyes blinked and something like an electric current seemed to shoot up my left arm.") As your partner continues to hold your wrist firmly, go on describing your sensations. Hold nothing back; it's important here and in the case of real blows to face your situation squarely, and to experience and acknowledge your feelings about it.

Once you've done this, lower your body by bending your knees slightly and return to a balanced and centered state, while your partner continues to hold your wrist. Consider the possibility that the wrist grab actually adds energy to your system, and that you can use that energy to deal with your current situation, maybe with plenty left over. Breathe deeply. Let the feeling of arousal and clarity, triggered by the release of adrenaline into your bloodstream, course freely through your entire being. Have your partner release your wrist. Walk around expansively. Consider the possibility that any sudden misfortune that befalls you during your journey can be converted to positive energy.

An introduction to ki. It's called ki in Japanese, ch'i in Chinese, pneuma in Greek, prana in Sanskrit, and, you might say, "the Force" in the Star Wars trilogy. In the ancient tradition, the word comes from the notion of breath, and is considered the fundamental energy of the universe that connects all things and undergirds all creative action. The Eastern martial arts share a common faith in this energy. By somehow controlling its flow in one's own body or projecting it toward external objects, the martial artist can supposedly achieve extraordinary powers. Legends abound of masters who can stop an opponent in his tracks from halfway across a room, or even throw him head over heels. Karate practitioners generally claim that ki, even more than muscular strength, makes it possible for them to break boards or concrete blocks.

Thus far, ki has proved difficult to measure, and skeptics tend to attribute its powers to suggestion, a sort of dynamic placebo effect. To the pragmatist, this distinction is unimportant. As a practitioner of aikido, an art in which ki plays an especially important role, I've generally found a strong correlation between my perception of personal ki and the effectiveness of my techniques (see Key Four: Intentionality, page 89). The idea of ki can offer the untrained person an effective way of gaining a sensation of increased power along with relaxation, especially during times of fatigue and stress, and thus is a useful item to pack for your journey.

Here's an exercise designed to demonstrate the power that can come from visualizing ki. Because the exercise involves rising from sitting to standing with a partner trying to hold you down, don't attempt it if you have any problems with your knees, back, or abdomen.

Sit in an armless, straight-backed chair with your hands on your knees. Try rising to a standing position several times, noting just how you do it. Now have your partner put his or her hands on your shoulders and push down. Using the same motions as before, try to rise with muscular force, pushing upward against the downward pressure of your partner's hands. Have your partner press down just hard enough to make it difficult for you to get up.

Have your partner remove his or her hands. Remaining seated, take a few moments to relax. Let go all the tension in your chest and shoulders. Feel your feet making a firm connection with the floor. Place the palm of your left hand on your abdomen and feel it expanding with each incoming breath. Put your left hand on your knee and continue breathing in the same way.

Now imagine a radiant ball of ki energy about the size of a grapefruit in the center of your abdomen. Imagine that it expands and contracts with each breath. Make this ball of ki the center of your attention. Have your partner push down on your shoulders again, with the same amount of pressure as before. This time don't pay any attention to the pressure. Assume the ball of ki will provide the power you'll need to stand. Keeping your attention on the ki in your abdomen, rise to a standing position using the same physical motions as before.

Notice the difference between the two experiences. Whether the ki is "real" or only a psychological aid is perhaps less important than the results you achieve. In any case, you didn't *create* the ki. According to the best thinking on this subject, the ki was already there. It's everywhere.

Relaxing for power. The word power springs from French and Latin roots meaning "to be able." At best, this ableness applies not to achieving dominance over other people but to realizing your own potential for mastery. Power, in any case, is closely allied with relaxation. Just as a tense muscle loses in strength, so a rigid, tense, and overbearing attitude eventually fails.

Start by standing and extending one arm to a horizontal position directly in front of you. Either arm will do, but let's say it's the right arm this time. The hand should be open with the fingers spread and the thumb pointing straight up. Have a partner stand at the right of your arm and bend it at the elbow by pressing up at your wrist and down at your elbow. Don't resist. Note that this exercise involves bending the arm at the elbow, not the shoulder.

Now that your partner has practiced bending your arm without any resistance on your part, you'll try two radically different ways of making your arm strong and resilient. After each of these, your partner will attempt to bend your arm at the elbow, adding force gradually. Your partner should not add so much force that a struggle ensues. Bear in mind that this isn't a contest but rather a comparison of two different ways of being powerful. The point is to see how much effort is required to keep the arm straight under pressure.

THE FIRST WAY: Hold your arm rigidly straight. Use your muscles to keep your arm from being bent. Have your partner gradually apply force in an attempt to bend your arm. It might bend or it might not. In either case, note how much effort you exerted in the process. Perhaps even more important, note how you feel about this experience.

THE SECOND WAY: Let your arm rise to the same horizontal position as before. This time, sense the aliveness of your arm and the energy flowing from your shoulder to your fingertips. Now visualize or feel your arm as part of a powerful laser beam that extends out past your fingertips, through any walls or other objects in front of you, across the horizon and to the ends of the universe. This beam is larger in diameter than your arm, and your arm is an integral part of it. Think of the beam as ki if you wish. Your arm is not rigid or tense. In fact, it's quite relaxed. But remember: being relaxed is *not* being limp. Your arm is full of life and energy. If anyone tried to bend your arm, the beam would become even more powerful and penetrating, and your arm, without effort, would also become more powerful.

Now have your partner gradually apply exactly the same amount of force as before in an attempt to bend your arm. Note how much effort you exerted in this case. How do you feel about the experience?

An overwhelming majority of people who have tried this exercise find the second way, the "energy arm," far more powerful and resilient than the first way, the "resistance arm." Electromyographic measurements of the electrical activity in the muscles indicate that this subjective judgement is correct. The energy arm might give a little but is far less likely to collapse than the resistance arm.

The implications for physical performance are obvious: relaxation is essential for the full expression of power. If we take the body as a metaphor for everything else in our lives, the implications are even more significant. Just think what kind of world it would be if we all realized that we could be powerful in everything we do without being tense and rigid.

These parting gifts, I hope, will be of use to you on your journey of mastery, as will the other information provided in this book. At this moment, however, I am struck by the insignificance of anything I or anyone else could give you compared with what you already have. You are the culmination of an extravagant evolutionary journey. Your DNA contains more information than all of the libraries in the world; information that goes back to the beginnings of life itself. In potentia, you are the most formidable all-around athlete who has ever roamed this planet. Many creatures possess more highly specialized sense organs, but no total sensorium is so well equipped and integrated as is yours. (The unaided human eye can detect a single quantum of light—the smallest amount possible—and discern more than ten million colors.) Your brain is the most complex entity in the known universe; its billions of twinkling neurons interact in ways so multitudinous and multifarious as to dwarf the capacity of any computer ever yet devised or even imagined. The best way to describe your total creative capacity is to say that for all practical purposes it is infinite.

Whatever your age, your upbringing, or your education, what you are made of is mostly unused potential. It is your evolutionary destiny to use what is unused, to learn and keep on learning for as long as you live. To choose this destiny, to walk the path of mastery, isn't always easy, but it is the ultimate human adventure. Destinations will appear in the distance, will be achieved and left behind, and still the path will continue. It will never end.

How to begin the journey? You need only to take the first step. When? There's always now.

Epilogue

The Master and the Fool

"I want you to tell me how I can be a learner."

It was not so much a query as a demand, almost a threat. He was a mountain man, with the long black hair, bold moustache and rough-hewn clothing of a nineteenth-century outlaw, one of a breed that lived illegally in the rugged hills of the Los Padres National Wilderness Area along the Big Sur coast of California—a place of buzzards and hawks, mountain lions and wild boar. Having just turned in the final proofs of a book on education (it was in the late 1960s), I had driven four hours south from San Francisco for a weekend of relaxation at Esalen Institute.

As I approached the lodge—a rustic building built at the edge of the Pacific on one of the few areas of flat land between the sea and the mountains of the Los Padres—I heard the sound of conga drums. Inside, the mountain man was sitting at one of the

169

drums, surrounded by eight other people, each also at a drum. He was apparently giving an informal lesson to whoever cared to participate. One of the drums was unoccupied. I pulled up to the unoccupied drum and joined the others, following the instruction as well as I could. When the session ended I started to walk away, but the mountain man came after me, grasped my shoulder, and fixed me with a significant look.

"Man," he said, "you are a *learner.*"

I stood there speechless. I'd never met this person, and he certainly had no idea I had just finished a book about learning. My conservative city garb had probably led him to think that I was a complete novice at the conga drum, the instrument of choice of the counterculture, and thus he must have been impressed by my seemingly rapid progress. Still, I was so pleased by his words that I didn't inform him I'd played before. He proceeded to tell me that he was a sculptor who worked metal with an acetylene torch, and that he was badly stuck and had been for a year; he was no longer a learner. Now he wanted me, a learner in his mind, to come up to his place in the Los Padres, look at his work, and tell him how *he* could be a learner. He was leaving right away and I could follow him in my car if I wished.

The invitation baffled me, but I realized it was a rare opportunity to visit the forbidden haunts of one of the legendary mountain men of Big Sur, so I immediately accepted. I followed his battered sedan up a steep and tortuous dirt road, then across a mountain meadow to a driveway that was nothing more than two tire tracks through a forest of live oak, madrone, and bay trees. For what seemed a long time, the car lurched and labored steeply upward, coming at last to a clearing near the top of the coast range. In the clearing stood several wooden structures: a two-room cabin, a tool shed, a crude studio for metal sculpture, and something that might have been a chicken or rabbit coop. At one point during my visit, I spotted a slim young woman with flowing blonde hair and a long dress standing like a ghost near the edge of the clearing. He never mentioned her.

The mountain man showed me into a sturdily built cabin with a large front window looking 4,000 feet down to the Pacific, now shining like a sheet of metal in the late afternoon sun. We sat and made disjointed conversation for a while. I found myself somewhat disoriented. But for the presence of several conga drums, we might have been sitting in an early nineteenth-century pioneer's cabin. It was all like a dream: the unlikely invitation, the rugged drive, the mysterious woman, the expansive gleam of the ocean through the trees.

When the mountain man announced that we would now go and look at his work so that I could tell him how to be a learner, I dumbly followed him out, having no idea of what I could possibly say that would be of any use to him. He walked me through his sculpture chronologically, showing me the point at which he had lost his creative spark, had stopped being a learner. When he finished, he fixed me with his eyes, and repeated his question one more time.

"Tell me. How can I be a learner?"

My mind went absolutely blank, and I heard myself saying, "It's simple. To be a learner, you've got to be willing to be a fool."

The mountain man nodded thoughtfully and said "thanks." There were a few more words, after which I got into my car and went back down the mountain.

Several years were to pass before I considered the possibility that my answer was anything more than a part of one of those slightly bizarre, easily forgotten sixties episodes. Still, the time did come when ideas from other places—all sorts of ideas—began to coalesce around my careless words of advice, and I began to see more than a casual relationship between learning and the willingness to be foolish, between the master and the fool. By fool, to be clear, I don't mean a stupid, unthinking person, but one with the spirit of the medieval fool, the court jester, the carefree fool in the tarot deck who bears the awesome number zero, signifying the fertile void from which all creation springs, the state of emptiness that allows new things to come into being.

The theme of emptiness as a precondition to significant learning shows up in the familiar tale of the wise man who comes to the Zen master, haughty in his great wisdom, asking how he can become even wiser. The master simply pours tea into the wise man's cup and keeps pouring until the cup runs over and spills all over the wise man, letting him know without words that if one's cup is already full there is no space in it for anything new. Then there is the question of why young people sometimes learn new things faster than old people; why my teenage daughters, for example, learned the new dances when I didn't. Was it just because they were willing to let themselves be foolish and I was not?

Or you might take the case of an eighteen-month-old infant learning to talk. Imagine the father leaning over the crib in which his baby son is engaging in what the behaviorist B. F. Skinner calls the free operant; that is, he's simply babbling various nonsense sounds. Out of this babble comes the syllable da. What happens? Father smiles broadly, jumps up and down with joy, and shouts, "Did you hear that? My son said 'daddy.'" Of course, he didn't say "daddy." Still, nothing is much more rewarding to an eighteen-month-old infant than to see an adult smiling broadly and jumping up and down. So, the behaviorists confirm our common sense by telling us that the probability of the infant uttering the syllable da has now increased slightly.

The father continues to be delighted by da, but after a while his enthusiasm begins to wane. Finally, the infant happens to say, not da, but dada. Once again, father goes slightly crazy with joy, thus increasing the probability that his son will repeat the sound dada. Through such reinforcements and approximations, the toddler finally learns to say daddy quite well. To do so, remember, he not only has been allowed but has been encouraged to babble, to make "mistakes," to engage in approximations—in short, to be a fool.

But what if this type of permission had not been granted? Let's rerun the same scene. There's father leaning over the crib of his eighteen-month-old son. Out of the infant's babble comes the syllable da. This time, father looks down sternly and says, "No, son, that is *wrong!* The correct pronunciation is *dad-dy.* Now repeat after me: *Dad-dy. Dad-dy. Dad-dy.*"

What would happen under these circumstances? If all of the adults around an infant responded in such a manner, it's quite possible he would never learn to talk. In any case, he would be afflicted with serious speech and psychological difficulties.

If this scenario should seem extreme, consider for a moment the learnings in life you've forfeited because your parents, your peers, your school, your society, have not allowed you to be playful, free, and foolish in the learning process. How many times have you failed to try something new out of fear of being thought silly? How often have you censored your spontaneity out of fear of being thought childish? Too bad. Psychologist Abraham Maslow discovered a childlike quality (he called it a "second naivete") in people who have met an unusually high degree of their potential. Ashleigh Montagu used the term neotany (from neonate, meaning newborn) to describe geniuses such as Mozart and Einstein. What we frown at as foolish in our friends, or ourselves, we're likely to smile at as merely eccentric in a world-renowned genius, never stopping to think that the freedom to be foolish might well be one of the keys to the genius's success—or even to something as basic as learning to talk.

When Jigoro Kano, the founder of judo, was quite old and close to death, the story goes, he called his students around him and told them he wanted to be buried in his white belt. What a touching story; how humble of the world's highest-ranking judoist in his last days to ask for the emblem of the beginner! But Kano's request, I eventually realized, was less humility than realism. At the moment of death, the ultimate transformation, we are all white belts. And if death makes beginners of us, so does life—again and again. In the master's secret mirror, even at the moment of highest renown and accomplishment, there is an image of the newest student in class, eager for knowledge, willing to play the fool.

And for all who walk the path of mastery, however far that journey has progressed, Kano's request becomes a lingering question, an ever-new challenge:

Are you willing to wear your white belt?

About the Author

George Leonard is the author of nine other books, including *Education and Ecstasy* and *The Ultimate Athlete,* as well as scores of magazine articles. He served as senior editor at *Look* magazine from 1953 to 1970, where he earned an unprecedented number of national awards for education, and is currently a contributing editor for *Esquire.* He holds a third-degree black belt in the martial art of aikido and is co-owner of an aikido school in Mill Valley, California, where he lives. He also lectures widely and has developed Leonard Energy Training, a practice inspired by aikido, which he has introduced to more than forty thousand people throughout the United States and the world.

THE IRON MARSHALL

THE
IRON MARSHALL

LOUIS L'AMOUR

BANTAM BOOKS

NEW YORK · TORONTO · LONDON · SYDNEY · AUCKLAND

THE IRON MARSHAL
Bantam paperback edition / June 1979
Louis L'Amour Hardcover Collection edition / January 1985

ISBN 0-553-06269-7

Published simultaneously in the United States and Canada

Bantam Books are published by Bantam Books, a division
of Bantam Doubleday Dell Publishing Group, Inc. Its trade-
mark, consisting of the words "Bantam Books" and the
portrayal of a rooster, is Registered in U.S. Patent and
Trademark Office and in other countries. Marca Registrada.
Bantam Books, 1540 Broadway, New York, New York 10036.

PRINTED IN THE UNITED STATES OF AMERICA

0   9   8   7   6   5   4   3

THE IRON MARSHALL

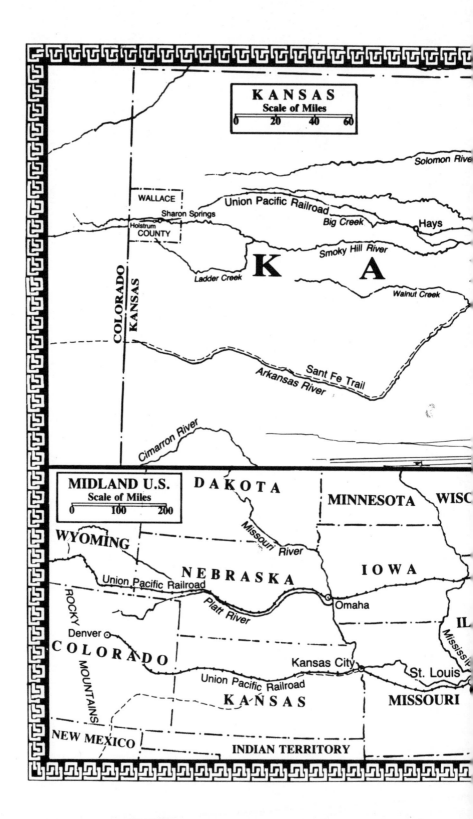

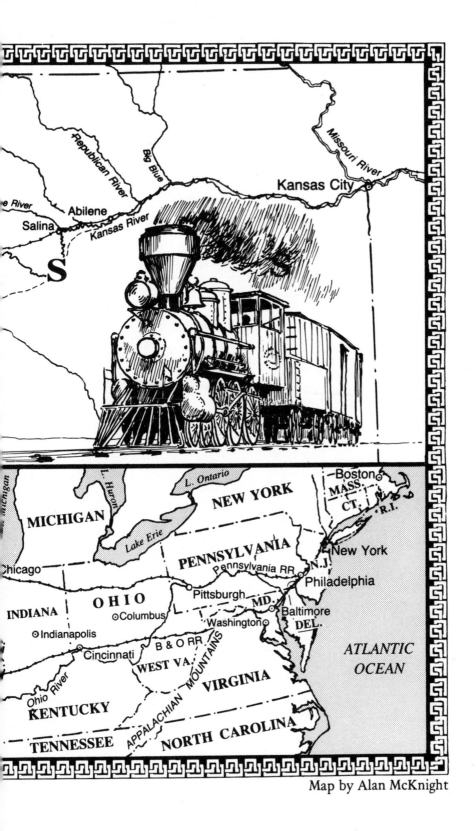

Map by Alan McKnight

ONE

A brutal kick in the ribs jolted him from a sound sleep and he lunged to his feet. The kicker, obviously a railroad detective, stepped back and drew a gun.

"Don't try it," he advised. "Just get off."

"Now? Are you crazy? At this speed I'd get killed."

"Tough. You either jump off or you get shot off."

Shanaghy looked at the gun. "Ah, what's the use? For two-bits I'd take that away from you and make you eat it, but I'll take the jump."

He turned and swung over the edge of the open gondola, hung for an instant to gauge the speed, then dropped from the ladder. He hit the ground knees bent and rolled head over heels down the embankment, coming to his feet in a cloud of dust to hear a fading shout.

". . . an' take your dirty duds with you!"

A bundle came flying from the train and hit the ground several hundred yards farther along. Then the train was past and he watched the caboose disappearing down the singing rails.

Shanaghy spat dust and swore at the disappearing train. "Ah, me lad!" he said bitterly. "There will come a time!"

1

He dug sand from his eyes and ears, muttering the while, and then he looked slowly around.

He stood on the bank beside the tracks in the midst of a vast and empty plain, nothing but grass, rippling in the wind. It reminded him of the sea when he crossed from Ireland.

He was thirsty, he was hungry, and he was mad all the way through. Moreover, he was bruised from the fall, adding to the bruises from what had gone before. He stared around again. At least, they would never find him here. He started to walk.

Suddenly he thought of the bundle thrown from the train. Dirty duds? He had no clothing but what he wore, and no possessions but the few things in his pocket. All else had been abandoned when he fled.

He had been on the dodge, unable to meet his friends for two days before he grabbed the freight train in the yards. He had not seen his enemies but he heard them coming. He was unarmed and the freight offered his only chance. He took the fast-moving train on the fly and once aboard he had fallen asleep. With daylight he awakened but, dead tired, he dropped off to sleep again while the train rumbled on its way. For most of two days and nights they had traveled, so now where was he?

He walked on until he came to the bundle. He paused, looking down at it as it lay among the weeds and brush near the foot of the slight embankment. A canvas haversack and a blanket-roll. He had never owned anything of the kind.

Shanaghy slid down the embankment and picked it up. Heavier than he expected. For a moment he considered leaving it but the blankets decided him. In a few hours darkness would be upon him and unless he was mistaken the nearest town was far, far away. Despite what the railroad bull had shouted, the blankets looked remarkably new and clean. Kneeling on the track he opened the haversack. The first thing he found was a slab of bacon wrapped in cheesecloth, then a small packet of coffee. "Some bindle-stiff's outfit," he told himself, then changed his mind. There was a packet of letters, a notebook with some loose papers tucked into it and a map.

In the compartment behind the letters was a carefully folded suit of black broadcloth, two clean shirts, a shirt-collar, cuff-links and a collar button. There was a suit of underwear, just off the shelf, a razor, soap, a shaving-brush, comb, pair of scissors and some face lotion.

What was more important, there was a .44 pistol and a box of ammunition. He checked the pistol. It was loaded.

Strapping up the bag, he slung the outfit over a shoulder and started on.

The hour was early, just after daylight. He plodded on, traveling, he presumed, at a rate of about two-and-a-half miles an hour. He walked beside the track to avoid the nuisance of trying to walk the irregularly spaced ties.

He saw many rabbits, a snake, and several buzzards. There was nothing else. Not a tree, not an animal, not even a large rock. Not until the middle of the afternoon when he had walked nearly twenty miles did the country begin to change. Twice the railroad crossed ravines on trestles, and finally he came to a shallow wash that seemed to rapidly narrow until it turned a bluff. He went down the embankment and followed the wash around the bluff to where it opened into a tiny basin where there were a few willows, a cottonwood or two.

On a flat place under the trees there was grass, a circle of stones for a fireplace, already blackened by use, and much broken wood. After gathering sticks and bark he got a fire started. Then he cut slices from the slab of bacon and broiled them on a stick over the fire.

He cooked and ate as he cooked, looking around. It was a snug, comfortable place. For the moment he had food, the water was good to drink and he could rest and relax. He had no idea where he was except that he was west of New York. He had never seen a map of the United States, and since arriving from Ireland when he was eleven he had never been further west than Philadelphia. He knew New York, and he had spent at least two weeks in Boston.

They would never find him here, but they'd be looking. Well, so let them look.

Nobody had ever said Tom Shanaghy was a nice man. From boyhood he had been a tough, iron-fisted bruiser, starting at six when he had helped his father in their blacksmith shop, shoeing horses, mending carts, sharpening plow-blades or whatever needed it.

His father, accepting a cash payment for joining up, had become a farrier . . . a horse-shoer . . . for the army and had gone out to British India. According to reports, he was killed there. Tom and his mother had emigrated to America, but she died on the way over and Tom Shanaghy landed in New York alone, without friends and without money.

He had walked off the boat into trouble. A boy about his own age, standing with a group of boys, called him "a dirty Mick," and Shanaghy replied the only way he knew. He went in swinging. His first swing dropped the boy who had yelled at him, his second swing dropped a companion, and then they were all over him.

He was alone and there were seven or eight of them. He slugged, kicked, bit and gouged, fighting with all he had because he was alone. Then suddenly another boy was beside him, a boy he had seen on the ship but had not known.

They were getting the worst of it when he heard a harsh voice. "Stop it, damn y'! Let the lads up!"

The boys who had started the fight scrambled to their feet, took one look and fled.

He was a big, burly man, almost six feet but strongly made. He wore a handlebar mustache and his nose had been broken. His knuckles were scarred with old cuts.

He took the cigar from his teeth. "What's y' name, bye?"

"Shanaghy, sir. Tom Shanaghy."

"Well, you're a fighter. A good fighter. Y' can take 'em as well as hand 'em out." The man turned sharply and looked at the other boy. "And who are you, m' lad?"

"Pendleton, sir. Richard Pendleton."

"Aye. Well, you've a way with your fists, too, and you're a friend of Shanaghy's?"

"Not exactly, sir. We came over on the same vessel, but did not meet until now. He was in a bad fight, sir, and it seemed only fair that I should have a part of it. I do not like seeing such an unequal fight."

"Nor I . . . unless it's on my side they are. You're a strong lad. But you two be off wi' you now. It's not a good place for you."

Shanaghy wiped the blood from a cut over his eye. "Sir? It's an important man y' are, as anybody with half an eye can see. Have y' no friends that might need a strong lad? It's alone I am, for my good mother died on shipboard."

The big man took the cigar from his teeth, his eyes glinting with a cynical humor. "Ah? A smart lad, an' not above a bit o' the blarney." From a pocket he took a slip of paper, and on it wrote a few words. "Here's a street an' the number. You'll be askin' for a man name of Clancy. Tell him Morrissey sent you."

"And my friend as well?"

Morrissey started to speak but Richard Pendleton interrupted. "No, thank you. No need to speak for me. I've a place to go and people who will be meeting me. Thank you."

Morrissey walked away and the two boys looked at each other. Shanaghy was strongly built with black hair and blue eyes, a sprinkling of freckles over his nose. Pendleton was wiry and had light brown hair, somewhat the taller.

"Thanks," Shanaghy said. "You're a fine fighter and you saved me a beating."

"It was Mr. Morrissey saved us both. Did you notice? They are afraid of him. He had only to speak, and they ran."

"He's a big man."

"I think he's more than that. I think he is John Morrissey, the prizefighter and gambling man."

"Never heard of him."

"My father told me of him, among others. He is . . . or was . . . the heavyweight champion at bare-knuckle fighting."

The boys had then shaken hands and parted, Shanaghy to seek his job.

It was a restaurant and saloon. There were a dozen men in the place and he asked for Clancy. "Yonder, by the door. But speak softly, he's in a foul mood."

He crossed the room to Clancy and stopped before him. "I'm Tom Shanaghy. I've come for a job."

"You've come for a job? Beat it, boy! I've no jobs and no time for ragamuffins in off the street."

"Mr. Morrissey gave me this. It is for you." Shanaghy handed him the note, and as he glanced at it the tall, thin man beside him looked over his shoulder.

"You know Morrissey?"

"I do."

"Clancy, don't argue with the lad. That's Old Smoke's fist . . . No other could write like him. You've no choice."

"All right," Clancy said irritably. "Make yourself useful." Abruptly, he walked away.

The tall man smiled. "It's all right, boy. Clancy doesn't like being told what to do, and least of all by Old Smoke. However, he'll stand by it. You've a job, then." As an afterthought, he added, "I'm his partner here . . . Henry Lochlin. You get into the kitchen and help with the dishes, clean up around. There'll be plenty to do, and don't worry about Clancy. He isn't as mean as he sounds."

That was the way of it. He washed dishes, swept floors, peeled potatoes and ran errands.

A week later Henry Lochlin stopped beside him. "You're a good lad and you're doing well. You've worked before this, I take it?"

"Aye . . . My father was a farrier, sir. We shod the horses of all the gentry, and I raced some of them."

Lochlin looked at him again. "You've ridden races?"

"Aye, on the dirt and on the turf, steeplechase as well. I rode first when I was nine, sir. That is, my first race was then. I've been up eleven times, sir."

"Good stock, those Irish horses."

"The best, sir. The very best."

"Did you win at all?"

"Three times, sir. We were in the money seven times, Mr. Lochlin."

"You're small for those big Irish horses."

"But strong, sir. I helped my father with the work. I have shod horses myself, a time or two."

Lochlin nodded. "One of these times, drop in on McCarthy. He's got a blacksmith shop down the block. He might need help."

McCarthy was a pleasant man, and a good smith. Shanaghy recognized that at once, and watched him with pleasure. His own father had been good or else they'd never have let him shoe all that racing stock, but this man was good, too.

"If a man would live he must be the best," McCarthy said, one day. "There's many a smith in New York City, and there's more than two hundred thousand horses in the town, bye. Two hundred thousand! Did you think of that? Each horse will drop twenty-five or -six pounds of manure per day, and there's a stable in near every block on Manhattan! Think of that! The day will come when they will not tolerate a stable or a kept horse in the city! You'll see!"

"But how will they get about?"

"There'll be a way. Steam cars . . . someway."

"But what of you, then?"

"Ah, lad, there be three to four thousand on Manhattan who say they shoe horses, but there's but a few to whom I'd trust a good horse." He looked sharply at Shanaghy. "Your pa was a farrier? What happened to him?"

"He went out to India with the soldiers. He was needed, they said. He turned up missing after an attack and is thought to be dead. Many were killed that time, and I am sure he was, too. With the hot weather and all, they don't let bodies lie about waiting to be identified."

"Aye, 'tis the way of war. Many go and few return, and what happens to some of them you never know." McCarthy glanced at him. "What is it you want for yourself? To be a waiter in a saloon? It isn't much, lad. Better your father's trade and to go west."

"West? Where is that?"

"Ah, lad, there's a wide land beyond us here! A far, beautiful land. They do be sayin' there's gold yonder, and silver, and all manner of things. Mostly there's land free for the taking."

"And the savages."

"Aye. They be there, but there's savages enough in the city, too." He paused, hammer in hand. "It is a rough place where you be workin', lad. There's mostly women of no account, and among the men there's thieves and worse. 'Tis no fit place for a lad."

"It is what I have, and Mr. Morrissey sees after me."

"Aye . . . when he's of a mind to, and when he's sober. I like old John, don't you forget that, but he's a rough 'un, battered his way up with two hard fists and his wits and now he walks among the swells. Some of them sneer at him behind his back, but it is behind his back. They are all afraid of him, and when election comes he can get out the votes. Why," he added grimly, "it is said that even the dead come to life and vote when he speaks, and well enough it can be true, for I've seen the names of those dead these three years, and still voting!"

Tom Shanaghy chuckled, shaking his head. "He's the canny one!"

McCarthy spat. "Aye, but a man'll get nowhere if he's dishonest. Chickens come home to roost, me bye. Ride a straight trail and y'll get farther and feel better, and have no worry about what someday will be discovered.

"Those who are dishonest will be dishonest with you, too,

and when it suits them will turn on y'. Among such folks y' trust no man . . . and, particularly, no woman."

Shanaghy shrugged. Who was McCarthy to talk? He ran a blacksmith shop he did not even own. Morrissey had a saloon, a restaurant, and who knew what else? People walked wide around him and spoke to him with respect.

His mother, he reflected, had sounded just like McCarthy, but what did she know? She'd never been three miles from her own village until they went to the ship. A fine woman, a decent woman, but she did not know much about life.

He was remembering all that as he made his camp. He took his blanket-roll back under the trees in the deepest shadow. He liked being close to the fire but was a little afraid of it, too. In New York they sometimes talked of the West and the Indians and he knew they were canny at hunting. He did not wish them to come upon him in the night.

He unrolled the blankets and it was then he found the shotgun. It was in two pieces, needing merely to be put together, and there was a tube container evidently made to contain the two pieces of the shotgun. Now it was filled with shells. He put the shotgun together and loaded it.

Lying on his back, hands clasped behind his head, Tom Shanaghy listened to the rustle of the leaves and watched the fire dying. Tonight, for the first time in a long while, his thoughts kept returning to Ireland.

It had been good there. Hungry, those years after his father went away, but good years in a green and lovely land. At first his father had sent them a little, then came the news that he was missing in action.

Almost twelve years now he had stayed in New York, and that, too, had been hard . . . from the very first. Nearly every day he had a fight, and the boys he met were tough and streetwise, as schooled in fighting as he, but they lacked his natural quickness and the strength developed from the black-smith's hammer and the hard work on the farm. He whipped them all.

All but Pegan Rice. The larger, older boy had whipped him four times. But while he was getting whipped, Tom Shanaghy was learning. Pegan had a bad habit of dropping his left after punching with it, so one time they fought Tom took the left going in and swung with his right. The punch went over the left to Pegan's chin, and the timing was right. Pegan went down hard. He got up, Tom feinted, Pegan threw the left and Tom slipped it and crossed his right to the chin again. After that he saw no more of Pegan Rice.

Shanaghy became a runner for John Morrissey, taking the word to gamblers and gambling houses, to the women on the line and to the ward heelers who did his bidding.

Yet two or three times each week he managed to work with McCarthy for an hour or two, sometimes the whole day. Despite the hard work, or perhaps because of it, he enjoyed himself. And he liked McCarthy. The old Irishman was a tough, no-nonsense sort of man, untouched by the corruption about him.

When not with McCarthy, his haunts were the saloons and dives.

Men such as Morrissey, who could swing the Irish vote, were important to Tammany Hall and, shrewdly, Morrissey had worked hard to make himself even more so. Admired for his fighting abilities, he was also a politician who found newcomers a place to live. He found them jobs, kept them out of trouble. His thugs and "shoulder-strikers," as they were called, frightened opposition voters away from the polls, protected their own voters, and occasionally stuffed ballot-boxes or engaged in all manner of trickery and deceit.

Basically, it was Morrissey's personal popularity that usually carried the day for him.

Shanaghy was thirteen years old when he glimpsed an old friend. He was coming up through the Five Points, walking the middle of the street as behooved one who knew the area, when he saw the Maid o' Killarney . . . She was hitched to a butcher's wagon.

He walked to the curb and stopped. Appearing to pay no attention, he looked the horse over carefully. The same scar on the inside of the fetlock, identical markings. It had to be.

The horse, left standing while a delivery was being made, suddenly took a step forward, stretching its nose to him. "Aye, Maid, you remember me, don't you?" He patted her a little, and when the driver came bustling from the house he commented, "Nice horse."

"Feisty," the delivery man said testily, "too feisty."

Tom had glanced at the sign on the side of the wagon, then

waved a hand and walked up the street. Once he was out of sight, he ran.

Morrissey, Tom knew, had a meeting at his gambling house at No. 8 Barclay Street, and he should be there now.

Tom entered the gambling house and saw Morrissey seated at a table with several other men, a beer and a cigar clutched in his big hands. Tom hesitated, then walked to Morrissey and spoke up.

"Sir? Mr. Morrissey?" Old Smoke did not like to be interrupted, and he turned sharply. When he saw the boy, some of the irritation left his eyes. "What is it, bye? What's wrong?"

"Sir, I must speak with you. Now, sir."

Astonished, Morrissey stared at him. In the year and a half since he had first seen Tom Shanaghy, the boy had never ventured to speak unless spoken to. He had kept out of the way, had done what he was told and kept his mouth shut.

"What is it, then?"

"Alone, sir. I must speak to you alone."

Morrissey pushed back his chair. "If you'll excuse me a moment, gentlemen?"

Taking his beer in one hand and cigar in the other, he led the way to a secluded table. He sat down and gestured for Tom to sit opposite. "Now what is it, bye? I am a busy man, as you can see."

"Sir, I've just seen the Maid o' Killarney!"

"The who? Who or what is this Maid o' Killarney?"

"A horse, sir. A racehorse. She's drawing a butcher's wagon in the Five Points."

Morrissey put the cigar in his teeth. "A racehorse drawing a butcher's wagon? She must be no good. Must have busted down."

"I don't think so, sir. She looked fit . . . only not cared for, sir. I know the mare, sir. She was uncommonly fast, and even if she's not in the best of shape she could still be bred, sir."

"All right, lad. Take your time and tell me about her . . ."

How long ago was that? Tom Shanaghy, hands clasped behind his head, looked up at the rustling leaves. Ten years? A long time back, a very long time.

Slowly and carefully he had explained to John Morrissey about the Maid. How he had been present when she was born, how he had ridden her as an exercise boy around the stables, and ridden her in her first race.

"The Maid won," he explained. "Then she won again. She won twice more with somebody else up, then the man who owned her got in debt over gambling. He lost her and she was sold to an American."

Morrissey dusted the ash from his cigar. "You're sure of the horse?"

"I am. It was my father fitted the first shoes to her. I played with her as a boy. I'd not make a mistake. And she remembered me."

"How old would she be?"

"Five . . . a bit over."

Two days later Morrissey called him in. "Tom, me bye, how would you like to drive a butcher's wagon?"

"Whatever you say."

"You've got a job, then. You'll drive the wagon and you'll check the horse. As I understand it the deliveries are over by noon. You'll take the horse to Fenway's after you've finished. Tomorrow is Saturday. Sunday morning take her out on the track and give her a light workout. Easy does it. See how she moves, if anything is wrong wi' her.

"Lochlin will be there, and he's a fine horseman. He will be watching. No trying for speed now, for she's been living poorly and will have to be taken careful. Above all, don't y' touch her with a currycomb or anything of the kind.

"And not a word of this to anyone, y' understand? Not a word!"

Sunday morning the air had been cool with a touch of fog in the air. He led the Maid out to the track and Lochlin gave him a leg up.

"Once around. Just see how she moves, lad. Maybe we have something and maybe we don't."

When they turned into the track, the Maid remembered. Her head came up and she tugged at the bit. "Not now, baby. Take it easy . . . easy now!"

She moved into a canter and went once around the track. Lochlin was waiting for them when he pulled up near the gate.

"Moves well. Seems a little stiff, that's all."

Tom took her around again, a little faster. She was eager and wanted to run and he had to restrain her.

"How was she when you rode her?" Lochlin asked when they returned.

"She's a finisher, Mr. Lochlin. She likes to come from behind, and if she's anything like she used to be she can really run."

For a week he drove another horse, much alike in outward appearance, with the butcher's wagon. In the afternoons he worked out the Maid. She had a natural affinity for the track, loved running, and liked to win. What Morrissey had in mind he had no idea, except that he expected to make a lot of money.

"Tom," Morrissey said one day, "don't come around to Barclay Street." He lit a fresh cigar. "There's a man who comes there to gamble. Quite the sharper he thinks himself, and he has a horse. He's been doing a bit of bragging about that horse, and I've a friend wishes to take him down a bit."

It had been a week later that Tom was driving the Maid with the butcher's wagon. He had a delivery that morning that took him to Barclay Street and he had stopped to get packages of meat from the wagon when he saw Morrissey. Several men were with him and he heard one of the men say, "What? Why, that Wade Hampton horse of mine could beat either of them! Either of them, I say!"

Shanaghy heard the arrogance in the tone but did not look around, although he wished to.

"Bob," another voice said, "you've been doing a lot of talking about that Wade Hampton horse. We hear a lot but we don't see any action. I think you're just talking through your hat!"

"Like hell, I am! He's won his last six races, and he'll win the next six. If you want to put your money where your mouth is, Sweeney, just find yourself a horse!"

"Bah!" Sweeney was contemptuous. "I don't own a horse, and you know it, but I think you're full of hot air! Why, I'd bet that milk-wagon horse could beat yours!"

"What?"

The Maid, in blinders and a fly net, stood waiting while Tom poured milk into a can, her head dropping as she snuffled at the dust along the curb.

"Don't be a fool, Sweeney!" another of the men protested.

"That mare is all stove up. Anyway, an animal like that can't run. All she can do is pull a wagon."

Lochlin emerged from the gambling house. "What's that? What's going on?"

"Sweeney just offered to bet that milk-wagon horse could beat Bob Childers's Wade Hampton. He wasn't serious, of course, but—"

"The hell I wasn't!" Sweeney said angrily. "You're damn right I'm serious! Bob carries on about that nag of his like it was the only horse in the world! Well, I think Bob's full of hot air!"

Lochlin shrugged. "You can't be seriously suggesting that that old nag could outrun a racehorse? You've got to be crazy, but if you're serious I'll lay twenty to one that Wade Hampton can beat him."

"Twenty to one? I'll take it!"

Sweeney hesitated. "Well now . . . See here. I don't know if—"

"Going to welsh on it, Sweeney?" Bob Childers asked. "You said I was full of hot air, what about you?"

"I'll be damned if I am! I said I'd bet and I will. Twenty to one . . . And I've got a thousand dollars says the milk-horse wins!"

"*A thousand dollars?*" Morrissey spoke for the first time. "That's serious money, Sweeney."

"I've got it and I'll bet it," Sweeney said stubbornly. "Bob, you an' Lochlin can put up or shut up."

"Think what you're doing, Sweeney. Bob has a racehorse. That old milk-wagon horse is stiff and old. Hell, if she ever could run, she can't any more. I'd say forget it."

"He made his bet," Lochlin said, "and I've accepted. I will put up my money on one condition. That we run the race tomorrow."

Lochlin turned to Childers. "Bob," he spoke softly, "this will be the easiest money we ever made. I knew Sweeney was a damn fool, but I didn't realize how *much* of a damn fool he was! This will be a cinch. I'll pick up a cool thousand for an investment of twenty thousand, and all in a matter of minutes." He paused. "How much are you betting, Bob? You can take him for plenty because he's too bullheaded to back out, and you know Sweeney . . . he's got it to bet."

"I don't know," Childers frowned. "I've got to think about it."

"He's good for plenty, Sweeney is, and he's that much of a damn fool. You'll never have a chance like this again. I would guess he's good for twenty or thirty thousand, and I can come up with another twenty. If you can come up with sixty thousand we can win it all. It's a cinch."

"It's a lot of money," Childers muttered.

"Of course, but it will take you a year to clear that much . . . Hell, it would take three good years to clear that much in your saloon. If the man's a fool, let's get his money before somebody else does."

"Where does Morrissey stand? Is he in with us?"

Lochlin shrugged. "He's not involved, so far. You can bet if he sees what we've got, he'll be in for a piece, but John was never much of a gambler. He operates the places but he doesn't gamble."

That was ten years ago or better! Shanaghy remembered the day of the race. He had been up on the Maid and they purposely tossed dust over her, and brought her on the track looking like the milk-wagon horse she'd been. But Shanaghy was nervous, for it was impossible to disguise the clean lines of her.

Wade Hampton had started fast and well and was leading by three lengths when the horses rounded the back turn. Then Tom let the Maid go. Filled with joy at the chance, the horse began to run. When they came under the wire she was running easily and won by half a length.

Morrissey had cautioned him. "Lad, if you look to be winning, don't make it by too much, understand? We can use this horse again."

The Maid won, and Sweeney, Lochlin and Morrissey split sixty thousand dollars among them.

Shanaghy told McCarthy about the race, and the old blacksmith straightened up from his work. "Aye, I heard of it, lad. And you were a part of that? You should be ashamed. It was a swindle. All of them should be ashamed: Ah, if their old mithers but knew of it!"

"But Mr. Lochlin lost money, too!" Shanaghy protested.

McCarthy spat. "If you believe that, you're more innocent

than I believed. Did you see any of Lochlin's money? Did anybody?"

"Gallagher was holding the bets. He said—"

"Aye, Gallagher! One of the same lot! Believe me, lad, Lochlin was the come-on, he was the pusher. Lochlin talked a good bet but he was in it up to his ears. And as for Morrissey, he was the brains of the lot—and seemed to be out of it all so he'd not be suspected. Old Smoke is a shrewd man, lad, and don't you forget it. Running for the state Senate, he is, and he'll be elected, too. You fight shy of that lot, lad, or you'll end in jail!"

Morrissey had given him five hundred dollars for tipping them off to a good thing and riding the horse. It was more money, Shanaghy reflected, than his poor pa had seen in his lifetime. With it, Shanaghy bought some new clothes and a better place to live. He put three hundred of it into a bank McCarthy suggested.

He had ridden the Maid in three more races before he grew too heavy for riding. By the time he was sixteen he was five feet nine inches, as tall as he was ever to be, and he weighed an easy hundred and sixty but looked lighter. Sometimes he sparred with Old Smoke himself, but the iron-fisted Irishman was rough, with both height and reach on Shanaghy, who learned to ride and slip punches, to bob and weave and move in and away.

Although a middleweight in size, he had the shoulders and punching power of a heavyweight, and several times they rang him in on unsuspecting country fighters larger than he.

Of Bob Childers or his family he saw nothing more until several months later when, emerging from the Five Points, he came upon a man who looked like Bob Childers's son standing on a corner with two other men.

"There's one of them now," one of the men said, pointing at Tom. "He rode the horse."

The burly young man who resembled Childers called out to him. "You! Come here!"

Shanaghy paused. He knew he should keep going, but something in the young man's tone irritated him. "You want to see me," he said, "come to where I am."

"I'll come, an' be damned to y'!"

Shanaghy was convinced this was Bob Childers's son. He was

a powerful young man, yet too heavy. Shanaghy stood waiting, watching the other two men as well. When the young man was almost to him he saw the others start, and he knew it would be not the one but all three he must fight. The first one stepped up on the curb. "You're one o' that pack o' thieves," he said, "and I'm going to teach you!"

"Your pa bought himself a horse race and he lost," Shanaghy said to the young man. "That's all. He asked for it with his loud mouth."

"Loud mouth, is it?" The young man lifted a ponderous fist threateningly. "I'll teach . . ."

If you are going to fight, Shanaghy had learned long since, don't waste time talking. As young Childers stepped up on the curb, Shanaghy went quickly to meet him. He smashed a left to Childers's mouth; then swung a right into his belly. The punch caught Childers moving in and was totally unexpected. A strong young man, Childers knew little of fighting and always had much to say before he swung a fist. This time he never said it. His wind left him with an *oof* and he staggered and fell back into a sitting position. Shanaghy wheeled and dove into the space between two buildings, ran their length and, turning sharply, mounted the stairs to the upper story.

This was an area he knew well. Emerging on the rooftop, he ran along the roofs, jumping the walls that divided one from the other. Soon he was blocks away. Coming down from the final rooftop, he went to his room.

A few days later he saw John Morrissey. "Aye," John said, "we bought ourselves a packet, lad. Bob's a beefhead himself, but some of the money was from his brother, Eben, and that's another thing. Eben Childers is uncommon shrewd, and a mean, mean man. The one you hit was not Bob's son but Eben's, so you've made an enemy. Be on your guard, lad, for they'll stop at nothing until you're killed or maimed. He believed that big son of his was unbeatable and you felled him with a blow."

Shanaghy shrugged it off. So he had made an enemy . . . Well, he had made enemies before this one. Yet it was little he knew of Eben Childers then, and he cared even less, for he had been fighting for half his life and knew nothing else.

"He's a hater, lad, and don't forget it. He lost money, but

worse than that he was made to appear a fool, and he's a proud, proud man."

The word got around that Childers was recruiting men for an all-out war with Morrissey, and Childers had influence where it mattered. Unexpectedly, Morrissey found doors closed to him that had always been open, but Shanaghy knew little beyond the casual barroom gossip that he picked up.

Then, one night, as he was coming up the Bowery, he was set upon by a gang of thugs who emerged suddenly from a doorway. "Break his legs!" somebody shouted. "Break his legs and his fingers!"

Again they reckoned without his knowledge of the area, for Tom lunged suddenly, meeting them as they came, and his iron-hard fist clipped the nearest man. The man fell. Leaping past him Shanaghy darted up a stair with the men hot after him. As he topped the flight, he turned. Then grasping a rail in either hand, he swung both feet up and kicked out hard. The boot heels caught the nearest man in the face and he toppled, knocking those behind him backward down the stairs. Again Shanaghy escaped over the roofs.

When he came warily down from the roofs, a few doors from his room, he held himself still in the doorway while he looked carefully around. He was hot and tired. He wanted nothing so much as to climb the stairs to his own room and fall on the bed, yet he was wary.

He had started to leave the doorway where he was hidden when he caught a flicker of movement in the shadows up the street. Was it a harmless drunk sleeping it off in a doorway? Or some of Childers's men waiting for him?

No use taking the chance. He went back to the roofs. Almost a block further along, he descended to McCarthy's blacksmith shop. The place was locked and silent, so he crawled into a wagon, pulled a spare canvas wagon sheet over him and went to sleep.

Shanaghy awakened to the clang of McCarthy's hammer. He sat up, rubbing his eyes. The sides of the wagon were high, and he could not see the wagonyard or the doorway to the shop. He stood up, grasped the side of the wagon and swung himself over. As his feet hit the ground he heard a rush of feet behind him. Instantly he ducked under the wagon and came up on the other side.

A man started under the wagon after him, and Shanaghy kicked him in the head, then turned to face the two who had come around the end of the wagon.

One of them yelled, "There he is! *Get him!*"

Suddenly McCarthy was in the door of his shop, holding a hammer. "One at a time!" he shouted. "Or I'll bust some skulls!"

The man who came at him was a beefy shoulder-striker from Childers's crew. It was a big, broad man with blond hair and a florid face who rushed at Shanaghy. The moment he put up his two hamlike fists, Shanaghy knew he might be good in a rough-and-tumble, but he was no boxer. The man came in, looping a wide right for Shanaghy's chin, and Shanaghy crouched and came in whipping two underhanded punches into the bigger man's belly.

The two punches were perfectly timed. A right to the belly, a left to the same place and then an overhand cross to the chin, and the man went down. He tried to get up but slumped back down into the dirt.

Turning sharply, Shanaghy hit the other man before he expected it, knocking every bit of wind out of him. As the man doubled up, Shanaghy gave him a knee in the face.

The first one was crawling out from under the wagon, a streak of blood on his face. He held up a hand. "No! No! I quit!"

"Be off with you, then," Shanaghy said, "but don't come looking for me again."

When they had gone, Shanaghy went into the blacksmith shop and pumped a bucketful of water from the well. He stripped to the waist and bathed his chest and shoulders, then dampened his hair and combed it out.

"Well," McCarthy said dryly, "it seems you can fight a little, and it seems you must. They be upon you, lad."

"Aye. I slipped them last night when they lay waiting at my house." Tom dried his hands. "I think I must take it to them a bit."

"Be careful, lad. There's a mean man there, that Eben Childers. He's a hard one, and cold. And his boys . . . You met the least of them in Bob. There's others . . . worse."

McCarthy watched Tom put on his shirt. "Lad, why don't

you go west? There's a deal of land out there, and a chance for a young man."

"Land? I'm no farmer, Mac."

"Aye, that you aren't. But what are you, then? A shoulder-striker for Morrissey? A street thug? A bum? Look at yourself, lad, and look well. Just exactly what are you? A fine broth of a lad who is nothing . . . Nothing, do y' hear me? And if you stay here hanging about with thugs, cardsharps and the like, you'll be nothing more until they pick you from the gutter some day."

Shanaghy glared at him. "Have a care, old man."

"Old man, is it? Well, *I've* grown old . . . Will you ever? You'll end with a broken skull some night and they'll have you off to bury in potter's field.

"What are you that any bum along the street is not? There's ten thousand like you in Five Points and they'll all die and come to nothing. You're young, and the land is wide. Why stay here where there's few chances? Why not go west? You could study law, study anything, make a man of yourself."

"I'm not a man?" Tom doubled his arm. "Look at that. Eighteen inches of biceps. Who can say I'm not a man?"

"Aye, you're strong, but what else are you? Have you got the brains God gave you? Or a head fit only for butting, like a billy goat?

"If a man is to be something, if he is to be a man, he's got to be more than muscle. He's got to do something wi' himself. Get an honest trade, a bit of land, a house of your own, if it is only of sod. Here your friends pat you on the back and let you buy them drinks or whatever, but when you get old and fat and sloppy they'll drop you for others. Men like you are born to be used and tossed aside . . . *if* you let it happen."

"What are you? A priest? When did you start preaching, Mac?"

"It's a bit of warning, that's all. You're a fine lad, so why become what you're becoming? There's a bigger, wider world than any slum, and a man only stays there because he hasn't the guts to get out. There's other people, other places, and you can make new friends, worthwhile friends."

Shanaghy stared at McCarthy with disgust. He picked up his coat and slung it over his shoulder. "Thanks for keepin' them off me," he said, and walked away into the sunlight.

He strode down the street, heading for Morrissey's nearest saloon . . . the Gem. Talking to himself as he walked along, he growled angry retorts at the distant McCarthy, saying all the things he had not said. But suddenly they began to sound very hollow and empty.

What was he, after all? He'd ridden a few races but he was too heavy for that now. He'd won a few fights in the ring, but he'd no desire to make a profession of that. He was at the beck and call of Morrissey and Lochlin, who were important men, in their way. But what was he, himself?

He shook himself irritably. It was not a subject on which he cared to dwell. McCarthy . . . well, what did he know? Who was he to talk?

Yet even as Tom thought this, his good sense told him that McCarthy wasn't worried about anybody laying for him when he came home of a night, and he was sleeping sound. Nor was he beholden to anybody for the money he made. He did his job, he did it well, and he took his pay and went home.

Now Shanaghy remembered that time all too well. He had stopped on a street corner, thinking about it. He was no farmer, he'd considered, but still there were towns out west. And if he went to one of them, knowing what he knew, he could become a big man, as big as Morrissey or bigger.

He had fiddled around with the idea and decided he liked it. What was that place out west? San Francisco? He'd heard of it . . . There was gold out there, they said.

Maybe . . . he'd give it some thought.

Two days later he approached Morrissey. "Mr. Morrissey? Have you got some kind of a job for me? A permanent job?"

Morrissey rolled the cigar in his teeth, then spat into the spittoon. "That I have, lad." He paused. "Did you ever do any shooting?"

"Shooting? With a gun?" Shanaghy shook his head. "No, I haven't."

"You can learn. I've got a shooting gallery. Man who handled it for me turned into a drunk. You learn to shoot, you get one-fifth of the take." He paused. "You try knocking down on me, bye, an' I'll have your hide off."

"I never stole anything from anybody," Shanaghy protested.

"That I know, bye. That I know. I've had my eye on you,

bye. Honest men are hard to find. Not many of them amongst
my lot."

Morrissey took a slip of paper from his pocket. "Take this.
You go along down to this address and give them this. I'll send
a man along who will teach you to shoot. Practice all you like,
and when you're good enough we'll let you win some money
for us, shooting with customers."

The shooting gallery was on the Bowery amid dozens of
other such establishments, pawnbrokers' shops, third-class hotels,
dance houses, saloons, cheap clothing stores. Up near Prince
Street was Tony Pastor's Opera House, and further down the
street the Old Bowery Theater. In between was all manner of
vice, trickery, and swindling, a scattering of beggars and pick-
pockets alert for the unwary.

At five cents a shot, there were prizes to be won—twenty
dollars to anyone who could hit a bull's-eye three times in
succession, and knives to be given to anyone who could hit a
bull's-eye once. There was a trumpeter who, if struck in the
heart, gave vent to a frightening blast on his trumpet.

Shanaghy liked the noise and confusion. Many of the sharp-
ers he knew by sight or by name, and the same with the girls
who paraded themselves along the street.

On the third morning an old man walked up to the shooting
gallery. He was a lean, wiry old man with white hair and cool
gray eyes. "How much for a shot?"

"Five cents . . . Twenty dollars if you hit the bull's-eye three
times."

The old man smiled. "And how many times can I win the
twenty?"

Shanaghy started to say, "As many times as you . . ." Suddenly he hesitated, warned by the amused look in the old
man's eyes. "Once," he said. "If you hit it three times."

"Down the street," the old man said, "they let me win three
times."

"Nine bull's-eyes?" Shanaghy grinned. "You're puttin' me
on."

The old man took up a pistol and placed three five-cent
pieces on the counter. "I'm good for business, young fellow."
He placed another fifteen cents on the counter. "Six shots in
here?" he asked mildly, and before he finished the words he
fired. His first shot hit the trumpeter who let go with a pierc-

ing blast. People stopped and stared. Instantly, he fired again, another blast.

"Now," he said, "I'll win my breakfast money."

Without even seeming to look or to care, he fired three bullets dead center into the main target. "There . . . I'll take your twenty."

Shanaghy paid it out while people crowded around. "You got easy targets, boy. Never picked up an easier twenty in my life!" He half turned toward those gathered around. "I don't see how he can afford to operate. That's the easiest twenty I ever picked up!"

The man turned away, winking at Shanaghy. "I'll be back, son, when I need more money."

Men crowded to the counter, eager for a chance. For over an hour he was busy loading guns and handing them to customers. Once the trumpet sounded and a street-boy won a knife. It was good business, but Shanaghy kept thinking back to the old man . . . He had never seen anybody shoot like that, without even seeming to aim. The man just glanced at the target and fired . . . It was uncanny.

On the third day the same man returned and walked up to the counter, when there was nobody around. "Howdy, son. I'm short of cash."

Shanaghy, who found himself liking the old man, said, "I expected you sooner."

"You did, did you? Well, son, it don't pay to kill the goose. All I want's a livin', an' you fellows can give it to me. Costs me only twenty, thirty dollars a week to live well enough to suit me, and I can pick up that much at one stop. There's fourteen shootin' galleries along the Bowery, an' I call on each of you ever' two weeks. This time I needed some extry."

He paused. "Down the street I don't even have to take up a gun. They know I can do it, so they just pay me."

"Not me," Shanaghy grinned at him. "I like to see you shoot. I never knew anybody could shoot like that."

"Where I come from, son, you'd better be able to shoot."

"How come you're back here? Too much for you out there?"

The man's eyes chilled. "Ain't too much for me anywhere, son. I got me a sister back here. I come to visit, but there ain't nothing I can do back here but shoot. I punch cows some, yonder. And I was a Texas Ranger for a spell—have to make a livin' somehow. Then I found these here shootin' galleries. I don't want to make it hard for any of you, so I sort of scatter myself around."

"Come here whenever you're of a mind to," Tom said. "You're good for business, and I like to see you shoot. I'd give aplenty to shoot like that."

"A body needs a mite of teachin' and a whole lot of practice. You got to get the feel for it first."

The old man put both hands on the counter. "This here is an easy livin' for me. My pa used to give me four or five ca'tridges an' I was expected to bring back some game for each loading, else he'd tan my hide for being wasteful. When it's like that, you get so's you don't waste much lead. You don't shoot until you're sure of your target and you make sure you don't miss.

"It was like that for most youngsters growin' up along the frontier. Their pa's were generally busy with farm work or whatever, so if they ate it was the meat the boys shot . . . or sometimes the girls. We had a neighbor girl could outshoot me with a rifle, but the pistol was too heavy for her."

"You didn't ever miss?"

"Oh, sure! There for a while I got my hide tanned right often."

"You never miss here."

"At this distance? How could I? A man gets to know his gun. Each one is somewhat different, some shootin' high and to the right, some low an' left. You got to estimate and allow.

"But a man who knows guns, he wants the best, so he just naturally swaps and buys until he gets what he wants. There's more straight-shootin' guns than there are men to shoot 'em, although some of those gents out west can really shoot.

"A good many western guns been worked over. I mean, most western men doctor their guns to fit their hands better, or to shoot better, or to ease the trigger-pull . . . although 'pull' is the wrong word. No man who knows how to shoot ever pulls a trigger. He squeezes her off gentle, like you'd squeeze a girl's hand. Otherwise, you pull off target. More missin' is done right in the trigger-squeeze than anywhere else."

"I hear those redskins can't shoot worth a damn."

"Don't you believe it! Some shoot as good as any white man. And they're almighty sly about it. They don't see no sense in setting themselves up as targets, so they just pop you off from behind any rock or tree."

That was the summer when Shanaghy learned how to shoot.

TWO

S hanaghy awakened in the cool hour of dawn. For a moment
he lay still, trying to remember where he was and how he
came to be there. He recalled being kicked off the open
gondola, then went back to his thoughts about New York.

John Morrissey had gone to upstate New York on some
political business, and Shanaghy, now promoted to a position
as one of Morrissey's lieutenants, had dropped around to the
Gem to check receipts. According to plan he had met Lochlin
there. They had barely seated themselves at the table when
Cogan, a bartender, stuck his head in the door.

"Mr. Shanaghy, sir? There's some men comin' in that look
like trouble."

Leaving Lochlin at the table, Shanaghy stepped over to the
door. He glanced quickly around. There were four men at the
bar, all standing together, and there were others scattered
about the room. They all had beers, but there was something
about them . . . .

The place was crowded, but somehow the men Cogan had
mentioned stood out, and one of them . . . Shanaghy turned
sharply. "Lochlin! Look out! It's Childers's men!"

He stepped quickly out into the saloon and pulled the door

24

shut behind him. He had started around the bar when one of the newcomers deliberately knocked the beer from the hand of a bricklayer who stood beside him. The bricklayer turned to protest and the man hit him. Then they started to break the place up.

Shanaghy ducked a blow and drove a fist into the middle of the nearest man, and kicked another on the kneecap. The door crashed open and he saw a dozen men coming in, all armed with pick-handles and other clubs.

Too many! "Cogan! Murphy! *Run!*"

Shanaghy spun a table in the path of the advancing men, and when several fell he crowned them with a chair. Ducking around the bar, he armed himself with bottles which he threw with unerring aim.

Another man went down, screaming. A bottle missed Shanaghy by inches and he ducked through the door to find Lochlin. The man was gone. He had scooped up the money he was to count and scrambled out the back door.

Slamming the door into place, Cogan, who had joined him, dropped a bar across it and they ran for the alley. There were too many to fight, too many altogether.

They had almost reached the back door when there was a shot and Lochlin staggered in, bleeding.

"Upstairs!" Shanaghy told them quickly. "Over the roofs!"

He stopped and lifted Lochlin bodily from the floor, holding him in place with one arm while he scooped up the moneybag with the other. He ran up the steps, blessing his good luck for all the years at the blacksmith's anvil, and then they came out on the roof, barring the trap behind them.

The sky was covered with low clouds, and it was beginning to rain.

Murphy, another aide of Morrissey's, had joined them. "There's a rig at Kendall's," he gasped.

Suddenly, from behind a parapet of a roof, a group of men raised themselves up. Shanaghy's glance counted six. He turned. As many more were coming across the roofs behind them.

"This time," somebody yelled, "ye'll not get away!"

Shanaghy dropped the moneybag and drew a snub-nosed pistol from a waistband holster. "I'm givin' y' fair warnin'," he said, "git to runnin' or somebody dies!"

"Hah!" a big roughneck shouted, lifting a club in one hand

and a half-brick in the other, ready to throw. "Y'll not git away this . . . !"

Men had been killed with sticks and stones for millions of years before a firearm was invented, and Tom Shanaghy did not hesitate. He had been well taught, and during the four years he had operated the shooting gallery he had practiced daily.

He palmed the gun and he fired even as the big man spoke. The gun was a .44 and Shanaghy fired three times.

The big man cried out and staggered. Another fell, and then they were all running.

Somehow Shanaghy and his men got to Kendall's, got into the rig and fled. Cogan was holding Lochlin while Shanaghy drove, and never would he forget that wild night drive through the dark, rain-whipped streets.

Where should they go? Shanaghy wondered. His own place was known and would not be safe. Lochlin's bachelor quarters would be unsafe, too. Yet there was a hiding place, a place Morrissey kept off Broadway. He drove there.

There was a floor safe in Morrissey's bedroom and that was where Tom took the money. He withheld a handful of bills, made a hasty estimate and dropped a note into the safe with the remainder of the money.

Giving Cogan and Murphy each $100 running money. They will hide out in Boston . . . you know where. I am taking $500 and leaving $500 with Lochlin. He's hurt bad but I'll get Florrie in to take care of him. Watch yourself.
Shanaghy

He gave money to each of the men and told Cogan to get word to Florrie to come and care for Lochlin. Then he reloaded his pistol and went to Morrissey's desk for another . . . There were two there and he took one.

He got Lochlin on the bed and bound up his wound as best he could. He'd been shot in the side and was unconscious, his clothing soaked with blood.

Florrie came to the door and he let her in, giving her Lochlin's money. "Tell nobody he's here and keep out of sight. I don't think you're known to them anyway."

"What will you do?"

"First, I've got to get that horse out of sight and into a stable. If they see it they'll trace Lochlin to this place. I'll think of myself after."

He went out through the kitchen window and down the back stairs. All was dark and silent. Thunder rumbled in the distance and there was occasional lightning. When he came out of the alley, the horse was standing there, head hanging. Shanaghy looked carefully around, then crossed the walk and got into the rig, turning the horse down the street. The top and sides kept most of the rain off. He dried his right hand and felt for his guns.

He had killed a man up there . . . perhaps two. But they were coming for him and would have killed him. His quick shooting had saved many other lives . . . probably.

He drove down the dark streets.

John Morrissey was a man who had lived with trouble, and so he was constantly aware of its proximity. Wisely, he had prepared hideouts where he could hole up until softer winds blew, and stables where horses could be found. It was to one of these that Shanaghy now drove.

All was dark and silent. There were two horses in the stable and several empty stalls. Shanaghy led his horse inside, dried him off and put oats in the bin. The rig he put into a carriage house out of sight and then he went to the house hard by. Over a cup of hot coffee he considered the situation.

Eben Childers had planned well. Obviously they had known that John Morrissey was out of town. The place on Barclay Street had probably been hit as well, and Childers's men would be on all the streets. It was no time to be out and about.

Morrissey would know of what had happened within a matter of hours, but Shanaghy, knowing his man, doubted that John would make any move until the force of Childers's drive was spent. Knowing such men as Childers used, Shanaghy knew that within hours, when victory seemed complete, they would begin to drink. Some would simply turn in to rest, others would scatter to find their doxies or whatever. And that would be the time to strike.

Sitting alone in the empty house with a coal-oil lamp on the table beside him, Tom Shanaghy plotted the strategy of the days to come. He would have to get in touch with Boynton and

Finlayson, and they would gather the boys for him so they
could be ready to strike back.

He paced the floor, muttering to himself, trying to plan the
counterattack as John would plan it, trying to foresee all that
must be done.

First, he must get word to Morrissey. Then, when Boynton
and Finlayson had gathered the gang together, they would
choose their targets and strike.

Finally, weary with planning, he went to sleep. He awakened in the light of a chill, rainy dawn and dressed. He
checked his guns and then went down to the street. There was
nobody around, but he had not expected to see any people.
This was a quiet neighborhood and it was Sunday.

Boynton would be in the Five Points. Shanaghy went through
the streets until he reached Broadway and there he hired a
hack. When he mentioned the Five Points the driver refused
flatly. "No, sir, I'll not be goin' yonder. Not for any man.
They'd steal the fillin's from your teeth, yonder. I'll take you
within a street or two, that's all!"

No argument would suffice, and Shanaghy didn't blame him.

He found Boynton sleeping off a drunk and shook him awake.
Shanaghy made coffee and forced a cup on the reluctant giant.
Slowly, word by word, he filled Boynton in on all that had
happened. "You're to get twenty good men . . . tough men."

He went ahead carefully with the planning. They would
gather in three positions, then strike fast and hard.

John Morrissey had made enemies, and Childers had tied in
with some of them. Mostly they were former followers of
Butcher Bill Poole, the only man who ever bested Morrissey in
a rough-and-tumble fight. Sometime later, Poole had been shot
and killed by Lew Baker. That was in 1855, and the funeral
procession for Poole had been the largest in the city until that
time.

Several hundred policemen had led the procession, followed
by two thousand members of the Poole Association, a political
faction. That was followed by nearly four thousand of the Order
of United Americans, and hose-and-engine companies from
New York, Boston and Baltimore, as well as Philadelphia. As a
special honor guard were two companies of militia named for
Poole, the Poole Guards and the Poole Light Guards.

When the rites were completed, the various sections broke

up, but the Guards and the Light Guards stayed together. It was evening before they reached Broadway and Canal Street, where a building was undergoing demolition. There, unknown to the Poole men, a number of the Morrissey faction had concealed themselves. The Original Hounds and a crowd of the Morrissey shoulder-strikers waited until the Poole men came within easy range, and then they cut loose with a shower of bricks and stones. Several Poole men went down, but they were the better-armed and charged the Morrissey faction with fixed bayonets.

Scattering, the Morrissey men took to the alleys and roofs. Yet all of them were not to escape, for later that night the Poole men attacked the engine-house where some of the Original Hounds were holed up, destroying the place and putting them to flight.

Despite the victory, the Poole forces were never again to wield their former power. Some of them, filled with hatred for Morrissey, had joined Childers.

Although Morrissey still maintained an interest in the old Gem Saloon, he no longer owned it. After operating other gambling houses, he had confined his interests to places on Barclay and Ann Street.

From Boynton's place, Shanaghy had gone on to find Finlayson. A thin, wiry man, he stared at Shanaghy and shook his head. "John's been beaten this time," he said, "beaten! They waited until he was out of town and then they moved. They've too much power."

"You believe that an' you'll believe anything," Shanaghy said. "Old Smoke has power where they've got none, an' Tammany will help him . . . if he needs it. But if we move fast—"

"Time ain't right," Finlayson objected. "They've got it all goin' their way. If John was only here . . ."

"You won't help?"

"Time ain't right," Finlayson shook his head. "You'll get yourself killed. I—"

"Forget it." Shanaghy could see that the man was frightened, his confidence shattered. "We'll do it without you."

He left on the run. He moved fast. He found O'Brien and then Larry Aiken and Linn. They were ready to move and glad somebody was doing something.

"At ten," Shanaghy told Aiken. "Don't wait for me, just move. By that time most of them will be drunk or sleeping it off."

Seated over a table he showed them on a sheet of paper how each move would be made, and when. Little did he guess that he would never be there to take part. Yet Larry Aiken was a good man, a tough man.

He remembered the night well. After leaving Aiken, he had come out on the street and started for a livery stable. He needed a rig now. There was a place up the island where he could get some guns. Unless he missed his guess, all of Childers's men would be armed.

He hired a rig. As he was hooking the trace chains, the hostler whispered to him. "Bye, I'm a friend of McCarthy's, so watch your step. Eben's got five hundred dollars for the man who brings you in alive—to him."

The hostler paused, looking around warily. "They're after you, bye. He aims to cripple you and blind you. He's said as much."

"I'll be careful," Shanaghy said. He stepped into the rig and gathered the reins. "Open the door, then. And thanks. I'll not forget, nor will Morrissey."

He drove into the street and turned uptown. No hurry, now, he told himself. Take it easy. *Five hundred?* That was enough to turn all of the Five Points after him, and many another besides. Who could he trust?

He left Delancey Street behind him and felt better. He drove on, holding the speed down so as not to attract attention. He put his hand on his gun. It was there. He felt for the other . . . it was gone! Dropped from his pocket, probably, while he hitched up the horse. He swore softly, bitterly.

Well, now. If he could get to that man on Twenty-fourth Street, he'd have guns aplenty.

Almost an hour later, after driving around the block and seeing no one, he pulled up in an alley and stepped down. Suddenly, he was uneasy. He knew about this source of weapons, so might not Childers as well?

It was dark and silent, with only the rain whispering on the street. He put a hand on the horse's shoulder. "You wait, boy. I'll be back."

Yet he did not move. The bricks of the street pavement

glistened wetly. He saw the dark maw of an alley opening toward the north, and beyond it a row of houses, each with steps and iron railings. He felt for the gun again, still irritated with himself. When had he ever trusted to a gun? Yet if there were too many of them, he must.

He studied the house where he must go. A faint light showed from under the shutters. What was the man's name?

Schneider . . . He stepped around the horse and went quickly up the steps. There were eight steps and an iron railing on either side. Under the steps there were other steps leading down.

He lifted the knocker and rapped, not too loud. There was a sudden movement within. A chill went up his spine. Was that a movement behind him? He turned sharply . . . nothing.

Within there was a rustle of movement, and then a voice through the door. "Who is it?"

"Shanaghy," he said.

A chain rattled and the door opened . . . not a crack, but suddenly thrown wide.

There were three men! They had him then . . . No, by the . . . !

Behind him there was a scurry of feet, and Shanaghy did the unexpected. Instead of trying to turn, of trying to escape, he went at them.

He was shorter than any one of the three, but he was stronger. He went into them with a lunge, and he swung a fist at the nearest. He had hit for the man on the right, knocking him into the way of the others. Then he had the gun out and he fired.

There was a muffled blast and the hit man screamed. Turning sharply he fired into the crowd suddenly closing in behind him, then darted down the hall. He smashed open the first door he came to, saw a frightened blonde woman catch up a blanket and hold it before her, and then he was past her and throwing a chair through a window. He went out, hung for an instant, then leaped across the areaway and crashed through the glass of the window opposite.

The room was empty. He ran through it, tried to gauge the best way to go, then ran down a hall. Behind him, somebody yelled and a door slammed open. "Stop, thief!" a woman shouted.

He went up the steps three at a time, turned at the landing

and ran on up. At the end of the hall he saw a gap, then a slate roof opposite him. It was wet and slippery. Behind him he heard screams and curses. He stepped to the windowledge and leaped, catching the edge of the gutter with his hands. It broke loose at one end and he clung to the metal as it swung him toward the ground. He dropped the final ten feet and ran through a gap between the buildings.

After running down an alley, he ducked across a street, up another alley, then along a street toward the north. He paused there once, to listen. They were coming, all right. They were scattering now.

Think . . . he must think.

The railroad yards, with all those cars standing, it would be dark there. He ran.

With all his hard work, he was in good shape, in better shape probably than any of his pursuers, unless some of Childers's footracers were among them. Footracing was a popular sport, and most gamblers had one or two on the payroll.

He ducked down another alley and turned into a street lined with trees. He paused, then walked on, catching his wind. He felt for the gun.

It was gone . . .

It must have fallen from his pocket back in an alley somewhere. He hoped they had not found it, that they wouldn't know he was unarmed.

Somebody crossed the street behind him and he heard a shout. He ducked into an alleyway . . . blind!

He turned back and went up the street, but they were closer now. They were spreading out, coming at him. Ahead of him there was a low fence, and he smelled wet cinders and coal smoke. Then he saw the cars. Over there was an engine, puffing thoughtfully as it waited. He dropped a hand to the fence rail and vaulted it easily, then slid down a bank and lost himself in the darkness.

A train whistled and he heard the *chug-chug* of a starting engine. Somebody fired a shot and it ricocheted over a car ahead of him.

He ducked under a row of standing cars and saw some moving cars ahead of him. He ran, caught the ladderrung and swung himself up and over into an empty gondola.

The train gathered speed.

Behind him there were shouts and yells. They were searching. A shot . . . not aimed toward him, apparently. Gasping, he dropped to a sitting position against the side of the car.

God, was he tired!

The train whistled and he looked up to see roofs going by. It was raining harder now.

THREE

When Shanaghy awakened again he lay for some time, just thinking. There was no sound but the trickling of water from the small creek and the chirping of birds. Somewhere the birds were singing an endless variety of songs. He did not know much about birds.

After a while he sat up and looked around. He wrapped his arms around his knees and rested his chin on his arms. He had never known a morning so still . . . Yes, he had—when he was a boy in Ireland and walked to the upper pasture to bring the horses down. It had been quiet in Ireland, too.

He got up, went to the stream. After taking off his shirt, he bathed his face, head and shoulders in the cold water. It felt good. Then he rolled up his blankets. Finding a few coals left in the fire, he rekindled it and broiled some bacon.

Then he examined the guns. The pistol was a good one, brand-new, apparently. Whose outfit did he have, anyway? He belted on the gun, tried it for balance and feel. It felt good.

He had to get back to New York. That meant returning to the railroad and finding a town or a water tank. Some place where a train might stop. He had to get back. Morrissey would need him.

Shanaghy walked back to his blanket-roll, but instead of picking it up he sat down again. Damn, it felt good! Just the stillness, the peace. After the hectic life he had.been living . . .

He knew the sound of horses' hoofs when he heard them, and he heard them now. For a moment he remained where he was, just listening. Then he got up, moved the blanket-roll out of sight near a tree and leaned the shotgun against the tree. The coat he wore effectively concealed the pistol.

Shanaghy walked down to the ashes of the fire. Now maybe he could find out where he was and how far away was the nearest town.

There were four of them and they came down the slope toward the stream, riding together. One man, on a gray horse, trailed a little behind.

"Hey!" He heard one of them speak. "Somebody's . . ."

They rode through the stream and pulled up about twenty feet away from him.

"Look," one of them said, "it's a pilgrim!"

"How are you?" Shanaghy said. "I wonder if . . ."

"It's an Irish pilgrim," another said. "What d' you know about that?"

Three of them were about his own age, one of them probably younger. The fourth was a lean, wiry older man with a battered, narrow-brimmed hat and an old gray coat and patched, home-spun pants. This man had his hands behind him.

Shanaghy squatted on his heels, stirring the ashes and adding a few sticks. "Headin' for town," he said casually. "How far is it?"

Some of the sticks caught a small fire.

The heavier-set of the riders took a coil of rope from his saddle and shook out a loop. He moved toward a large cottonwood. "How about here?" he suggested.

"Wait a minute," another said. "What about *him*?"

A man in a white buckskin vest had looked on but not yet spoken. He had sat, staring at Shanaghy. Then slowly he smiled. "We can always make it two," he said.

The heavy-set one looked startled. "But we don't even *know* him. He ain't done any harm."

"How do we know? He looks to me like a sinful man." He turned his full attention to Shanaghy. "Where's your horse?"

"I don't have one." Shanaghy was wary. He was in trouble

but he did not know how much, nor had he quite understood what they were talking about. "I dropped off a train."

"Out here? You must be crazy! It's forty miles to the nearest town."

"I can walk."

"*Walk?* Now I know you're crazy."

The man in the white vest spoke again. "He shouldn't be here. He's in the wrong place at the wrong time."

Shanaghy was growing irritated. "This looks like a good place to me," he said. "I like it."

"You hear that?" White Vest said. "He says he likes it."

There was a moment of silence, then the man on the horse with his hands behind him said, "I always knew you were rotten, Drako."

"Bass?" Drako glanced at the man with the coiled rope. "Take him."

Shanaghy had never seen anybody rope steers, but he had heard stories from his old friend who taught him to shoot. He saw the rope go up, saw the loop shoot at him and as the horse gathered itself to leap he threw himself toward a tree. The trunk was no more than six feet from him and he was quick. For Shanaghy, to think was to act. He threw himself past the tree, then around it in a lunge.

The loop caught him as he had known it would, but as the horse leaped to drag him he had a turn around the tree, then a second. The horse hit the end of the rope with a lunge and the girth parted. The horse charged on, then man, saddle and rope hit the ground hard.

Drako swore and the third man grabbed for a gun.

Shanaghy never knew how he did it but he had not stopped moving. When the girth broke he had thrown off the rope and when the third man grabbed for his gun, Shanaghy shot him.

He intended to shoot him through the body but the man was moving and the bullet caught his left arm at the elbow, breaking it.

"Next time," Shanaghy covered his miss, "I'll break the other arm. Now get out of here . . . all of you."

"Mister?" The man with his hands behind him spoke softly, desperately. "Mister, I never begged for anything in my life, but—"

For the first time Shanaghy realized that the man's hands were tied behind his back.

"Leave that man here," Shanaghy said. "Let go of that lead-rope and leave him."

"I'll be damned if I will!" Drako shouted.

"You'll be dead if you don't," Shanaghy replied. "I was mindin' my own affairs. You come bargin' in here an' you just tried to sweep too many streets all at once. If you want to live long enough to see sundown you'll get out, and if you come back you'll deserve what you get."

"Oh, we'll be back, all right!"

Drako dropped the lead-rope and turned his horse away. "We'll surely be back!"

Shanaghy watched them ride away and then he walked over to the bound man and cut his hands loose. "Don't know what they had you for, chum," he said, "but that's a bad lot."

The man rubbed his wrists. "You're new in this country," he replied grimly. "They was fixin' to hang me. If you hadn't been here I'd be dead by now."

Shanaghy walked to the tree where he had concealed his blanket-roll and the shotgun, and took them up.

"My name's Tom Shanaghy," he said.

"Josh Lundy," the older man said. Then he added, "We got but one horse. No use killin' him carryin' double. You ride awhile, then I will."

Lundy reached for the bed-roll but stopped abruptly, his eyes on the shotgun. Then slowly he took the roll of blankets and tied it behind the saddle. "You carry a shotgun all the time?" he asked. Something in his tone drew Shanaghy's attention.

"No . . . Why?"

"Wondered."

Yet suddenly Lundy's manner had changed. The friendliness was gone from his tone and he was somehow cool and remote.

"You come far?" he asked suddenly.

"New York."

"On a train, you said?"

"Uh-huh. Railroad bull bounced me off back yonder a ways. I walked for a while, then saw this stream and followed her to here."

"Got you an outfit there. Didn't figure you fellers in New York carried blanket-rolls."

"We don't."

"You were almighty quick with that gun," Lundy said. "I never seen a man no quicker."

"Fellow taught me. I never used a gun very much. Where I come from it's knuckle-and-skull, the boots if you go down."

Tom Shanaghy was used to walking and he stepped off briskly. He was puzzled by all that had happened and waited for Lundy to explain, which he seemed in no hurry to do. In fact, since seeing the shotgun he had said very little.

Shanaghy looked around as he walked. As far as he could see there was nothing but grass and sky and the twin ruts of the trail cutting through the grass ahead. Here and there along the road there were sunflowers in bloom.

He paused suddenly. "Lundy, what in God's name do they do with all this country? There's no farms."

"Cattle country," Lundy replied, "grazin' land. Used to be buffalo."

Something moved in the distance, a moment of tawny-red when caught by the sun's rays, then a flicker of white and they were gone.

"What was that? Cows?"

"Antelope," Lundy said. "There's a good many of them."

"Who they belong to?"

Lundy glanced at him. "God, I guess you could say. They're wild."

"Can you hunt them?"

"Uh-huh. Not the best eatin' though. They're good enough, but not so good as buffalo or deer meat." He walked the horse in silence for several minutes and then asked, "What do you aim to do now?"

"Me? Catch a train back to New York. I piled on that train in a hurry and I was dead tired. I never wanted to get this far away." He hesitated, suddenly thoughtful. "Say, how far is it to New York, anyway?"

Lundy shrugged. "You got me. Maybe a thousand miles."

Shanaghy pulled up short. "A thousand . . . ? It can't be!"

"It is. Maybe more. This here's Kansas you're in." Lundy pointed ahead. "Colorado's right over there. You must have been really knocked out when you hit that train."

"Well . . . I'd been movin' a lot. Hadn't slept much, that's true. I was dead beat." He scowled, thinking back. "I woke up now and again but it seems the train was always movin'. One time I looked out and there was nothing but four or five buildings across the street and some riders . . . I don't know where that was."

"Least, you had you an outfit."

Shanaghy offered no reply. He was growing increasingly uneasy. The best thing he could do was get to a station and buy a ticket for New York. There, at least, he knew what was going on.

"Those lads back yonder," he said suddenly, "what were they going to hang you for?"

"I stole a horse. That's hanging out here. But this one I stole back. Belongs to a girl-kid. That Drako . . . he wanted the horse."

"The girl got the horse now?"

"Uh-huh."

Shanaghy looked at the saddle. "That's a heavy piece there. That saddle, I mean."

"Stock saddle. It's a work saddle. A man handlin' cattle and rough stock needs a good saddle to work from and this here's the best. Most cowhands spend most of their lives settin' in saddles just like this.

"I seen some of those eastern saddles . . . like postage stamps. They're all right for somebody who spends an hour or so in the saddle, but a cowhand is up in the leather sixteen to eighteen hours a day. He's roping stock from the saddle and needs a pommel where he can either tie fast or take a turn, depending on how he was raised and where he learned his business. A saddle is a cowhand's workbench."

Lundy pulled up. " 'Bout time you took a turn, although I ain't much at walkin'."

Shanaghy mounted and settled himself in the strange saddle. It felt good. The seat was natural, and although the stirrups were longer than he was used to he did not take time to shorten them.

"Town up ahead," Lundy commented, after a while. "You keep that gun handy. Drako may be around. That's a rough crew he runs with and they don't like anybody messing with them."

"What about you?"

"When we get close to town I'm goin' to cut an' run. I've got friends there, somebody who'll lend me a gun. I ain't huntin' trouble. You being a stranger . . . you be right careful. From what I've heard they fight with fists back east. Well, out here it's like in the South. We settle our troubles with guns."

Shadows were long when they rode into town. Shanaghy was again in the saddle when they reached the town's edge and he stepped down. "Here's your horse, Lundy," he said. "See you around."

"Shanaghy?" Lundy hesitated a moment as if reluctant to speak. "Better keep that shotgun out of sight. Somebody will recognize it."

"Recognize it? How?"

"I don't know how you come to have it," Lundy said, "but that shotgun is known by sight in at least twenty towns out here. That shotgun belonged to Marshal Rig Barrett."

"I never heard of him."

"Well, ever'body out here has. Rig was his own army. When he moved into a place folks knew he was there. He cleaned up towns, outlaw gangs, train robberies, whatever. And he never let anybody even handle one of his guns."

"So?"

Josh Lundy gathered the reins and stepped into the saddle. "Marshal Rig Barrett had a lot of enemies, Shanaghy. He had a lot of friends, too. And they are going to be asking questions and wanting answers."

Lundy looked up the dusk-filled street. He wanted to be away, but he stalled. "Shanaghy," his tone sharpened with irritation, "don't you see? They're going to want to know how you came by Rig's shotgun. They're going to tell themselves the only way you could lay hands on it would be over Rig's dead body, and they just aren't going to believe any eastern pilgrim could kill Rig in a fair fight."

"I didn't kill him. I never so much as saw him."

"Who's going to believe that?"

"Nobody will have to. I'll be out of town on the next train. This town will never see hide nor hair of me again."

"If they see that shotgun and figure you killed Rig, you'll never get a chance to leave. They'll hang you, boy. They'll give you the rope they planned to use on me."

"When's the next train leave? You know this town."

"Nothing out of here in either direction until tomorrow noon, and that one is westbound. There will be an eastbound train tomorrow evening about nine o'clock."

Lundy turned his horse and rode off. When he had gone about fifty feet he called back. "Was I you I'd not wait for that evening train."

Tom Shanaghy stood alone in the dusty street and swore, slowly, bitterly. Then he unrolled the blankets, took down the shotgun, and rolled it up again.

He would get something to eat, then a ticket and a bed.

FOUR

It was suppertime in town and the streets were almost empty. Not that there was much to the town, only a row of stores, saloons, gambling joints and a hotel or two facing a dusty street from either side. Here and there were hitching rails and there were boardwalks in front of most of the buildings.

He walked to what looked like the best hotel and went in. The clerk, a tall young man with a sallow face and hollows over his cheekbones, pushed the ledger toward him. He signed it *Thomas Shanaghy, New York,* and pushed it back.

"That will be fifty cents, Mr. Shanaghy. Will you be staying long?"

"Until the eastbound train tomorrow night," Shanaghy said.

He paid for the room with a ten-dollar gold piece and received his change.

"If you are interested in a little game, Mr. Shanaghy," the clerk suggested, "there's one going in the back room right here in the hotel."

"Thanks." Shanaghy had been a shill himself and was not to be taken in. "I never gamble."

"No? Then perhaps—"

"I don't want a girl, either," Shanaghy said. "I want something to eat, some rest, and a New York newspaper if you've got one."

The clerk did not like him very much. He jerked his thumb toward a door from which there was an occasional rattle of dishes. "You can eat in there." He indicated the opposite direction. "And there's a saloon over there. As for a New York newspaper . . ."

He shuffled through some newspapers on the desk, all well read by the looks of them. "I am afraid we haven't any. Occasionally some drummer leaves one in the lobby, so you might look around."

Shanaghy considered that and decided against it. He took his key, listened to the directions of the clerk and took up his blanket-roll and went up the stairs. Chances are there would be nothing about the New York gambling war in the paper anyway, he decided. There were always brawls, gang fights and killings, and the newspapers reported only a small percentage of them. John Morrissey was a popular figure, of course, but Eben Childers was scarcely known away from the Five Points, the Bowery and a scattering of places in the vicinity of Broadway.

The room offered little. A window over the street, a bed, a chair, a dressing table with an oval mirror, and on the table beneath the mirror a white bowl and pitcher. There was water in the pitcher. On a rack beside it there was a towel.

On the floor there was a strip of worn carpet. Shanaghy removed his coat, rolled up his sleeves and bathed his face and hands, then put water on his hair and combed it.

He studied himself critically. At five-nine he was a shade taller than average, and he was stronger than most, due to the hard work in the smithys. The girls along the Line were always telling him how handsome he was, but that was malarkey. They knew he was a friend of Morrissey's and the Morrissey name stood for power and influence in the world they knew, so they were always buttering him up. Not that he saw much of them. He had always been on the gambling, roughneck side.

Brushing his coat with his hands, he put it on and picked up his hat and went down the stairs. The restaurant was open, and he went in, ordered some beef and beans and began to relax.

The waiter was a portly man with slicked-back hair who wore

a candy-striped shirt and sleeve garters. He filled Shanaghy's cup and slopped a liberal portion into the saucer.

A screened window was open on the street and Shanaghy heard the clang of a blacksmith's hammer. He jerked his head toward the sound. "Workin' late, ain't he?"

"Lots of work," the waiter put down the coffeepot. "Soon be time for the cattle drives, too. There's always riders who need horses shod when the drives are on. He keeps busy."

The waiter took his pot and moved away and Shanaghy relaxed slowly. It felt good just to sit. For days now . . . weeks, actually, he'd been on the go. Now he had nothing to do until this time tomorrow night. He'd better buy that ticket right away. If anything happened he would at least have his ticket, and once in New York again he'd be all right.

What could happen? He shrugged a shoulder in reply to his own question and looked up to see the waiter returning with a steaming plate. "If you want more, sing out," the waiter said. "We're used to hungry men."

Shanaghy was halfway through his meal when the door from the street opened and a man came in, spurs jingling. He crossed to a table where two other men sat eating. Pulling back a chair he dropped into it. "Ain't no sign of him," the new-comer said. "He's three days overdue. That ain't like Rig."

Shanaghy was cutting a piece from his steak, and at the name he almost stopped.

Rig? Rig Barrett?

"Last word we had he was in Kansas City. That was last week."

"He may be here, scoutin' around. You know how he is, never makes any fuss."

"I'm worried, Judge. You know what Vince Patterson said, and Vince ain't a man who blows off a lot of hot air. Last I heard he was hirin' hands down around Uvalde and Eagle Pass, tough hands. Joel Strong rode in a few days ago and he said Vince had hired twenty-five men . . . Now you know he doesn't need more than half that many to bring twenty-five hundred head over the trail. So why's he hirin' so many men?"

"Maybe worried about Indians."

"Him? Vince would tackle hell with a bucket of water. No, this time he figures to get even. When his brother was killed, Vince promised us he'd be back."

"He can't blame the whole town for that."

"He does, though. Vince is a tough man and he doesn't fool around. Rig Barrett could make him see the light, but you know and I know that Vince won't back down for no man."

The judge sipped his coffee, then lit a cigar. "I know Vince. He's a hard man, all right. It takes hard men to do what he did. He came out from Kentucky and started roping and branding cattle. He made friends with some Indians, fought those who wanted to fight, and he built a ranch. He worked all by himself, the first two years. Then his brother came out and worked and fought right beside him. That was the brother Drako killed."

Drako?

Tom Shanaghy heard only snatches of the conversation from there on, no matter how he strained his ears. He was curious, naturally. Rig Barrett had evidently planned on riding that freight west and somehow had gotten off again and left his gear behind . . . But why should such a man ride a freight? To come into town unseen? Maybe, but Rig didn't seem like a man who would care. He might even want the townspeople to see him arrive.

So what had become of him? Shanaghy wished there was a train that night. Right away. He began to feel hemmed in. His old friend of the shooting galleries had told him much about the West. If you shot a man in a fair fight there was no argument. If you shot a man in the back, or murdered him otherwise, you could get hung. You had a choice . . . run or be hung.

If Shanaghy was found with the shotgun and blanket-roll that belonged to Rig, he would be presumed guilty.

He finished his coffee and got up, then paid for his meal and left. Two-bits . . . Well, that wasn't too bad. And the food was good.

The air was fresh and cool in the street and there were few people about. The sound of the blacksmith's hammer drew him forward and he strolled down the street.

The wide doors of the shop were pushed back. The fire on the forge glowed a dull red, and there were several lanterns hung about to give light. The smith glanced up as Shanaghy stepped into the door.

"Workin' late," Shanaghy commented. "Buy you a drink?"

"Don't drink."

"Well, neither do I. Have one now and again." He glanced at the work the smith was doing. "Makin' a landside? I haven't made one of those in years. Seen my pa do it many's the time."

"Are you a smith?"

"Now and again. My pa was a good one."

"Want a job?"

Shanaghy hesitated. "I'm leavin' town tomorrow night, but if you're crowded with work I could work nine, ten hours tomorrow. What is it, mostly?"

"Shoeing horses, a couple of wagons to fit with new tires, some welding."

"I can do that. I'm not experienced with plows or plowshares. I've been living in New York City and it has been mostly shoeing, driving or riding horses . . . putting tires on a few wagons and buggies."

"You come in at six o'clock, you've got a day's work. Wish you could stay. I've got enough work for three men, and everybody wants his work done right now."

The smith mopped his brow. "Here," he pulled an old kitchen chair around. "Time I took a rest. You set for a while. New York, eh? I've never been there."

"You got you a tire-bender?"

"Heard of them. Are they any good?"

"Some of them. I never saw one until last year, but a mighty good smith I worked with in New York, name of McCarthy, he used one. Liked it."

"Maybe I should get one. Might save some time."

"Been smithing here long?"

"Long? Hell, I started this town! Man down the road a piece saw my gear when I was passin' along the trail, and he asked me if I could bend a tire. Well, I did four wagons for him, and meanwhile several people brought horses to be shod.

"Out here folks do most of their own shoeing, but it leaves a lot to be said for it. Most of them do a pretty slam-bang job of it.

"Well, I worked there for about two weeks and then I moved back under that big cottonwood, and between times I put up a shed. Then old Greenwood came along with a wagon loaded with whiskey, and he pulled in and began peddling drinks off the tailgate of his wagon.

"I'd taken the trouble to claim a quarter section, so he was on my land. I told him so and he made me no argument but started paying rent. Then Holstrum came in, and he found where my quarter ended and filed on the quarter section right alongside. He put in his store and we had a town.

"Today we've got the stockyards and the railroad, so there's eighty-odd people livin' here now."

"Much trouble?"

"Some . . . Them Drakos are trouble. They settled down over west of here. There's the old man and three, four boys. Unruly. That's what they are, unruly. Greenwood, Holstrum an' me, why we want this here to be a *town*. We got it in mind to build a church and a school . . . maybe both in one building until we can manage more.

"We made a mistake there at the beginning. We chose Bert Drako for marshal and he straightened out a few bad ones who drifted in . . . killed one man.

"Then it kind of went to his head. That killing done it, I guess. He's got to thinking he's the whole cheese hereabouts. Him and those boys of his. They've begun to act like they owned the town, and we don't need that. Don't need it a-tall! This here's a good little town.

"Four or five of us got together and formed ourselves a committee. We've transplanted several small trees to start a park, and we're diggin' a well in our spare time . . . a town well, and then one for the park, too."

He got up. "Well, back to work. If you're still of a mind to do some smithing, you come around. I'll be in here shortly after sunup."

Tom Shanaghy walked back uptown and stopped in front of the hotel. For a moment he stood there, looking up and down the dim street, lighted only here and there by windows along the way.

He shook his head in disbelief. This was a *town*? It was nothing, just a huddle of ramshackle frame buildings built along a railroad track, with nothing anywhere around but bald prairie. Yet the smith had sounded proud, and he seemed to genuinely love the place. How, Shanaghy wondered, could anybody?

As for himself, he couldn't get out of it fast enough. He would help the smith tomorrow, as it would serve to pass the time. Besides, he liked the feel of a good hammer in his hand, the red-glow from the forge and the pleasure of shaping something, making something. Maybe that was why these people liked their town, because they had built it themselves, with their own hands and minds.

He went upstairs, turned in and slept well, with a light spatter of rain to aid his slumber and cool things off. Awakening in the morning he thought of the letters and papers in the blanket-roll. He should look at them, as there might be some clue in them as to Rig Barrett and what had happened to him.

The sun was not yet up, although it was vaguely gray outside. He lay still for a while, gathering his wits and somewhat uncomfortable. The bed was good enough, and the fresh prairie air through the window was cool and pleasant. The discomfort, he realized, was only within himself, yet he could find no reason for it.

Oddly, New York, to which he would be returning, seemed far away and he had a hard time placing it all in his mind. Every time he tried to bring the city within focus, it faded out, and the feeling irritated him.

He bathed, dressed, prepared his things for a quick departure, and then went down to breakfast. The citizens of the town ate at home, and only transients such as himself ate at the hotel. On this morning there was only one other person in the dining room . . . a young woman wearing a gray traveling outfit, a very cool and composed young woman who took him in at a glance and then ignored him.

She was quite pretty, an ash-blonde with very regular features. Obviously awaiting someone, she was impatient now, and she glanced often at a tiny watch she carried in her purse. Curious, Shanaghy took his time, wondering whom she was to meet and what such a girl was doing in this place.

He knew little of women. Most of those he knew had been the girls off the Line or those who walked the streets on the Bowery, and he knew them only by sight or the casual contacts made in dance halls where he went often to collect for Morrissey, who owned several.

It was early for such a woman to be around. Had she come in from the country? That was unlikely. Had she got off a train? The first of the day had not arrived yet.

A new man entered. He was slim and dark, wearing a Prince

Albert coat and a planter's hat. He was neat, his gray vest spotless, the striped gray pants hanging down over highly polished boots.

Shanaghy glanced at him. Though he had never seen the man before, he knew the type, a con man and a four-flusher. He was smooth and handsome, with a face that seemed to have all the right lines but somehow missed something.

The girl started up, then sank back. "George! Of all people!"

She acted surprised, but Shanaghy was sure this was the person she had waited for. Why the act then?

Shanaghy refilled his cup. The smith could wait just a little longer.

FIVE

Whatever was happening here was none of his business, but Shanaghy knew breeding when he saw it, and the girl had it. The man did not. He was simply a flashy tough who had put on the outward manners of a gentleman, and Shanaghy knew that something was in the wind.

Seeming to be unaware of them, he accepted a plate of steak and eggs from last night's waiter. Scarcely had the waiter gone when Shanaghy heard George say, "Don't worry, ma'am. I promised you he'd never get here and he will not."

"But what if they get someone else?"

The man shrugged. "There's nobody else. Barrett had the reputation, and he knew how to handle such situations. With him out of the picture it will happen just as we want it to."

After that there was only an overheard word here and there, but Shanaghy understood nothing. Barrett must be Rig Barrett, but how could George be sure Rig would not show up?

The couple turned suddenly to look at him, but he was seemingly oblivious to their conversation and they could not know they had spoken loud enough to be overheard. Anyway, from Shanaghy's dress he was obviously not native to the town, but a stranger.

50

Despite himself, he was puzzled. Who were these people? Why was it important to them that Rig Barrett not be present? And how could George be so sure Rig would not show up . . . unless he had made sure he would not?

Murder? Why not, if the stakes were great enough? But what stakes could be, in such a place as this? Yet . . . Shanaghy didn't know. This country was new to him and he did not know where the money was.

Cattle, someone had said. Grazing land. There was a shortage of beef in the eastern states. He had heard talk of that. Yet if it was cattle, where were they? And why was it necessary for Barrett to be out of the picture?

Tom Shanaghy was a cynic and a skeptic. The world in which he had lived in New York was a world where only the dollar counted. If people were after something, it had to be money or a commodity that could be turned into money. Such a girl as this was not meeting such a man unless there was money in it. No doubt she thought she was using him, and probably he believed he was using her.

Cattle came from Texas. Vince Patterson was coming up from Texas with cattle. He was coming to revenge himself upon the town where Drako had been marshal.

Hence it was possible that this girl was somehow connected with Patterson, or hoped somehow to profit from his arrival in town.

Too bad he was leaving for New York. He would like to see what happened.

He got up, paid for his meal and walked down the street to the blacksmith shop. The smith was using the bellows on his fire. "Couple of wheels to be fitted with tires," he commented. "Hank Drako's wagon. He brought it in last week and was mad when I wouldn't fit the tires right off. Now I know Hank. He fords three little streams coming in here, and in one of them he always pulls up in midstream to let his horses drink. So while he's settin' there those tires and wheels are soaking up water. You can't fit a tire unless the wheel is all dried out and I told him he'd have to leave it. He was mighty put out about it."

He pointed with his hammer. "There's the wheels. I made the tires. You go ahead and fit them."

Shanaghy took off his coat and shirt and hung them on nails inside the smithy. Then he built a circular fire outside in the yard at a place where such fires had been built before. When he had a small fire going, he laid the tire in it and put some of the burning sticks on top to get a more uniform heat.

After a few minutes he tried the iron with a small stick and, after a few more minutes, tried it again. This time the stick slipped easily along the tire as if oiled, and a thin wisp of smoke arose from it.

In the meantime he had placed the wheel to be fitted on a millstone, fitting the hub into the center hole. Putting the tire in position, Shanaghy pried it over the wheel with a tiredog, aided with a few hefty blows from a six-pound sledge. The tire went into place, the wood smoking from the heat of the iron tire, the wood of the wheel cracking and groaning as the tire contracted. The smith had a rack with a trough in which the wheel could be turned until the tire could be contracted to a tight fit. The cool water in the trough sloshed as he turned.

Shanaghy was busy with the second wheel when he heard a horseman ride up. He worked on, conscious of scrutiny, and when he finished driving the tire into place he added a few taps for good measure and then turned.

A thin, stoop-shouldered man with a drooping mustache sat on a buckskin horse, watching him. The man wore an old blue shirt, homespun pants tucked into boots, and a six-shooter. He also carried a rifle in his hands. His hat was narrow-brimmed and battered.

"Ain't seen you before," he said.

"Good reason for it."

"What's that?" The man sat up a little, not liking Shanaghy's tone.

"I haven't been here before."

The man stared at him and Shanaghy went on about his work. He had some strap-hinges to make, and he went about it.

"You the pilgrim had the run-in with my son?"

Shanaghy looked up. He was aware that the smith was watching. So were a couple of men on the boardwalk across the street.

"If that was your son," Shanaghy suggested, "you'd better advise him not to try to take in too much territory. I was minding my own affairs."

"My son's my deputy. So was the man you shot."

"Deputy? You need deputies to handle a town this size?" Shanaghy straightened up from the anvil. "A man who couldn't handle a town this size by himself must be pretty small potatoes."

"What's that?" Drako reined his horse around threateningly. "You sayin' I don't amount to much?"

"Mister," Shanaghy said, "if I couldn't handle a town this size without deputies, I'd quit. Also, if I were you I'd advise your son that hanging a man without a trial is murder, no matter who does it."

Shanaghy thought he had Drako pegged, yet he knew he was taking a chance. For that he was prepared. Since childhood he had been facing boys and men, some of whom were tough, some who just believed they were. He did not like this Drako any more than he had liked his arrogant son, but it had never been his way to dodge a fight. He had discovered long since that such men accept dodging as cowardice and it only invited trouble.

One way or the other, he didn't care. Within hours he would be riding the cars back to New York, where enough trouble already awaited him.

"You talk mighty free," Drako said.

"Mister, I have work to do. If you've come here hunting trouble, step right in and get started. If you aren't hunting trouble, I'd suggest you get on down the street while you're all in one piece."

Shanaghy had a light hammer in his hand and he knew what he could do with it. Long ago he had learned how to throw a hatchet or a hammer with perfect accuracy. He knew that before Drako could put a hand on his gun, he could have that hammer on its way. And once thrown, Shanaghy would follow it in. It was a chancy thing to do, but he had been taking such chances all his life.

Drako hesitated, then reined his horse around. "I'll see you again!" he blustered, then rode off.

"You do that," Shanaghy called out. "Any time, any place."

The smith heaved a sigh when Drako was gone. "Figured he was goin' to shoot you," he said.

"And me with this hammer? I'd have put it right between his eyes."

"Just as well you're leavin' town," the smith said, "although I surely wish you weren't. You're the best I've seen in awhile. You must have you a girl back there to want to go so bad."

"A girl? No, I've no girl." Yet the thought reminded him of the girl in the gray traveling outfit.

"Speaking of girls . . ." Shanaghy began, then went on to describe her. "Do you have any idea who she is?"

"I surely don't, but I know she didn't come in on the train, like you'd expect. She rode in a-horseback . . . side-saddle. She rode in early so I doubt she came far."

The smith paused. "She's a handsome young woman. You interested in her?"

"Not that way. Kind of curious, though, about who she is and where she found that man she was talkin' to."

They returned to work. At noon, Shanaghy hung up the leather apron and washed his hands in the tub. As he dried them, he thought about the girl, Drako, and Barrett.

"Smithy," he asked, "this man Barrett, who has been sent for? What if he doesn't show?"

"There'll be hell to pay. Vince Patterson is a hard, hard man, and from all we hear he's coming up the trail loaded for bear. Short of a shooting war there's no way we can stop him. He knows how many men we've got and he will have more."

"And Rig Barrett could stop him?"

He shrugged. "Who knows? He could if anybody could. Rig's been there before, and they know it. He's a strong man, and they know if shooting starts somebody will die. Somebody may die anyhow, but with Rig shooting it's no longer a gambling matter.

"What we hope for is that he'll be here, and that his mere presence will stop them. He's a known man."

Later, when Shanaghy walked to the door to cool off in the light breeze, he looked down the street at the town and shook his head, wonderingly.

It was nothing. A collection of ramshackle shacks and frame buildings stuck up in the middle of nowhere, and yet men were willing to fight for it. He took out his heavy silver watch and looked at it. There were hours yet before the train was due.

The smith came out and stood beside him.

"It ain't much," Shanaghy said.

"It's all we've got," the smith replied. "And it's home."

Home . . . how long since he had a real home? Shanaghy wondered. His thoughts went back to the stone cottage on the edge of moors in Ireland. He remembered the morning walks through the mist when he went to the uplands to bring the horses down. How long ago it seemed! He turned away from the dusty street and walked back to the forge.

Yet the thoughts of home had altered his mood. He finished a lap weld in a wagon tire, and returned to making hinges, but suddenly he was feeling lost and lonely, remembering the green hills of Ireland and the long talks with his father beside the forge. His father, he realized now, had been a strange man, half a poet, half a mystic.

"A man," his father said once, "should be like iron, not steel. If steel is heated too much it becomes brittle and it will break, while iron has great strength, boy. Yet it can be shaped and changed by the proper hammering and the right amount of heat. A good man is like that."

What had Rig Barrett been like?

Shanaghy took a punch and made holes in a hinge, thinking about Barrett. The smith stopped, straightening up and putting a hand across the small of his back.

"This man Barrett," Shanaghy said. "Tell me about him."

The smith hesitated, thinking about it. "A small man," he said. "He rode with the Texas Rangers during the war with Mexico. Fought Comanches, drove a team over the Santa Fe Trail. As a boy, they tell me, he drove turkeys or pigs to market back east—drives that would go for more'n a hundred miles.

"He's been over the trail a time or two and folks know him. They know he's an honest man who will stand for no nonsense. We figured if anybody could make Vince Patterson see the light, why, he was it."

The smith glanced at him. "You're a good hand. Why don't you stay? What's back in New York that makes it so important?"

"New York? Hell, man, that's my town! I . . . ." Shanaghy's voice trailed off. Who was he fooling? New York was not his town. Chances were, by now they'd forgotten all about him. In a country town like this if a man turned up missing, like Rig Barrett, for example, he left quite a hole. Back in New York, if one Irish slugger stepped out of line or got lost, somebody else stepped right into his place and nobody even remembered.

McCarthy might remember. Morrissey might even give him a thought.

"See here," the smith said suddenly. "You're a good man. If you didn't want to work for me, I could sell you a half-interest."

Shanaghy smiled. "I think not, I'd not make light of your town, Smith, but I am a city man. I like the lights and the bustle. Besides, if this Vince Patterson is all you say he is, your town may not be here much longer. That man who was talking to that young woman . . . I heard part of something this morning . . . I got the impression he didn't expect Rig to ever get here."

The smith had turned back to the forge, but now he turned sharply around. "What's that mean?"

"Well," Shanaghy replied lamely, "I can't really say. Maybe they were talking about somebody else, but I got the idea they were talking about Rig. I also got the idea that steps had been taken to see that he never got here."

The smith took off his apron. "You stay right here, Shanaghy. I've got to see a man."

The smith left, almost running.

"Now what the hell have you done?" Shanaghy asked himself. "You and your big mouth. You don't know anything, you're just surmising. And why should they care, anyway?"

The fact remained that they did care. Whatever that girl had in mind she cared a lot, and so had the man with her. They had not wanted Rig Barrett to be around when Vince Patterson reached town. Shanaghy took out his big silver watch. It was still hours until train time.

Well, this was the town's problem, if it could be called a town. He took up another set of hinges and placed them on the pile, then started all over again. He liked the feel of the hammer in his hand, checking the heat of the iron on which he worked by the color.

He walked to the door and looked up and down the street. There were two buggies and a wagon standing at the hitching-rails. Several horses, saddled, were tied along the street, usual, he supposed, for this time of day.

Suddenly the man called George appeared on the street. He glanced up and down, then strolled slowly along, lingering here and there as if to see into the various stores. When he reached the blacksmith shop he paused and taking a thin cigar from his pocket, he lighted it, glancing at Shanaghy.

"Where's the smith?" he asked.

"Around."

"Back soon?"

"Soon. Can I do something for you?"

George smiled. His teeth were white, his smile pleasant. Yet only the lips smiled. The eyes were cool, calculating. "I didn't know the smith had a helper."

"Occasionally."

"You from around here?"

Shanaghy shrugged. "Who is? This is a new town, mister. Everybody here is from somewhere else. Like you . . . Where do you come from?"

George threw him a sharp, hard look. "I thought that was a question that wasn't asked out here."

"You asked me."

"Ah? So I did. Well, I'm from Natchez, on the Mississippi."

"Gambling town," Shanaghy commented. "At least Natchez-Under-the-Hill is. They tell me there are a lot of shysters and con men around there . . . and more crooked gamblers than anywhere."

George's eyes took on a hard, ugly look. "It seems to me you know a good deal about Natchez. You've been there?"

"Heard about it."

"You hear too much."

Shanaghy suddenly felt good. He did not know why he felt so good, but he did. Maybe it was the prospect of a fight, or maybe it was because he simply did not like George.

He looked at George, and he smiled.

Angered, George turned sharply away, yet he had not taken two steps before Shanaghy spoke.

Why he said what he did he would never know. It would have been wiser to let well enough alone, yet the words came out uncalled for.

"Really doesn't make much difference whether Rig comes or not," he said. "Everything's ready."

SIX

G eorge stopped so abruptly it was a wonder he didn't fall on
his face. He turned slowly and for a moment they stared at
each other.

George, Shanaghy reflected, did not like him. He didn't like
him at all. Yet George's tone was even. "Who was that you
mentioned? Rig, did you say?"

"Rig Barrett," Shanaghy said, "a careful man. Leaves nothing to chance."

He didn't know what he was talking about, but he didn't like
George any better than the gambler, or whatever he was, liked
him, and he spoke merely to irritate him. Yet there was more,
for the townspeople were worried about Vince Patterson and
George, he knew, was somehow connected with all that might
happen.

Most of the people he had known made crime a profession,
and there were many such around the Bowery, the Five Points
and lower Broadway. Many believed all honest men to be
stupid, and usually were overly optimistic about their own
plans, believing they couldn't fail. Nor did they ever seem to
realize they were risking their lives or, at the very least,
several years of their lives against sums of money that could in

no way pay for the time they were losing or the pleasures they would be missing.

The man called George was such a one, sure that he was much smarter than those with whom he dealt. And even when he was being used, he would be certain he was using them. But who was the girl? What was her part in all this?

"Rig Barrett? I don't believe I know him." George's left hand unbuttoned his coat. "Is he from around here?"

"Figured you knew him," Shanaghy replied blandly. "Everybody's talking about him. Folks seem to be expecting trouble when the cattle come up the trail, and they're figuring on Rig to handle it. If he gets here, that is. Personally, I think he's just keeping out of sight until the right moment, as he's not the kind of man to let people down."

George shrugged and turned away. "Sometimes a man can't help it," he suggested.

Shanaghy picked up his hammer again and went to the forge. He looked at the iron heating there. He put down the hammer, took the tongs and lifted the iron from the fire.

"A man like that," he said, "if he couldn't make it, would surely send somebody in his place."

George walked away, ignoring him, and Shanaghy chuckled, continuing with his work. He was punching holes in a hinge when a man came from across the street and stopped in the door.

"Where's Carpenter?"

"Carpenter?"

"The smith."

"Oh? I didn't know his name. Just called him Smith."

The man nodded. "Many do. Where is he?" He stepped forward, holding out his hand. "I'm Holstrum."

Shanaghy held up his. It was black with soot. "Sorry. I'm Tom Shanaghy. I've just been lending a hand here for a few hours."

"Glad to have you. We need good men."

"Drako still the marshal?"

"He is."

"Best fire him then, if Vince Patterson is hunting him. You'd best find a man the town will stand behind."

"Rig Barrett will fire him. Then there won't be any gunplay. We don't need any shooting."

"And if Rig doesn't get here?"

Holstrum hesitated, not enjoying the thought. Then he looked across the street, his face blank. "I will do it," he said. "It must be done before Vince Patterson arrives. Maybe if Drako had been fired, that will be an end to it, and if there is trouble let Drako handle it. He's been hunting trouble ever since the shooting."

"Suppose," Shanaghy wondered, "if Rig sent somebody in his place?"

"It wouldn't work. There is no other who would do as well. Rig is known. Perhaps Hickok . . . I do not know."

Shanaghy walked back to the bellows and worked at it, heating up the fire. "You can't know what will happen, Mr. Holstrum. Nor if Barrett will come. You had best be rid of Drako and have another marshal."

Holstrum shook his head. "That's the trouble. There are brave men here, but none of us are experienced at the handling of such trouble. All of us will fight, but it is not a fight we want. If there is shooting, there will be killing, and the more shooting the more killing. It is a job for Rig Barrett."

He paused. "There must be no trouble, for there are other herds coming, and there will be much business here and our town is young. We must have that business."

Holstrum walked back to the forge and watched the glowing embers, and the irons heating. "The cattle-buyers will come on the noon train, and they will be buying the herds that come over the trail. In the next few weeks there will be two or three hundred thousand dollars paid for cattle, and the cattlemen will pay off their hands. And many of them will buy clothing, food, supplies, liquor, whatever they need in our stores. Such money will put the town on a solid footing. We will be able to build our church and our school."

Shanaghy took the iron in the tongs and walked back to the anvil. He took up his hammer. He struck a blow, then another. He stopped. "Two or three hundred thousand dollars? Where would a town this size get that much money?"

"Oh, we don't have that much! Not by far. But we have sent for it and it will be here. We must pay off the drovers, you know, and the buyers will want checks cashed, and—"

"Two or three hundred thousand? It is coming by train?"

"How else? It will be here, and Rig Barrett is coming with it. I tell you, there must be no trouble."

Holstrum walked away and Shanaghy went on about his business. There was no bank in the town, although there was a building on which some ambitious person had painted "BANK" a sign, no doubt with the best of intentions. Banking, such as there was, was handled by Holstrum himself or by Greenwood. No doubt the money for cashing checks written by the cattle-buyers would come from the safe of one or the other.

Carpenter did not return, so Shanaghy continued to work. One of the things he had always enjoyed about blacksmithing was the time to think. Once a man knew what he was doing, he could work swiftly, smoothly, and there was time to ponder.

The smith was a good man with tools—not so good as either McCarthy or his father, but good enough. He laid out his work well, and Shanaghy fitted two more rims to wheels and added to the supply of hinges.

In the corner of the room, fastened to a timber brace, he found a soot-stained sheet of paper listing work to be done. He studied it, then went ahead with what was needed, but his thoughts kept reverting to the girl in the restaurant and to George. What did they want? What were they after? Surely, the two could not be . . . no . . . whatever she was, she was not that type. Larceny maybe, prostitution, no.

The more he considered the situation, the surer he was that somehow or other George had contrived that Rig Barrett not be present when Patterson arrived with his cattle.

Was Barrett dead? Even the shrewdest of gunfighters can be shot from ambush . . . especially if it were done at some unexpected time or place. He thought again of the letters, the map in his pack. They would surely tell him something of where Barrett had been and what he had been doing.

Why a map?

Shanaghy had no answer to that. Suddenly he was restless. He must look at those letters.

Why had he not read them before? He hesitated over the answer to that, and then admitted that he felt a curious reticence about invading the privacy of another person.

A gentleman, his father had told him once, did not read another person's mail. Whatever these letters were, they were not addressed to him but to Rig Barrett . . . Yet Rig Barrett was not here, or didn't seem to be, and this was an emergency. He knew little of Barrett except what he heard, but he tried to put himself in Barrett's place.

What would Rig do? What would John Morrissey do? What would his father have done?

They would read those letters and plan accordingly. Look at the situation, Shanaghy told himself. These people expect Barrett. He has not come. George believes he will not or cannot come. Yet Shanaghy himself had Barrett's clothing, his blankets and his prized shotgun.

Damn it, he swore softly. Where are you, Carpenter?

He worked, but as he worked he wondered where George was and where that girl was. He also thought of those cattle with twenty-five tough cowhands moving north, mile by mile, coming closer and closer to that inevitable hour.

And what about Drako? Drako would also know of that, he and his tough sons. What were they doing? Were they going to run or fight?

Fight, he decided. They were too proud or too foolish to run. But they would need help . . . and probably knew where to get it.

At last Carpenter returned, and Holstrum was with him.

Shanaghy stripped off his apron. "Got to go up the street," he said. "I'll be back."

"Wait just a minute," Carpenter suggested. He turned to the storekeeper. "Holstrum, you tell him."

"Shanaghy, we don't know you, except that Carp here says you're a mighty fine smith and a good worker. He also says you backed down Drako."

Shanaghy shrugged. "I wouldn't say that. Drako likes to know who he's fightin', and I'm kind of unknown. He wasn't scared . . . He just wanted to think it over some. Just the same—" he paused— "I don't think Drako is as tough as he'd like to have people think, or as tough as he'd like to believe he is."

"Nonetheless, you stopped him. He stood off when you showed yourself ready. Now, we've been expecting Rig Barrett and something's happened, because he hasn't showed."

"I don't think he's going to show," Shanaghy said.

They looked at him, suddenly attentive. Tom remembered, too late, about Josh Lundy's warning.

"I heard this man George tell a woman he wouldn't show." It

sounded weak, he knew. There was suspicion in their eyes now.

"How could he know that?" Holstrum asked.

"He couldn't . . . unless he knew somebody had made certain of it." Shanaghy hung up the apron, took down his shirt and put it on. The two men watched him until he donned his coat, then somewhat reluctantly Holstrum suggested, "Shanaghy, I don't know you but Carpenter has respect for you, and he liked the way you stood off Drako. Well . . . if Rig doesn't show, how about you? Would you take on the job? Rig being a known man, he had the battle half won. It will be tougher for you."

Shanaghy smiled. What would Old Smoke say to that? Offered a job as marshal! Old Smoke, he realized suddenly, would have taken it, and he would have been right out there in the street to stop them. John Morrissey never backed water for any man. And come to think of it, he never had either. He'd run a couple of times, but only from numbers and when he knew he was coming back.

"Thanks," he said. "I have a ticket on the night train. I'm heading back to New York, where I've trouble enough waiting and some old scores to pay."

"Shanaghy," Holstrum protested, "we're in serious trouble here. Patterson's liable to burn our town. He has said he would."

"Sorry. When that train goes, I'll be on it."

He walked away up the street. Damn it, this wasn't his fight! What did they take him for? He just showed up in town and . . . What did they know about him, after all? And if they did know about him, what would they think then? It was like McCarthy said, he was nothing but a Bowery thug. Would they want him for marshal if they knew that?

Shanaghy went to his room and opened the haversack. For the first time he looked at the shirts. They were much too small for him, with his seventeen-inch neck. The cuffs were frayed and worn. Mr. Rig Barrett did not make much of being a peace officer, for the outfit was that of a poor man. Only the guns were neat and well kept.

If Rig Barrett had been less than an honest man, these shirts might have been made of the striped silk the gamblers wore—or some of them, at least.

Shanaghy took out the packet of letters, the notebook with the loose papers tucked inside, and the map. He put them down on the bed, then walked over and locked the door. He took out his six-shooter and placed it on the bed beside him as he sat.

There were four letters in the packet, and he put them aside, reluctant to open them. First, he looked at the loose papers.

The first was a carefully written description of the town, all compressed into about three lines, with a list of the stores, saloons and other buildings, and a diagram showing their locations along the street.

Below it were brief written outlines of several people, the first being: *Patterson, Vincent, age 36, height five feet ten inches, hair brown, eyes brown. M. Marcella Draper, 2 sons, 1 daughter. Father to Texas with Moses Austin. Mexican War 1 yr. service; Texas Rangers, 2 yrs. Veteran several Indian battles. Runs about 6,000 head. Rarely drinks. Strong, stubborn, fearless. Never leaves a job incomplete. Honest, a driver of men but feeds them well. Always has the best cook on the range. Excellent stock in remuda. Cattle always top grade. Can be reasoned with if in the mood. Once started, no stopping.*

Drako, Henry, age 41, five feet eleven inches, black hair, mixed gray. Mustache, often unshaven. Believed wanted in West Virginia for horse theft; 3 sons, Win, Dandy, and Wilson. No record on boys. Suspected horse theft. Cattle theft. Movers. W. Va. to Ohio; to Illinois; served in Blackhawk War; to Tennessee, trouble with man named Sackett whose horse Drako "borrowed." Sackett recovered horse, suggested they leave. They did. Marshal killed V. Patterson's brother. Victim apparently under the influence.

Pendleton, Alfred. Brn Suffolk, Eng. Age 44 yrs. Six feet. Hair blond, eyes blue, slender build; 1 son, 1 daughter. Widower. Buys cattle, feeds, ships. Occasional buyer from Patterson. Win Drako suspected of stealing Pendleton calves. Quiet man, avoids trouble. Son, Richard, strong, athletic, attended William & Mary College 2 years. Now 25. Good horseman, good shot. Pendleton suffered reverses due to drouth, cattle theft.

There were brief listings on Carpenter, Greenwood and Holstrum that told Shanaghy nothing he did not already know.

There were notes on several other businessmen and, at the end:

Josh Lundy, cowhand, five feet eight inches, slender, age 29. Brn Texas. Presently employed by Pendleton. Witness in cow theft against Win Drako. Claimed horse in possession of Drako was stolen from Pendleton range, horse Lundy said owned by Jan Pendleton.

That must be the horse Lundy had been accused of stealing. He said he had stolen a horse, stolen it back, for a girl.

Lundy's father killed by Indians when he was twelve, supported mother and three sisters herding cattle, raising a few on his own. Wounded in Indian fight. Wounded again in fight with border bandits. Cattle drive to east, swam herd over the Mississippi. Right arm broken when thrown from bad horse. Good man with a rifle. Short arm makes handling pistol difficult. Reliable.

Obviously, Rig Barrett was no fool and left little to chance. He wished to know what kind of men he must deal with.

Pendleton . . . Why did that name hold his attention? Lundy might have mentioned it when he spoke of stealing the horse. Jan Pendleton was obviously that girl.

The second page was a simple list of expenditures for supplies, ammunition and such items, along with a note of fifty dollars sent to "Maggie."

A third sheet was the beginning of a letter to Mag, evidently Barrett's wife:

Dear Lady:

I taken pen in hand to inform you of my whereabouts and destination. Unfortunately, the prairie town to which I go offers employment for two months only, making it impractical to send for you, Dear Lady. I shall ride down the trail to meet Mr. Patterson before he is close to town. Perhaps we may reach an understanding.

The trouble I foresee will not come from him. There are other elements entering into this, which accounts for my presence in Kansas City. Be assured that when this task is complete I shall come to you at once, in St. Louis.

Do you remember Mr. Pendleton? The gentleman who loaned you the handkerchief on the train? He is here—in the town, that is—and, I fear, is having trouble.

I shall write aga . . .

The letter ended there and Tom Shanaghy put it down with the others. It wasn't much help except to indicate that Barrett had not anticipated trouble from Patterson that he couldn't handle. What worried him was something he had apparently come upon in Kansas City, or something that led him to go there.

What?

Shanaghy glanced through the packet of letters, but none of them seemed of consequence. They were from friends and business associates, but offered no clue to what might have been the trouble in Kansas City.

There was one other note, another unfinished letter written by Barrett to somebody:

> I shall not ride the cushions, as I did before. This time I'll speak to a conductor I know and arrange to ride a caboose into town. That way I might arrive unseen . . .

Shanaghy put the letters down, and glanced at the notebook. Probably nothing there but he would have to see. The trouble was, he was hungry. He had been up since daylight and had put in a hard morning's work at the smithy. Yet he sat still, thinking.

Tom Shanaghy had never considered himself a bright man. He had not even thought about it. He had survived in a hard, rough world along the Bowery and in the Five Points, and he supposed he was shrewd after a fashion. Most of his problems he had solved with his fists, but they did not help much now.

Rig Barrett, now, how about him? Barrett was supposed to be here and was not. Yet he was the kind of man to keep appointments. Hence he was either here and hiding out somewhere, or he was not here. If he was not here, he must be unable to be here. And that meant he was either a prisoner, which was unlikely, injured or dead.

His gear had been on the train and in the gondola in which Shanaghy was riding. That meant he had either put the gear there himself, and had not followed it, or that the stuff had been thrown there by someone else.

Of course, Barrett might have gotten on the train and, for some reason, gotten off again. But that was unlikely, because if he had arranged to travel by caboose he would have gone directly to it.

"The way it looks," Shanaghy muttered, "is that Barrett was headed for the caboose when somebody laid one on him. Probably conked him on the noggin and then tossed his gear aboard a passing train, figuring to leave nothing that would name him when they found the body."

That also looks, he told himself, as though Mr. Rig Barrett is not going to arrive in town, and that means whoever plans to pull something off is going to have mighty little trouble doing it.

There was a sharp rap on the door. Shanaghy got to his feet and opened it.

Four men stood there and they all held guns. One of them was Holstrum. "They tell me," the big storekeeper said, "that you have Rig Barrett's shotgun."

Shanaghy glanced from one to the other. Nobody needed to tell him that he was in trouble. Just like Lundy had told him. He started to step forward and their guns lifted. One of them held a rope in his hand.

SEVEN

Tom Shanaghy was in trouble, but he had been in trouble before. He smiled, suddenly, thinking that he could remember few occasions when he had not been in trouble.

"That's right," he replied cheerfully, "I do have his shotgun. When he knew I was coming out here he said I might need it."

That was a lie, of course, but what he needed now was to keep himself from being hung, and he gave them the most likely story. They had already suggested that he might be the man to take Rig's place, so what better story than that Rig had actually sent him?

"Rig sent you? You know him?"

"Let's put it this way. Rig Barrett isn't here. I am. You need a man to take his place. I can do it. You want Drako fired, and I can do that, and will do it."

Shanaghy smiled again, at the thought. That, at least, he would enjoy doing.

"You mean to stop Vince Patterson?" Holstrum demanded. "You think you can?"

"It isn't Vince I'm worried about, gentlemen, nor was it Vince who worried Rig Barrett. Rig was quite sure he could talk to Vince and could reason with him. I mean to try the same thing."

"If he wasn't worried about Vince," Holstrum demanded, "then what did worry him?"

Now he had him. Rig had gone to Kansas City because of some suspicion he had, yet what that was Shanaghy did not know. He reached for the first thing that came to mind, and the moment it shaped into words Shanaghy was sure he had hit upon it.

"What worried him," Shanaghy paused, then suddenly decided to keep his mouth shut, "was something else entirely, but I am not free . . . I can't betray his confidence. Yet have no fear now. I shall handle it."

Yet all the time Shanaghy kept in mind that eastbound train that would get him out of all this. Would it come in time? Would he be able to get away?

Whatever else he had done, he had now made them unsure. So he spoke up with confidence. "Now, gentlemen, I am hungry. I want to eat and then get back to the smithy. But choose your time and if it is me you wish to be marshal here, let me know. I have work to do."

They turned to go and suddenly an idea came to Shanaghy. He said to Holstrum, "You know something of the railroad operations here. Is it customary to have a railroad detective riding the trains?"

Holstrum shook his head. "Never heard of such a thing. There's been no theft from freight cars, and we've had no goods lost."

When they were gone Shanaghy put his things together on the bed, then went down the stairs. This would be a good place to be away from if Rig Barrett did show up.

But that man who kicked him off the train? Just who was *he*?

"Shanaghy," he told himself, "you've come upon something. That was no railroad bull, that was somebody who wanted you off the train for fear of what you might see. And what might that have been, lad? What, indeed?"

Whoever he was, Shanaghy owed him one, but the thought nagged him that something was going on of which he knew nothing. Could that man have been tied in with George and the mysterious lady?

Carpenter himself was in the restaurant when Shanaghy

entered. "Wife's sick," he said, "I'm eatin' out." He waved a hand and Shanaghy joined him. "Right where we sit I killed a buffalo, only last spring. Skinned him out right on the spot.

"Them times, there was nothing anywhere a man might look on but grass waving in the wind. Now Holstrum has him a corn crop growing, and my wife has a vegetable garden. I tell you, my friend, this will be a town to be proud of!

"A few years ago some called this the Great American Desert. They just didn't know soil! This here Kansas country will grow the finest corn, wheat and barley a man could wish for! You mark my words, one day this prairie where only buffalo ranged will feed half the world!

"We have been killing the buffalo. Magnificent as they are, a man must decide what his values are and you can grow no crops where buffalo range. There's no fence will stop them.

"My folks came from Europe and never owned a bit of land to call their own. They were beholden to the lord of the manor for their living, yet before my old father died he owned more than the lord of the manor had.

"You see a few poor shacks now, but give us time. We have been shipping buffalo hides and bones to the eastern markets, and now we're beginning to ship beef. Give us a few years and we will be storing and shipping grain."

He lifted a finger at Tom. "Shanaghy, we need young men here, young men like you."

"Like me?" Shanaghy's grin was sour. "What do you know of me?"

"All we need to know, all we will ever ask. You can do an honest day's work and you take pride in what you do. No man who loves the working of iron as you do can be bad."

Their food was brought and when the waiter had gone, Carpenter said, "The wheels you fitted for Drako? Beautiful! You're a fine craftsman, Tom! A fine craftsman!"

Shanaghy felt himself flushing, and with pride, and embarrassment as well. Nobody had called him a craftsman before, and he relished the term.

"You take pride in your work. You have an eye for the color of red-hot iron such as only the true craftsman has.

"I tell you, Tom, a man who has never taken pride in a job well done is an empty man."

They ate then, and drank their coffee, but Carpenter had set Tom to thinking. Why not stay, after all?

What did he owe Morrissey, or any of them back east? Morrissey had given him a job when needed, but Tom had repaid him with an honest day's work and no shirking. He had fought Morrissey's enemies and made a few of his own in the process, but what had he to show for it? A little money in the bank, a tribute to his mother's advice.

Surely, there was not a soul there who would miss him past the week. Others had disappeared or gone away, and Shanaghy remembered well how little they were missed.

He could scarcely remember the Bowery for the grass blowing in the wind.

Carpenter put down his knife and fork. "Holstrum said you were taking the job as marshal, and that you were sent by Rig Barrett."

"In a way," Tom said, "and it doesn't look as if Rig is going to make it in time. . . . I shall do what he planned to do and ride out to meet Vince Patterson."

"You said you did not believe him to be the greatest trouble? What, then?"

"At this moment, I am not sure. I trust no man now, although you most of all."

"You won't be leaving on the train?"

Tom hesitated for a long time and then he said, "Not right now. Maybe later." He looked over at the smith. "I shall need a horse for a few days."

"I have one . . . the blue roan in the corral. There's the rig for him, too."

They went back to work then, and they handled their iron. And when the train came in, Tom was standing outside to see it stop. There was, he knew, still time. He could still make it. For a moment he hesitated, then went back into the shop and took off his apron.

"South of here," he asked Carpenter, "are there any ranches?"

"Nothing this side of Texas that I know of. Holstrum has a place about seven or eight miles southeast. Nothing but a cabin, shed and a corral. He runs a few head down there and usually has some horses for riding."

"Who takes care of the stock?"

"He's got a man there, but the stock doesn't drift much

because he has the best grass and water for miles. He's a canny man, Holstrum is. I've a place, too, but not as good as the one he found."

Carpenter considered the subject, then added, "Only other place around is about ten miles west. There's a two-by-four saloon over there and about three dugouts. Drako lives about three miles south of it, he and his boys."

"Who makes me marshal?" Shanaghy asks. "If I am to do anything I'd better be wearing a badge . . . or have one."

"Greenwood. You go see him. It was him suggested Rig Barrett. Greenwood's had experience with tough towns. He held out for Barrett and I backed him."

"What about Holstrum?"

"He was worried we'd get a worse Drako. So were some of the others. I could see his point, because Drako is bad enough."

Greenwood was leaning in his bar in the empty saloon when Shanaghy walked in. He was a pleasant-looking man who seemed to be in his late thirties. He smiled a little when he saw Shanaghy. "Talked you into it, did they? I hoped they would."

Shanaghy took the badge Greenwood pushed toward him and pinned it on his shirt pocket. "First time I ever wore one of them," he said.

Greenwood smiled. "You'll wear it with pride, son. I know your kind."

"My kind?" Shanaghy turned his eyes on him. "Mr. Greenwood, I've been a shoulder-striker for John Morrissey."

"Then you're a tough man, and that's what we need. It was never my luck to know Old Smoke, but I saw him fight once. A rough man, a hard man, and a tricky one when it came to elections, but I never knew him to go back on his word, and I know you will be the same. If there is any way in which I can help, let me know."

Shanaghy hesitated. "I don't know who I can trust."

"Who did you trust in New York?"

"Nobody . . . Maybe McCarthy, the smith."

"Then trust nobody here, not even me. Son, in the job you're taking you will stand on your own feet. You will get little help and no thanks from most people. They want the law, but they fear it, too.

"If you need a posse or riflemen, they will be sworn in, but they won't like it. Many men in this town have used guns and some are quite expert. But what a marshal needs is not men who are good with guns, but for himself to be good with men, with handling men.

"Take my word for it, son, a marshal must be judged not by the number of men he has killed in line of duty, but by the tough men he has handled without using a gun, even without violence."

"I don't know whether I am up to it."

"You are. Trust your own judgment of men and of situations. You must stand or fall by your own decisions."

"I think I know who—"

Greenwood lifted a hand. "Don't tell me. Don't tell anybody. Keep it to yourself. Gather your own facts, act upon them as you see fit. If you make a mistake you may be crucified for it. That's the job."

"Thanks."

"Let me buy you a drink," Greenwood suggested.

Shanaghy shook his head. "I don't drink."

Greenwood smiled. "Neither do I," he said cheerfully. "I sell it to those who do and I have no moral scruples against drinking, but I myself don't drink."

Tom Shanaghy walked back to the street. He was marshal of the town now, and he had no idea what the job paid. Nor did he care.

He stood there, looking around. How did a man go about being a marshal? Where did he start? Shanaghy grinned at his own ignorance. He reflected that one job he had was to fire Drako, but that could wait until the former marshall appeared in town wearing the badge.

That came first. Then he must ride down the country and meet Vince Patterson and talk to him before he arrived in town. And he must, if he could, convince Drako that he must stay out of town until the Patterson outfit was gone.

His thoughts returned to George. George was staying at the same hotel as he was, but where was *she*?

He walked down to the railroad station. The depot had three rooms, all connecting and with doors on both sides. The waiting room, which had four benches, the ticket seller's office (the agent was also the telegrapher and freight agent) and the freight room, where freight was held until shipped or picked up, if incoming. On the train side of the depot there was a rough plank platform, already weathered and gray, about sixty feet long.

Shanaghy stepped into the station and walked to the window. The agent looked around. He wore a black vest, a white shirt with sleeve-garters, and a green eyeshade. "Somethin' for ya?" he asked. Then he noticed the star.

"Hah? You're the new marshal. What's been done about Drako?"

"Haven't seen him since they gave me this. I am going to tell him when he rides in."

The station agent came to the window and leaned his elbows on the inside counter. "Don't envy you. He's a mean one, and so are those boys of his."

"I've met him, and one of them."

"Got your work cut out for you, and then Patterson comin' up the trail. Boy, I don't envy you! None a-tall!"

"Any railroad detectives working this line?"

"Nah! Why? We've had no trouble."

"If you had a valuable shipment, how would it be handled?"

The agent shrugged. "Same as anything else. It would come in and it would set until picked up. I s'pose if it was very valuable, I'd be wearin' my pistol and they'd be here to pick it up right off."

"You've got a gun then?"

"I have." The agent grinned. "Never fired a shot in my life."

"Then leave it alone," Shanaghy advised. "You'd probably shoot the wrong man."

Shanaghy walked out on the platform and looked down the track. Nothing but twin rails disappearing in the shimmering distance. He doubted if the agent knew about the shipment of money that would be coming in, and to mention it would be merely to start gossip.

He would have to see that men were here to meet the shipment on arrival.

Yet the moment he thought of that, he thought of another aspect. What if they decided to stop the train before it came to town? Chances were, the shipment would be in an express car and guarded only by the agent en route.

For the idea that this was what Rig Barrett guessed would happen had come to Shanaghy only a few hours before. When everybody in town was involved with what might happen when

Vince Patterson came to town, the thieves could steal the money brought to pay for the cattle and to pay off the hands.

Barrett might even have had a tip, being the man he was, with connections everywhere.

How many people were involved? And what would be their roles? Plan the job yourself, he suggested to himself, and see how you would do it. You've associated with crooks long enough to know.

The fewer involved, the larger the cut for each, and the less likely they were to be noticed. What if the supposed railroad detective had been a crook? Was the girl involved? And George?

Tom Shanaghy walked up the street to the blacksmith shop and Drako was standing by his horse, waiting. He was wearing a badge.

EIGHT

Tom Shanaghy walked on up and stopped, facing Drako. The man was smiling but he was wary.

"Wearin' a badge, hey? What do you think that will get you?"

Shanaghy had been facing such issues since he first walked off the boat in New York. "I've been appointed town Marshal," he said, "and one is all the town needs. I want your badge, Drako."

"You think I'll give it up? Just like that?"

"The authority is not the badge, it is in the vote of the council. They've chosen me Marshal. I want your badge, Drako."

"All right," Drako reached up to unpin the badge, and in that instant Shanaghy knew what the man would do, for it was just what he himself might have done.

Drako unpinned the badge and took it in his left hand and tossed it to him. "Here . . . catch!"

Shanaghy made no move to make the catch. He simply drew his gun, and he was an instant faster . . . Drako had tossed the badge and dropped his hand to his gun, but he was already covered by Shanaghy's pistol.

Drako's hand froze, gripping his gun. Startled, he hesitated, but Shanaghy's thumb was holding his hammer back. And slowly, carefully, Drako released his grip on his gun and moved his hand to the pommel of the saddle. "Smart, hey? We'll see how smart you are when Vince Patterson comes to town."

"He'll be looking for you, not me, and he will know where to find you."

"Maybe."

"You and your boys . . . Come to town whenever you like, only come unarmed."

"Are you crazy?"

"That's it. They can hang their pistols in the saloon, but if they wear them on the street I'll throw them in jail."

"What jail? You ain't got no jail!"

"My jail will be that hitching-rail right yonder. I'll shackle them to it and there they'll stay until their fine is paid . . . rain or shine."

Drako stared at him, then turned his horse sharply around and walked him out of town.

Shanaghy picked the badge out of the dust and put it in his pocket. He looked up to see Holstrum watching him. Greenwood was standing in the door of his saloon and Carpenter had stopped work. He ignored the others and walked over to Carpenter. "Be busy for a few days. After that I'll lend you a hand."

"My offer stands. You can buy a piece of my business."

"Maybe . . . later."

Shanaghy went to his room and checked the shotgun. Then, trusting to nothing, he reloaded it with buckshot.

Sitting down on the bed he studied the situation. First he must find out where Patterson might be. Coming up the trail, of course, but where was he now, and moving how fast?

What had he gotten himself into, anyway? There he was, just waiting for the train to take him back to New York, with everything settled in his mind, and now where was he? Marshal of a hick town with all the trouble in the world about to come down on him. What did he know about being a marshal?

Well, someone said, "Set a crook to catch a crook," but he had never been a crook, exactly, although he had known enough of them and had witnessed a lot of their activities.

He looked around the room. Only a bed, a chair and a small table with a lamp on it. In the corner a washstand with a bowl

and pitcher. Beside the table was a strip of what passed for a
towel, and at the end of the hall a bath.

First thing, he'd better step on down the street and buy
some clothes. All he had was what he stood up in, and that was
too little. He'd need some shirts, a new suit, and some of those
pants they wore around here . . . maybe a hat.

Give up his derby? Not by a damn sight!

That Drako would act. Somehow he was sure. The man was
not about to take this lying down, nor would his boys be willing
to do so. Shanaghy knew he could expect trouble from them,
and soon.

What bothered him, as it must have bothered the missing
Rig Barrett, was the mechanism of the robbery that he believed was to come. How did the crooks expect to handle it,
and how many were involved?

He could scarcely believe that the fashionably dressed young
woman was involved, and yet why would such a woman be
meeting with George? And who was she, anyway?

Tom Shanaghy walked down the street to Holstrum's. There
was another man in the store but Holstrum came to wait on the
new marshal himself. "You picked yourself a tough job, Marshal,
but we'll give you all the support you need."

"Thanks. What I need now is some clothes. I packed light
when I came west."

"This on credit?"

Shanaghy smiled. "Cash . . . I always pay cash, Mr. Holstrum.
I like to keep the decks clear."

Luckily, he found some shirts. "Most womenfolks make
shirts for their men," Holstrum explained. "Pendleton buys
shirts here and there's a few others."

He bought shirts, underwear, two pairs of pants, a thick
leather belt and some boots. He also bought one hundred
rounds of .44-pistol ammunition, a Winchester rifle and fifty
shotgun shells.

"Expecting a war?" Holstrum asked, curiously.

"No, I'm not. But if one comes, I'll be ready."

"Rig Barrett must figure you could do the job. I never heard
of him sending anybody in his place. Didn't know anybody was
that close to him."

"Rig kept his personal affairs to himself," Shanaghy replied.
"I intend to do the same."

Shanaghy thought for an instant of his past. There had been fistfights, knife fights and gun battles. He could scarcely remember a time when he had not been fighting.

"However," he added, "this is only a precaution. I don't think there will be trouble."

When he had taken his clothes back to the hotel and changed his shirt, Shanaghy came downstairs and went to the restaurant for a late supper.

George was not there, but the young woman was. She looked up as Shanaghy entered and her eyes fell to the badge. She stared at it, then lifted her eyes to his. He thought he detected a glimmer of anger or impatience.

"How do you do, ma'am?" he removed his derby. "Welcome to our fair city."

She regarded him cooly and then simply turned her head away, ignoring him.

A voice spoke suddenly from behind him on his left, and he looked around quickly. There was a table there, in the corner, and another girl sat there, a younger, perhaps prettier girl. "You're a stranger here yourself, aren't you, Marshal?"

"I am, and saddled with a job before I've got me feet on the ground. But then, by the look of the place, nobody has been here much longer."

The younger girl held out her hand. "I am Jan Pendleton and I want to thank you."

"Me? Wait until I've done something, miss. I am only just marshal."

"You saved Josh Lundy from hanging, and Josh is my very good friend."

"I can't take credit," he said. "They were going to hang me, too, just because I happened to be there. It seemed to me my neck was long enough, without getting it stretched."

"Thank you, nevertheless."

"May I join you?"

"Please do."

He sat where he could see the other woman. She looked annoyed, and that pleased him. He put his derby on the chair beside him and ordered what the restaurant had to offer. There wasn't much variety but he was accustomed to that and had always been a healthy eater.

"Glad you got your horse back," he told her. "Too bad

there's so many thieves about. Never could figure out why anybody, man or woman, would take to stealing. They never get as much as they stand to lose.

"You take a woman now. Suppose she was a thief and went to prison? They work 'em almighty hard there, and they've no chance to take care of themselves. And when they come out, they're not only old but they've lost their looks."

The young woman across the room looked up and their eyes met. He smiled and her lips thinned to a hard line.

"Biggest trouble with being a crook," he added, "is the company you have to keep." He paused. "If I saw myself getting involved in such a thing, I'd grab the first train out of town."

Jan looked at him curiously, her eyes flickering to the elegant and composed young woman across the room. She changed the subject.

"Are you going to be with us long, Mr. Shanaghy?"

"It is in my thoughts," he said, "although there be some who hope I'll not."

The cool young woman looked up. "Isn't the life expectancy in your kind of job rather short?"

"It is. Although while I live, the life expectancies of those who break the law will be even less."

He turned from her and began to talk to Jan Pendleton of horses, range, Josh Lundy. "Do you know Mr. Patterson?" he asked suddenly, remembering that her father sometimes bought cattle from him.

"Oh, of course! Uncle Vince is a lovely man! He can be very stern, I suppose, but I've never seen him that way. Whenever he is here he stays with us, and he has such wonderful stories to tell. He gave me my first horse."

"The one that was stolen?"

"The very same. I am glad Josh got it back before Uncle Vince returned, because he would have been furious."

"Seems to me he's already sore at Hank Drako."

"He is." She looked at him seriously. "Mr. Shanaghy, you must not let there be trouble. Father says Uncle Vince may burn the town. He holds all of them responsible for the killing of his brother."

"He'll not burn it," Tom said. "There will be no trouble."

The young woman across the room laughed gently, and Tom

Shanaghy felt his face flushing. Before he could speak, however, Jan interrupted. "My father is in town and I am sure he would like to meet you. He will wish to thank you for helping Josh."

Pendleton came in as she was speaking and crossed to the table. After he had talked a bit, Shanaghy said, quite casually, "Mr. Pendleton, you know much of what goes on around here. Do you know of any shipments that have come in during the last couple of days?"

Shanaghy's eyes were on the woman across the room as he spoke, and he saw her fork suddenly stop in midair. For just an instant she was absolutely still, then she continued to eat.

"What sort of shipments?"

"I am not quite sure, but I'd be guessing it would be something unusual, or to someone not well known here."

"No . . . I'm afraid not. But then I am not about town very much. What were you thinking of?"

Shanaghy had been talking only to see the face of the woman across the room, for he was but feeling his way. What could it be, after all? What made it important he be off the train?

Or . . . the thought came suddenly, what if it was not some*thing* but some*body*? Suppose there were others hidden on the train who did not wish to chance being seen by a hobo who might climb over the cars looking for a place to hide out?

That was it, that had to be it.

Alfred Pendleton spoke with a decided British accent. Although the Irish had no love for the British, it sounded close enough to home to have a pleasant sound. Pendleton asked where Tom was from and Shanaghy replied, "Killarney."

"A lovely place. We vacationed there once."

"And now we are all in Kansas," Jan said.

"And that isn't strange," her father remarked. "There are just two lines of railroad to the west, and most people who come out here stop along one or the other. I am constantly meeting people I knew in England or in the eastern states.

"The fastest development will naturally be along the railroads, and the best opportunities." Pendleton glanced at him. "I suspect you've run into some old friends, haven't you?"

Old friends? What friends did Shanaghy have who might come west? No friends, but what of enemies? Eben Childers was a hater, he had been told, and his men would guess that he took a train to escape them. Finding him would be no great problem. Shanaghy shook his head. "No old friends, and I hope no enemies."

Pendleton talked for a few minutes about the future of Kansas and the way the country was growing and then added, "I think you have chosen wisely, Mr. Shanaghy, in settling here. Carpenter says you are an excellent smith and that you may buy a share of his business."

There it was again. Everybody was taking it for granted that he was here to stay. Shanaghy was remembering John Morrissey and the Bowery, although the memories had been fading away in the warm Kansas sun and the demands of his new job. Then he remembered and looked around. The woman across the room was gone.

"She left a few minutes ago," Jan said, impishly.

"I was wondering who she was and what she was doing here."

"No doubt. She's very attractive, don't you agree?"

"I wasn't thinking of that. But she certainly was . . . is."

"If you are wondering who she is, you could check the register at the hotel," Pendleton suggested.

"She's not registered."

"Not here? But then where . . . ?"

"Exactly. Where else? She's not camping on the plains, and nobody sees her coming and going, although Carpenter did see her riding into town one day."

"You're *very* interested, aren't you?" Jan suggested.

"Yes, ma'am. When there's trouble expected, it is my business to know as much as I can. I don't want anybody to get hurt."

Shanaghy pushed back his chair. "Have you any message for Vince Patterson? I'm riding to meet him."

Pendleton shook his head. "If you're expecting to talk him out of it, forget it. We've tried. He's a stubborn, hardheaded man. But a good man for all of that, and no fool."

"I've got to try."

"You can tell him hello for me," Jan said, "and give him my love."

Well, that word did something to him. Shanaghy wished all of a sudden that he was a better man, and he said, "Miss, if that doesn't do it, nothing will."

Then he turned sharply and left, wondering why he was suddenly feeling all hot and embarrassed.

Tomorrow morning he would be riding out, and suddenly he did not want to go anywhere. He just wanted to stay right here.

When the door closed behind him, Pendleton glanced at his daughter. "An interesting young man," he commented.

"He's nice," she said, "and he's strong . . . very strong."

"Naturally. He's a blacksmith."

"I wasn't thinking of that," she replied. "Perhaps resolute is the word. I don't think he knows what he wants yet, but when he makes up his mind . . . he will get it."

NINE

The horse Shanaghy rode was a roan, a mustang with a Morgan cross, and the moment he hit the saddle he knew he had a horse. The roan trotted into the street, and the moment he had the room he went to bucking.

Shanaghy, who had ridden all his life, had never tackled anything like this. How he stayed with the horse he never knew, but stay he did. And when finally they loped away he heard a cheer from the few scattered people who had watched.

There had been last-minute advice from Carpenter. The herd would move about twelve miles per day, perhaps less now, as the grass was good and Patterson would want to bring them in fat for the market.

The country, which had appeared flat, proved less so than Shanaghy expected, for there were rolling hills and some deeper ravines. When he was well away from town, he drew up to look around.

As far as the eye could reach there was only grass moving in the wind. These were the fabled buffalo plains, but there were no buffalo now. Far off, he glimpsed a herd of antelope. There was no sound but the wind . . .

For several minutes he sat very still, feeling the wind on his face. The air was fresh, the sky was clear, and somehow the soft wind and the coolness smoothed the troubles from his mind.

Yet . . . the thought came again . . . what of that young woman? Who was she? What was she?

That she was not staying anywhere in town was obvious, and he doubted if she could be living with Hank Drako . . . She simply wasn't the Drakos' type.

That she might live in the town to the west was possible but doubtful, as she seemed too fresh when she rode into town in the morning. True, she had come but twice, but nonetheless she must have somewhere to live that was close by, providing her with a means to keep her clothes pressed and clean.

Where, then?

Puzzling over the question, he rode steadily south, a vast sky above him, a vast sea of grass all about. As he rode, some of the accumulated tension began to dissipate. For the first time in days he began to feel relaxed and rested. He talked to the roan, and the horse twitched his ears, apparently liking the sound of Shanaghy's voice. Shanaghy had always liked horses and he liked this one. Once, sighting a small seep, he turned aside for it and allowed the horse a slow drink while he sat in the saddle, studying the country.

He was riding away when he saw the tracks. He knew nothing of tracking, but he could see that at least three horses had passed that way heading for the seep. Turning, he followed the tracks back and found where the riders had dismounted and waited for some time. There were the tracks of the horses and a number of cigarette butts. Then he found the tracks of a fourth rider who had come in from the northeast. Thoughtfully, Shanaghy studied the tracks. Although he knew little or nothing about "reading sign," as the westerners called it, he did know a good deal about horseshoes and the shoeing of horses, and this looked like work Carpenter might have done.

This rider had not dismounted but had remained in the saddle while talking to the others, then had turned around and ridden back along the original trail.

Chances were, it was a casual meeting between some range riders who had stopped for a smoke.

By nightfall, Shanaghy had traveled a distance equal to three days for the herd, and he made camp under some cottonwoods in a little draw where he found the remains of a campfire. He was learning that most places suitable for camps had been used by others before him, but there was water here, some shade, fuel and grass, whatever any traveler might need.

At daybreak he was again on the trail. From what Carpenter and Pendleton had said, he surmised that Patterson would be no more than five or six days' drive from town, and so he rode with his eyes on the horizon to the south, looking for dust or any sign of moving cattle.

It was almost sundown on the second day when he topped out on a small rise and saw them.

They were still miles away to the south, but he could see the long dark line of the moving herd and a few smaller dots that would be outriders. He was still several miles from them when he rode down into a long, shallow valley and saw their chuckwagon, and the thin trail of smoke rising from the campfire. This, then, was where the herd would bed down.

As Shanaghy trotted his horse down the long slope toward the camp, he saw the cook, a man in a once-white apron and battered hat, draw a Winchester from the wagon and lay it across the corner of the tailgate.

He slowed down as he approached, and walked his horse up to the fire. "I'm looking for the Patterson herd."

The cook, a sour-looking man with a handlebar mustache, noted the badge on Shanaghy's shirt with no approval. "You found it."

"Mind if I wait?"

"Light an' set." Then after a bit of kneading at the dough on the board before him, the cook said, "Where's Rig Barrett?"

"I came in his place."

The cook glanced at him with grim, unfriendly eyes. "They sendin' a boy to do a man's job?"

Tom Shanaghy shoved his derby back on his head. "I been doing man's work since I was twelve," he replied calmly. Then he said, "You must be about the best trail herd cook there is."

The man straightened up. "I do my job." Then he added, "Where'd you get that idea?"

"They tell me Vince Patterson never has anything less than the best."

"Well," the cook's tone was now less surly. "I do what I can. Those are hungry boys, yonder."

"Hope there's enough left for a hungry marshal," Shanaghy said.

He looked up to see two men riding into the hollow. One of them, he immediately guessed, was Vince Patterson. The other was probably his trail boss.

Shanaghy got to his feet. He had decided long ago that he could not fight Patterson and hope to win. One look at the man told him he had decided well. But it had been said that Patterson was a reasonable man, although hardheaded.

"Mr. Patterson?" he said. "I'm Tom Shanaghy, and I need your help."

"Help?" Patterson was surprised. He had expected a warning or a challenge. "What do you mean, you want my help?"

He swung down from the saddle as did the other man. That second man was lean and hard, not a large man but wiry . . . and dangerous. Shanaghy sensed that at once. The man was a fighting man, probably hired for the job.

"When Rig couldn't make it," Shanaghy said, "I had to take over the job for him. But Rig was no damn fool, and he saw right away there was something else involved than a fight between a trail driver and a town."

"What's that mean?"

"Rig figured, and I think the same, that somebody decided to use you."

Patterson stiffened. "Use *me*? I'll be damned if anybody is using me or is going to use me. What kind of talk is that?"

"You're mad at Hank Drako, and rightly so. They heard you were coming up the trail to burn the town where your brother was killed. Now I never put any stock in that, because you're too bright a man to punish a lot of innocent people for what one damn fool did. But there are some others who figured you would do it and that the town would fight . . . which they would, of course."

"So?"

"So these other folks, and I'm not sure who they all are yet, decided that while you and the town were fighting they would steal the money brought in to pay for your herd and to pay off your hands."

Patterson stared at Shanaghy, then turned to the cook. "Fred, give us some coffee, will you?" Then he turned back to Shanaghy. "Sit down. I want to talk to you."

When they were seated, Patterson looked him over cooly. "I don't know you."

"No way you could. Like everybody else out here, I'm a newcomer. The people there in town decided they wanted me to be marshal."

"What happened to Hank Drako?"

"He's around, he and those boys of his." Then he added, "They told me to fire him, and I did."

"You *fired* Hank Drako?"

"I did."

"And he took it?"

"Well, I don't think he liked it very much."

The other man was watching Shanaghy, and Tom knew he was being sized up carefully by a fighting man who knew his business. That part was good. Such men were less apt to make mistakes than a cocky youngster or a would-be tough guy trying to show how bad he was.

"Rig knew something was crossways, Mr. Patterson. He went to Kansas City working on the case. Something happened to Rig there and I had to take over."

Patterson looked at him. "Did Rig feel you were up to the job?"

Shanaghy shrugged. "Well, that's Rig's shotgun over there tied to my saddle."

Somehow or other he had to win this man over to accepting him and his story. He had to get Vince Patterson to stop and think, to help if he would—at least to hold off on whatever he meant to do. And Tom Shanaghy meant to use every artifice he could.

"By the way, Mr. Patterson, I'm carrying a message for you."

"A message? For me?"

"Yes, sir. A very lovely young lady said to say hello and give her love to her Uncle Vince."

The rancher flushed. "That sounds like Jan." His tone was gentler. "Do you know Jan?"

"I've talked to her," Shanaghy said quietly, "I don't know her as well as I'd like to, but I'm quite sure I never will."

Patterson and his trail boss were both looking at Shanaghy and he flushed beet-red. "She's a mighty fine young lady and I'm nothing but an Irish lad who's been given a marshal's job nobody else wanted."

Nobody spoke for a few minutes. The slim man rolled a cigarette and Patterson finally said, "If nobody else wanted the job, why'd you take it?"

"First, because it had to be done. Second, because I thought I could do it. I knew damn well that while I might whip one of your men, or even two or three, I couldn't whip all of you. I was also relying on something Rig said."

"And what was that?"

"He said you were a stubborn, hardheaded man who was also a decent man, and that you were reasonable. He intended to do just what I've done, ride down the trail to talk to you."

"And if I don't listen?"

"I'll protect my town with whatever means I have. If I win, you lose some good men. If you win, you destroy a fine town that's just becoming something. And then you have to drive your herd a hundred and fifty miles across grazed-over ground to another market. And while you and the town are fighting, these other people will steal all that money and we will have aided and abetted them in their crime.

"I know you're an honest man, Mr. Patterson, and no matter how much you hate our town, you don't want to help a bunch of crooks steal the money that was to be paid to you and your men."

The herd was streaming into the valley, and Patterson's trail boss swung into the saddle to help turn them and round them up. Patterson drank his coffee, thinking, and Tom Shanaghy kept his mouth shut.

Finally, Patterson said, "These other people? Who are they?"

"Mr. Patterson," he said slowly, "I'm working on that and right now I just don't know. I think I have three of them spotted, but where they are holed up and just who or how many are involved, I don't know.

"There's a woman involved . . . I think."

"A *woman?*"

"Yes, sir. And the one thing that may be in our favor is that she thinks we are all a pack of fools."

"Maybe we are," Patterson muttered. "Maybe we are."

"Sir? I'm not going to let them get that money. Not one red cent of it."

"You said you wanted my help . . . In what way?"

"This is good grass. The grass around town, and west or east of town, is no way as good as this. I want you to hold off . . . let your cattle fatten while I get this thing worked out. All I need is a couple of days.

"I think," Shanaghy added, "they've got a schedule figured out. I think they know when you're coming in, or about when. I think they have it all set to start, quickly, quietly, efficiently, as soon as you come busting into town to take it apart. While you and the town are busy, they'll get the money and get out . . . Then they'll be gone and we'll be left holding the sack . . .

"If you hold back, three things happen. Your cattle get fatter, their timing is thrown off, and I get a chance to work on the situation before it develops. Personally, I think if their timing is thrown off, something is going to come unglued."

Patterson refilled their cups. "How did you get involved in all this?"

"Well, Drako's son and some others were fixing to hang Josh Lundy. They decided to include me. I persuaded them not to. And, of course, somebody had to take Rig's place."

"Where's Hank Drako now?"

"On his ranch, I expect. Your business with Drako is none of mine. He strikes me as part coyote and part weasel. I think he will kill anything that's helpless or seems so, but if you move against him, don't do it in town."

"You laying down the law?"

"Yes, sir. You lay down the law on your ranch. I do it in town. What you do outside of town is your business and not mine. I wasn't hired to protect the whole state of Kansas, just this town."

Vince Patterson finished his coffee and glanced at his cattle. Some were already lying down, most were still grazing. A few of his men were riding toward the fire. It would be sundown in a little while.

"You staying with us tonight?" Patterson asked.

"With your permission, sir."

Patterson stared at him. "Are you always this respectful?"

Shanaghy grinned. "No, sir. But you're a gentleman, sir, and this is one argument I can't win with my fists or a gun."

Patterson stared for a minute, then chuckled. "All right, damn you, stay the night. I'll sleep on it." He held out his hand. "No promises, mind you, but damn it, Shanaghy, I like you."

TEN

Slowly the hands drifted up to the fire, some of them to bed down, some to catch a quick supper and return to riding herd on the cattle. As they came in they regarded Shanaghy thoughtfully, noticing the badge first, then the derby.

One redheaded cowpuncher looked across the fire at him and said, "That there hat's a temptation. Anybody ever shoot it off you?"

Shanaghy pushed the derby back a little and grinned cheerfully. "Not yet. Maybe that's because they figured I wouldn't know if they were shooting at the derby or me."

He dipped into the stew. "Anyway, it seems a waste of lead. I didn't buy my gun for shooting hats."

He ate in silence for a moment and then said, "The way I figure it, the marshal of a town should be measured by the trouble he keeps clear of town rather than the gunfights he wins. The first thing I did when I took over," he spoke in a low, conversational tone, "was to study the arms situation and the shooters.

"First off I found the town has thirty-seven shotguns, and folks who can use them. We have nine Big Fifty Buffalo guns, two Berdan sharpshooting rifles, five Winchesters, and seven

91

Spencer fifty-six-calibers. We have fourteen assorted rifles from the Hawken to the Ballard, and every man in town and most of the women have pistols.

"Next thing, I looked over what kind of people we had to do the shooting. Five of the men in town were sharpshooters during the Civil War, one side or the other. Nine others fought in the war. We've got one old mountain man, and six veterans of Indian battles. There's only two men in town who haven't been in battle, but they're just a frettin' and a fumin' to prove themselves as good as the others.

"Long before I ever saw the place, they figured sometime there might be an Indian raid, so they built the town without any blind spots, front or back. The rifles and shotguns are kept loaded lest there be unexpected trouble, and they are stashed around town easy to hand.

"Most of the folks there want no trouble. They figure outfits like yours will have money to spend, and they're anxious to help. They want to do business with you, the cattle bosses and whoever comes up the trail. They are right friendly folks, but they love their town.

"Me, I'm just a driftin' stranger, and I don't quite see what they like about it but they know. When you boys ride into town I want every one of you to hang up his gun in Greenwood's place."

The redhead laughed, somewhat grimly. "Mister, you've got to be jokin'. I hang up my gun for no man."

"All right," Shanaghy replied cheerfully. "I was just telling you so's you'd know. You see, what worries me isn't you boys at all. It's two or three of the townspeople who are trigger-happy. A couple of those sharpshooters, for example, I've been having trouble convincing them this isn't an all-out war.

"They've agreed to hold their fire and sit tight, but if somebody should in the fullness of his spirits suddenly decide to discharge his piece into the air, that street would turn into a bloodbath.

"All those boys and girls with guns are going to be hunkered down behind log walls or brick walls, and they are going to be shooting into an open street without cover."

Tom Shanaghy shook his head woefully. "Of course, the street's dusty this time of year, and it soaks up blood real fast."

Nobody had anything more to say, and Shanaghy simply

finished his meal. After throwing the grounds from his cup, he walked to where his bedroll lay.

Vince Patterson had sat over at one side and heard it all. He struck a match on the side of his pants, lit a cigar, and approached Shanaghy. "Was that Rig's idea?" he asked mildly.

"Can't blame it on him. Folks there needed a little organization, but they'll go about their business like always unless trouble starts."

"You could be running a bluff."

"Yes, sir. That I could. Be mighty expensive, though, if it was called and I proved to be holdin' the pat hand I've told 'em about.

"Also," Shanaghy added, "I had to have a diversion."

"A diversion?"

"Something to trim the odds, sort of. You've got some loyal hands there. If trouble started in town and then something happened to your herd, I figure about half your men would cut and run to protect the cows."

"What could go wrong with my herd?"

Shanaghy shrugged. "Well, a few days ago some Kiowas showed up. Least that's what the old-timers said they were. I don't know one Indian from another.

"Well, these Kiowas had been raiding Pawnees up the country a bit, they caught the short end of the stick, and they were sore.

"We fed 'em, and I sort of suggested they stay around and keep out of sight. I also suggested that it might be worth a bunch of presents if they sort of listened for gunfire."

Patterson was looking at him. "Gunfire?"

"Uh-huh. If they heard gunfire from town, they were to stampede your herd."

Patterson swore.

"Stampede 'em, and scatter them all over the prairie."

Patterson swore again, and then he said, "But we have you, Marshal. What about that?"

"You would lose a man or two taking me, Mr. Patterson, but it would change nothing. You see, the way that plan of mine is set up, it works without anybody saying anything. They don't need me at all now.

"Things been pretty dull around town lately. No fights to

speak of, and the boys are kind of restless, kind of keyed up, if you know what I mean."

"You seem to have thought of everything."

"I've tried. You see, I've heard your boys ride for the brand. Well, that town is my brand. They hired me to do a job, and I'm doing it the best way I know how."

Later, Shanaghy lay in his blankets staring up at the stars. He had lied, of course. His plans were not nearly so thorough as he had implied. Nonetheless, they were good plans and he planned to put them into execution as soon as he got back . . . *if* he got back.

If he avoided trouble and saved some lives with his stories, all would be well. At least he had offered a little doubt, and nobody wanted to get shot down in the street. If what he had said was not true, it was all possible, and they could not know whether he was telling the truth or not.

When he heard stirring around the camp he got up. It was not yet four o'clock in the morning, he noticed by his big silver watch, but the camp was coming alive. He crawled out of bed, put on his derby and then got into his pants and boots.

Nobody was paying any attention to him, and he went to the fire for his grub along with the others.

Patterson was there. He glanced at Shanaghy, gave a short nod and went on eating.

The air was clear and cool. There was a smell of dust and cattle on the air, and off to one side a cowpuncher was letting his bronc buck the kinks out of his system. Nobody was talking until he went to get coffee and Red picked up the pot and filled his cup for him.

Red grinned at him. "You spin a good yarn, Marshal, but, you know, we didn't figure any of it was worth throwin' a loop over."

"I can carve it on your headstone," Shanaghy said.

"What?"

" 'He asked to be showed; we showed him.' "

"Hey," Red said, "that ain't bad! I've seen men buried with less."

"To tell you the truth, Red," Shanaghy said, "I'd rather buy you a drink than shoot you."

"Well, now," Red said cheerfully, "I'll remember that, Marshal. How many do you figure to set up for?"

"Hell," Shanaghy said, "I'll buy a drink for the whole crew. You're a good bunch of lads."

He finished his coffee. "Besides, you've got a good cook."

He saddled up. As he was tightening his cinch, Vince Patterson walked over. "Don't expect us for about four or five days, Marshal. And if you need any help with those hold-up people, you let us know. We'll ride with you."

Shanaghy held out his hand. "Rig sure had you figured. He said you were a decent and a reasonable man."

They shook hands. "Shanaghy," Patterson said, "I think Jan Pendleton is the finest girl I know, but she could do a whole lot worse than you."

Tom Shanaghy flushed. "Mr. Patterson," he said, "don't you even think that. I'm not the man for her, and I know she's given no thought to me. Why, she's only seen me once."

"I married my wife the second time I saw her," Patterson said, "and we've got twenty years of happiness behind us."

Tom Shanaghy turned his horse and rode away.

He had gone only two horse-lengths when Patterson called after him. "What about Hank Drako?"

"Hank's going to be hunting me, he and his boys. If they find me, you've got no problem. If you boys find them you can have them, just so it's out of town."

He rode hard. There were things he had to do, and time was short, and he did not think of Jan Pendleton. At least, he tried not to.

The town lay quiet in the late afternoon sun when Shanaghy rode into the street. He took his horse to Carpenter's stable and stripped off the gear. He gave the roan a good rubdown, thinking all the while, then took his saddlebags and walked over to the blacksmith shop.

Carpenter looked up. "Holstrum was by. Wanted to know where you were."

"Drako been around?"

"Not hide nor hair." Carpenter put down his hammer. "Had it for today." He took off his leather apron. "Oh, by the way! That young woman you're interested in. She came by. Wanted a horse shod . . . today."

"You do it?"

"Uh-huh. A different horse, too. Sometimes I wonder about eastern folks. Seem to think horses all look alike."

"Pendleton been around?"

"No, but his son was in. He was asking for you."

Shanaghy was not concerned about young Pendleton. His thoughts were on the robbery . . . Or was he simply seeing ghosts? What did he have, after all, but a lot of suspicions?

A strange girl in town for no apparent reason, who kept to herself. In other words, she was simply minding her own business.

Her odd association with a man who looked like a tinhorn gambler, and the puzzle about where she lived.

A man on a train who Shanaghy had believed to be a railroad detective and who apparently was not.

Rig Barrett's suspicions that something was in the wind, which Shanaghy was inclined to trust.

And the fact that somebody seemed to have taken pains to eliminate Rig before he could arrive in town.

And the knowledge that a lot of money, probably a quarter of a million in gold and bills, would be arriving on the train someday soon.

Who knew of that? Almost everybody in town who did not actually know could surmise. So could a lot of others. After all, there had to be money on hand. Such a town would not ordinarily have so much, so it would have to be brought in.

That man on the train now . . . Now that Shanaghy considered it, that man had not seemed western. Well, why should he? Neither was he, Tom Shanaghy.

The trouble with Vince seemed to have been averted, but nobody knew that but him. He decided nobody must know, not if he could help it.

He turned toward the hotel and halted suddenly. A man was riding toward him on a buckskin horse.

"Howdy!" It was Josh Lundy. "Remember me?"

"I do."

"Figured you might need some help. My boss give me a few days off and I thought I'd ride in to see if you needed a hand."

"You could get killed."

"You didn't seem to pay much mind down by the creek that day."

"I was saving my own hide."

"No matter."

Shanaghy liked the cowhand and remembered Rig's estimate

of him. The man was seasoned, tough, and had local experience, knowing local people whom Shanaghy did not. "Let's get over to Greenwood's and I'll buy you a beer," he suggested.

From where they sat, as Shanaghy had correctly remembered, they could look down the street. Besides, it was quiet here and they could talk.

"Watch yourself." Greenwood walked over to give the warning. "There's talk that Drako and his boys are coming into town after you."

He had started away when Shanaghy said, "Who told you that?"

"Holstrum . . . I guess somebody said something about it over at the store."

They sipped their beers and slowly, carefully, Shanaghy told Josh Lundy of the suspected plan to seize the money shipment.

His thoughts returned to the hoofprints by the seep. "Anybody running cattle in south of here?" He explained his interest.

"Drifters, more than likely. There's a lot of odd characters stop by Drako's place." Lundy paused. "Four of them, you say?"

"It looked to me like somebody brought them a message. He didn't get off his horse, just talked awhile and left."

"Mostly guesswork, Marshal."

Suddenly Lundy said, "Is that the girl you've been talking about, Marshal?"

It was . . . She came riding up the street, then dismounted in front of the café.

Shanaghy got to his feet. "Josh, I'm going to have a talk with her. Right now."

ELEVEN

It was cool and quiet in the restaurant and at this hour it was empty, something she had no doubt counted upon. When Shanaghy entered she looked up, a flash of annoyance crossing her face.

After crossing to her table, he said, "Mind if I sit down?"

She looked up. Beautiful, she undoubtedly was, but her features might have been cut from marble. "I do, indeed. I wish to be alone."

"I am sorry, ma'am, but I have some questions."

"And I have no answers. Must I call the manager?"

"If you like."

She looked at him with contempt. "If you wish to take advantage of your authority, ask what questions you will. I shall decide whether or not to reply."

"Fair enough. Mind telling me how long you've been here?"

"In this town? Slightly over a week."

"What's your purpose here?"

Her expression was one of exasperated patience. "I am looking for ranch property. My father was unable to come, and we share our financial interests. We are looking for good grass and a source of permanent water."

Shanaghy felt like a fool. Of course, what could be more likely? "Found anything that suits you?"

"No . . . There are two possibilities, that is all. Now, is there anything more?"

"Do you expect to be here long?"

She put her cup down sharply. "Marshal, or whatever you are called, I have told you why I was here, and I am on legitimate business. I am not the sort of woman who expects to be badgered by every small-town officer with an exaggerated sense of his own importance. Unless you have some kind of a trumped-up charge, I would prefer you to leave . . . now."

He got up. "Sorry, ma'am."

She did not reply.

He started to leave, then turned and seated himself where he could watch the street outside. She had made him feel a fool, and it was not a feeling he liked. Her story was perfectly logical. Of course, every really smart crook he had ever known had a good cover story. He had heard them discussed on a number of occasions. They had considered him as one of them and talked freely. Yet he couldn't see anything he could get a handle on.

One thing he had neglected to ask: where was she staying? No doubt she had a good answer for that, too.

The waiter brought his coffee and he stared out toward the street. Suppose he himself was planning such an operation, how would he bring it off?

By involving as few people as possible, so there would be less chance of loose talk. And keeping those few out of sight until they made their move, or else by using people who had a reason for being around town.

The plotters, if there were any, would want to make their move, as Barrett believed, just when Vince Patterson hit town.

Shanaghy swore softly and the girl glanced his way. It had suddenly occurred to him that they must know exactly when that cash shipment was to arrive, and that meant they had somebody on the inside at one end or the other.

How would they do it? They might strike just as the stuff was brought from the train, move in quietly, knock out or strangle the guards, and reload the stuff on the train to be taken off at some point further along.

That would be one way. Another would be to have a rig

standing by, or a wagon, and load the money on and move out while the shooting was in progress. Undoubtedly those ranchers who were in town would try to get away, and they could simply go with them.

There was still another way. Arrange to hide it right in town until the shooting was over, and until people had stopped looking for it.

If they should hide it in town . . . where? And how could they get it away, or be sure of getting it away, during the fighting they would expect to take place?

The way Shanaghy saw it was that the money must be taken right from the depot. If not on the train, then by a rig . . . but taken where?

There would be immediate pursuit when the robbery was discovered . . . or would there? Who would be apt to pursue? Who would first realize the gold was missing?

Suppose . . . just suppose there was no one who knew the gold was due to arrive?

Carpenter, Holstrum and Greenwood all knew, but supposing that during the fight they were killed or otherwise put out of action? If that were to happen the thieves might have several days in which to disappear.

If those men were marked for death, then he would also be on such a list.

When would these killings be carried out? Either at the time or just before the robbery, and probably under cover of the Vince Patterson raid on the town.

Suppose somebody actually riding with Patterson was involved? The cowman had taken on some gun-hands for this trip north, and among them might be one or more men involved in the theft.

As Shanaghy considered all that might happen, a rider approached outside and dismounted across the street and one door further along. He dismounted stiffly as if he had been riding for some distance. He whipped the dust from his clothes with his hat and then turned to loosen his cinch.

As he did so, another man crossed the street to the walk just beyond the rider and turned to walk past him. It was George.

When near the cowhand, George paused to light a cigar, and for a moment his hands were cupped around the match. Was he speaking? After a moment he shook out a match and dropped it, then walked on.

Off to his left where the young woman sat, Shanaghy heard a cup click hard against a saucer, as though it had been put down with some impatience or anger.

Shanaghy turned and looked at her, smiling. Her lips tightened and she turned her eyes from his. She was angry, without a doubt.

He glanced around again. The rider was walking toward Greenwood's. His horse wore a—p—connected brand . . . one of those used by Vince Patterson.

When Shanaghy looked back, the girl was gone. A moment later he heard the click of her heels on the boardwalk. He got up, leaving money on the table, and went outside.

Who was the rider? Had he actually spoken to George? Had the girl been angry because it all happened while he, Shanaghy, was watching?

Was the rider a messenger? If so, from whom? Did Patterson know he had come?

Shanaghy hesitated, then turned toward Greenwood's. No guns were to be worn in town, he had said. Well, that meant now.

Or was this man merely a bait for a trap? Perhaps today was the day they meant to eliminate *him*. Tom Shanaghy had served too long with Morrissey not to suspect such things.

If this man was bait, there would be others around. They would not be likely to trust such a job to one man alone, unless he was very, very good.

Even then they would have someone else. They would want some insurance. Which meant another marksman.

Would that be George?

For several minutes Shanaghy sat still, thinking it over. Wherever the girl had gone it was not to the street, for she had not appeared there. He finished his coffee and went back through the kitchen and out the back door—but only after a careful glance up and down to see if anyone lurked there.

At the corner of a building, he hesitated, looking around it toward the saloon. From there, he had a good view of the swinging doors. This rider was from Patterson's outfit and he had issued his ultimatum to them . . . no guns in town. Now this man had ridden in wearing his guns . . . Was it a test? A direct challenge?

Or maybe the man had gone to the saloon to hang up his guns?

If not, the challenge must be met, and he would meet it now.

From inside the saloon the patrons could see up and down the street, but approaching the building indirectly, Shanaghy could be crossing the street before they saw him. He was in the middle of the street and walking fast before he glimpsed the two horses tied in the alleyway beside Holstrum's store, and then he was going up the steps and into the saloon.

Two strangers sat at a table on the right side of the saloon. The Patterson rider was at the bar. Greenwood looked up and directly at him, but he said nothing.

Shanaghy walked to the bar. "Sorry, cowboy," he said, smiling, "while you're in town you will have to hang up the guns. Mr. Greenwood will take them for you."

"Hang up my guns?" the cowhand took a half step back. "You want my guns, you got to take them!"

The man was ready, and so were the other two. "Oh, well," Shanaghy replied cheerfully, "if you feel that way about it." He turned away and to the bar, as if no longer caring.

Frustrated in his attempt to start a fight, the cowhand let his hands fall away from his guns, and Shanaghy hit him.

It was a smashing backhand blow to the mouth, yet no sooner had the blow struck than Shanaghy's hand dropped to the cowhand's shoulder and grabbed him by the collar. Shanaghy jerked the man into a wicked left hook to the belly. Flipping the man around with his back to Shanaghy, the marshal flipped his guns from the twin holsters, covering the two men at the table.

"Get up!" he spoke sharply, but cooly. "Get up and unfasten your gunbelts!"

"Look here! You got no call to—!"

"Now," Shanaghy shoved the gasping cowboy toward them, rearing back both hammers. The clicks of the cocking hammers were loud in the room.

"All right," the shorter man said, "looks like you got—"

He drew, and Tom Shanaghy shot him through the tobacco

tag hanging from his shirt pocket. The man went down, and the left-handed gun was on the other.

His face yellow and sick-looking, the second man slowly, carefully, lifted his hands.

"Put 'em down," Shanaghy said, "and let go your gunbelt. If you feel lucky, you just play the fool like your partner did."

He shoved the cowhand he had grabbed over to the table. The cowhand was grasping his side, a pained expression on his face. "Damn you!" he said. "You busted a rib!"

"Only one? That punch is usually good for three. My best day it was five, but he was coming at me."

Without turning his head, he spoke to Greenwood. "See what you can do for that man, will you? He's hurt but he's not dead."

He gestured with a gun, shoving the other into his waistband. "Court ain't in session," he said, "so I'll handle it. Fifty dollars or fifty days."

"Hell, who's got that much money?"

"If you've got a friend who has," Shanaghy said cheerfully, "you'd better get word to him. Start walking now . . . outside."

The hitching-rail in front of the smithy was built with posts of good size set deep in the earth, and the rail itself was of oak, notched into the posts and spiked in place. He handcuffed each man to the rail by one wrist.

"How long you goin' to leave us here?"

Shanaghy did not smile. "Fifty days, unless you can come up with the fine."

"Fifty days? You're crazy! What if it rains?"

"Well," Shanaghy said, "the overhang will protect you if the rain comes from thataway. Otherwise, I'd say you're liable to get wet. The same thing goes for the sun."

Shanaghy pushed his derby back on his head. "You boys came in here asking for it. Maybe the man who sent you will put up your fines." He grinned suddenly. "But I've a notion he'll just let you rot. You're no good to him any more."

"When I get loose—!"

Shanaghy shook his head reprovingly. "That's the feelin' that got you into trouble. My advice is to just pull your freight and get out of here."

"Where'd a man who wears a derby learn to use a gun like that?"

Shanaghy smiled. "I had a good teacher, and a lot of time to practice."

He went back to Greenwood's. The place was empty and Greenwood was mopping the floor. "How is he?"

Greenwood shrugged. "If he's lucky, he'll live. If your bullet had been an inch or two lower, he'd never have made it to the doctor."

Greenwood took his mop and bucket to the back room and returned, drying his hands. "You don't waste around much, do you?"

"I do not. At such a time a man can only do what he must."

Shanaghy drank part of a beer and then remembered the horses. Leaving his beer on the bar, he went out quickly and hurried down the street. He rounded the corner into the alley beside Holstrum's store and pulled up.

The horses were gone . . .

TWELVE

Shanaghy stood for an instant, realizing that the horses might have belonged to someone other than the men in the saloon. But if such was the case, who did they belong to?

He glanced down at the tracks. One resembled a track seen at the seep where the unknown riders had met.

Turning, he walked back up the street, but as he went, he was thinking. If those horses had belonged to the men in the saloon, they were still in town . . . Nobody had ridden out, for in this wide-open country, except at night, it was impossible to enter or leave town without being seen.

He returned to Greenwood's. "Know any of those men?" he asked the saloonkeeper.

Greenwood shrugged. "They're strangers, Tom. The minute they walked in I had them pegged for trouble. A man in my business has to know."

"Mine, too."

"You acted like you knew what to do!"

Shanaghy shrugged. "I broke up fights and bounced tough guys out of Bowery saloons when I was sixteen. I've been through that a couple of hundred times."

"With guns?"

"Sometimes. More than likely slungshots, billies or chivs . . . knives, I mean. You take the mean one first . . . Then the others lose their stomach for it.

"That one," he added, "he was going to start trouble, and the others were going to shoot me."

"Rig Barrett couldn't have done it better."

Shanaghy looked at Greenwood. "No? Well, maybe. He'd more than likely have it all figured out now and know who the front man was."

"You believe there is one?"

"Look . . . Some of these boys came in from out of town. This job was planned out of town. Rig knew that. So how did they know about it? Either somebody tipped them off or they had a tip from the place that will supply the money."

"I wish I could have seen those horses," Greenwood mused.

"Seen 'em? Why?"

"I'd know if they were from around here. Hell, Tom, every western man knows horses and he doesn't forget them."

Suddenly, Shanaghy swore. "Damn! That must've been what Carpenter meant!"

"Meant? What was that?"

"Awhile back he made some comment to the effect that somebody didn't realize that horses could be remembered, or something like that. I think he recognized the horse that girl was riding."

"You surely don't think she's involved? That girl's a lady."

Shanaghy shrugged. "Anybody can want money, and I've seen some pretty cold-blooded ladies. I've seen them at cockfights and dogfights, real bluestockings, and enjoying every minute of it."

He walked out again on the street. Right now he was wishing he had a friend, any kind of a friend. He was wishing he could talk to McCarthy or Old Smoke Morrissey, or that old-timer who taught him to use a six-shooter. He needed somebody he could talk to . . . and he had no idea whether Greenwood could be trusted or not.

He thought of Holstrum, but the storekeeper was a quiet, phlegmatic sort not likely to be of any help.

Carpenter . . . ? He turned toward the smithy, suddenly aware that he had heard no ringing of the hammer for some time.

He walked more swiftly as he neared the smithy, and suddenly saw a woman standing in the entrance, shading her eyes with her hand as she looked his way.

"Are you Tom?" she said as he walked up. "I'm Mrs. Carpenter."

"I was looking for your husband."

"So was I. I brought his lunch and he wasn't here. The forge is almost cold. I can't imagine—"

"In this town? Where could a man go?"

"He might be at Greenwood's. He said something to me this morning about having a talk with him."

She paused. "Marshal? Would you go there for me? A lady can't go into such places."

"He's not at Greenwood's. I've just come from there."

"I'm frightened, Marshal. It isn't like him. He's . . . he's a very meticulous man . . . about everything. If he had been going anywhere he would have told me."

"Ma'am? Did he talk any about horses? I mean, did he say anything about a horse he'd recognized lately?"

"No . . . not that I can recall. He's been preoccupied, and that's unlike him. I think he has been worried."

"So have we all, ma'am. So have we all."

Shanaghy paused, then continued: "Ma'am?" She was a pleasant-looking, attractive woman. Had someone asked her what she was, she would have said, "housewife," and been proud of it. "Ma'am? I can use your help.

"You know the people in this town. I am still a stranger. Anyway, sometimes women are more perceptive about people than men are. Something's going on here. I think somebody is planning to steal the money that's being brought into town to pay for cattle and to pay off the drivers. Mostly it will be outside people, but I think somebody right here in town is in on it, and may have started the whole thing.

"There aren't many secrets in a town of this size, and I want you to think about it. Meanwhile, I'll have a look for your husband. If he comes back, let Greenwood know."

"Do you trust him? He's a saloonkeeper."

"I trust no one. Not even you. But I *think* he's an honest man."

"Enough money, that much money, would tempt many an

honest man. My husband worked very hard this past year, and he has made just over seven hundred dollars. That's pretty good. I doubt if either Mr. Greenwood or Mr. Holstrum has done any better, so think of what two hundred and fifty thousand dollars represents."

"Ma'am, I've known crooks most of my life, but the honest men I knew . . . well, I don't think some of them would sell out at any price. I don't believe your husband would."

She started to turn away, then hesitated. "Marshal? Who is that young woman who is staying at the hotel? The very attractive one we see riding about?"

"She says she's looking at land, that she and her father are prospective buyers." He paused. "But she isn't staying at the hotel."

"Not at the hotel? Then where—?"

"I've no idea, ma'am. Yet you've seen her. She's always neat, never dusty, her clothes always fresh and clean. She's not camping out, ma'am."

Holstrum was behind the counter of his store. He peered at Shanaghy over his glasses and smiled. "Ah? You come to my little store, Marshal? What can I do for you?"

"I'm looking for Carpenter."

"Carpenter, is it? Ah, no. Not today, I think." He waved a hand. "But who knows? We see each other often, one day is like the next. He is not at his shop?"

Shanaghy shook his head. He liked the store, and the pleasant smells of dry goods, slabs of bacon, fresh-cut chewing tobacco, new leather from the saddles and bridles, and coffee from the coffee-grinder.

"Sometimes, Marshal, I think you worry too much. When the men of Patterson come you can talk. Maybe he will listen to you."

"Maybe." He looked out of the window at the empty street. A hatful of breeze caught at the dust and swirled it, then dropped it reluctantly. He went to the huge circular cheese under glass and lifted it, slicing off an edge for himself, then he strolled back to the counter.

"Maybe I should go back to New York," he muttered. "Since coming here I've been thinking of other things than myself. I'm growing soft."

"It is a small place here," Holstrum agreed. "We have not much to offer."

"Where were you from, Holstrum? Another small town?"

"A farm," the older man said. "On a farm I was born. On a farm I lived. There was work, much work. Morning, noon and night, there was work. Always, I think of other places, better places than the farm. I think of women, too, of soft, warm, beautiful women mit perfume. On the farm I see no such women. My mama, she is gone before I know more than her face, and we are all men. My father, he drives us. Always it is work."

"So you came west?"

"I work on a boat on the canal. Then I come to Chicago, where I work. I save a little. I see always people with much. I envy them. I go where they go and stand outside and look in on them.

"They are rich people. Their women are soft and warm, and when they passed me going from their carriages, I smell their perfume. So I say, someday . . ."

He broke off. "A boy's foolishness, that's what it was. Now I have good business. Soon I shall be rich man."

"What happened to the farm? And your brothers who stayed?"

Holstrum shrugged. "My father is dead. The farm is now only one of five farms. They have done well, my brothers. One also owns a store. One has a bank."

Shanaghy finished the cheese. "You might have been a banker had you stayed, but you wouldn't have seen all this." He waved a hand.

Holstrum stared at him over his glasses. "I do not like all this. Sometime I will have a big business in a big town . . . You'll see."

Shanaghy grinned. "And maybe the woman with the perfume . . . or have you found her already?"

Holstrum lowered his head and stared at the marshal over his glasses. For a moment he peered at Shanaghy, then shook his head. "One time I think I meet such a woman. She wished to go to a fine place so I dress in my new black suit and take her there. We ate and we talked, but I do not know what she says . . . many words of things of which I know nothing." He paused. "I never see her again. And the meal," he added, "it cost me all I would earn in one week. For *one* meal.

"Someday," he added, "it will not be so! I shall eat many such meals, and I shall not think of cost! I will know many such women, and they will not think small of me."

"You think she did?"

"I never see her again. When I go to ask they say she is not at home, or is not 'receiving.' "

"Tough," Shanaghy said. "That could happen to anyone." He was thinking of Jan Pendleton. What a fool Holstrum was! But he wouldn't be. Not by a damned sight. He wasn't going to make a fool of himself.

By suppertime they all knew Carpenter was gone. None of his horses were missing. His saddle was in the barn. His pistol, rifle and shotgun were all in place. Yet Carpenter was nowhere around.

The judge was in the restaurant when Shanaghy came in. He remembered him from that first night when some man had come in to tell the judge that something must have happened to Rig Barrett. The judge nodded when he saw Shanaghy.

He held out his hand. "Marshal? I am Judge McBane. Judge by courtesy, that is. Once, back in Illinois, I was a judge. Out here I am merely another lawyer, trying to make a living."

"We need a judge, and we need a court. The nearest one is miles away."

"You may be right. Sometimes I think the fewer laws the better. We are an orderly people, we Americans, although others do not think of us so."

He was a short, heavyset man with a bulging vest, a heavy watch chain with a gold nugget and an elk's tooth suspended from it, and a thick mustache that covered his upper lip and most of his mouth. "I understand our smith has disappeared?"

"Well . . . he doesn't seem to be around. But there are no horses missing that we've heard of, and all his are in the corral."

The judge led the way to a table, seated himself and brushed his mustache with the back of his forefinger, first the right side, then the left.

"He was in to see me," the judge commented casually, his

eyes roaming the room. "Said the horses of those men you have chained down in the street had disappeared."

"They have."

Judge McBane turned his slightly bulging eyes back to Shanaghy. "Seems to me," he suggested, speaking quietly, "that a marshal looking for a missing man could go through every stable in town. If he didn't find Carpenter he might find those horses. Their brands might tell him something."

Shanaghy flushed. "Of course!" He shook his head ruefully. "I'm new at this business, Judge, but why couldn't I think of what's so obvious?"

"I do it all the time," the judge replied cheerfully.

Shanaghy got up suddenly. "Judge? If I may be excused—?"

Later, he thought, How did I remember to say that?

He had not realized there were so many stables in the town, but where horses are used there must be places in which to keep them.

In the ninth stable, near an abandoned corral, both by the smell and by struck matches, Shanaghy found fresh manure and places where the horses had stood. They were gone now.

He was turning away when he saw the boot-toe. It was barely showing above the hay in the long manger—hay with which a body had obviously been hastily covered.

Even before he brushed away the hay, Tom Shanaghy knew.

It was Carpenter.

THIRTEEN

He had been struck over the head, then stabbed at least three times. The blow over the head seemed to have come from behind.

Shanaghy thought of Mrs. Carpenter and swore softly, bitterly. He would have to tell her. It was something that must be done, and now.

Yet first, he must look around. Whoever had killed Carpenter had come here with him, or had come up behind him. It was unlikely that Carpenter had been killed elsewhere and brought here. Undoubtedly he had found the horses and been killed at that moment.

Why kill him for seeing the horses unless the horses pointed to someone? Yet from what he had gathered there were few local brands. There were but a few local people who ran cattle, and the farmers did not have any but a few milk cows which they kept up or picketed on grass so they could not stray.

Shanaghy straightened up and stood very still, thinking. He had started to strike another match when he heard a faint stirring . . . Was it outside? Or inside?

Careful to make no sound, he eased himself back into the stall and squatted on his heels.

The double doors of the stable stood open. Along one side was a row of four stalls, divided one from another simply by horizontal poles and floor-to-roof posts. The manger was simply a long trough that extended through all four stalls.

On the opposite side there was simply the wall. Nails had been driven into the boards on which to hang odd bits of old harness, links of chain, and whatever had been lying around loose. Near that wall was a wooden bucket and a pitchfork. On the ledge formed by a two-by-four that ran the length of the side between supporting posts, there had been a currycomb, a brush and some heavy shears.

At the back of the barn was a window. Here and there cracks allowed a glimpse of the lights of the town. The nearest building was about fifty yards off, the pole corral on the side away from the town.

Somebody had either come here with Carpenter or had followed him here. Perhaps had lain in wait for him. And Carpenter was dead.

Again, a faint stirring. Shanaghy cleared the thong from the hammer of his six-shooter. He heard a faint creak and looked up. One of the big barn doors was slowly swinging shut!

He started to rise . . . Was it a trap? Or just the wind?

He was in the fourth and last stall. He got up suddenly and started for the door. As he did so it swung shut and he heard a latch drop into place.

Rushing to the door, he pushed against it, but the door held firm. He knew the hasp on the door couldn't be very strong. He stepped back to lunge against it, hesitated, for fear of a shot, then threw himself at the barrier.

The door was immovable. Something was wedged against it from the outside. He turned quickly toward the window . . . It was too small!

For an instant Shanaghy stood perfectly still. This was stupid! What in the world could be the reason? Nobody could be kept locked up like this for long. He would get out on his own, or, when morning came and people began moving about, he could call out . . .

If he was alive.

Realization came to him one instant before he smelled the smoke.

Fire!

Destroying not only him, but Carpenter's body, as well—Carpenter's body with its telltale wounds.

Shanaghy was no fool to waste time in charging about or battering at walls. The closest buildings were stores, empty at night. The feeble sounds he could make, unless he started shooting, would attract no attention, and even the shots might be passed off as some drunk celebrating a little.

The smoke was coming through cracks from the north side of the barn, the side away from the town, and from the smell it was hay burning. Hay would create the most smoke, and might smoulder for some time before growing into flame, but it was smoke that killed most people in fires. Shanaghy knew that from the firemen working Morrissey's volunteer companies in New York.

He had to get out, and he had to get Carpenter's body out. He'd never get the doors battered down in time.

The smoke was getting thicker. As he ran to Carpenter's body, he started coughing. He lifted the smaller man from the manger . . . to the back of the barn.

The loft . . . the small loft where hay was stored for use during bad weather! There was a simple ladder of crosspieces nailed to a post that gave access to the loft.

Higher up, the smoke would be worse. No matter. It was the only way. Lifting Carpenter's body, Shanaghy slung it over his shoulder. Holding the body in place, he grasped the post itself with his free hand and climbed.

Five steps. He dumped the body on the little hay that remained. Then, coughing and gasping, he reached for the roof.

It was made of poles with a crude thatch of branches and straw. Almost unable to breathe, his eyes smarting from the smoke, he clawed at the poles with his bare hands. He ripped and he tore. He got hold of a branch and broke it free. Dust and dirt cascaded over him. He tore at the thatch, coughing with great, lung-tearing gasps. Suddenly, his hand went through and fresh air flooded around him. Below him, he heard the crackle of flames from inside the barn.

After ripping branches away, he grasped a pole and broke it by sheer brute strength. More dust and straw tumbled through upon him, but there was more fresh air, too.

Stooping, he grabbed Carpenter's body by the collar and

crawled through the hole onto the roof. Flames were leaping up behind him. None were yet visible outside, although there was considerable smoke.

After reaching the edge of the barn, he dropped the body and leaped down himself, falling quickly to one side, gun in hand.

Nothing . . . the would-be killer was gone, fearful of being seen close to the burning barn.

Tom Shanaghy gathered Carpenter's body in his arms and walked slowly away. Behind him the barn exploded into flame, and he heard shouts and yells from the town. The Carpenter home was but a hundred yards or so away, and he walked toward it.

She was standing on the step, looking toward the fire, and she saw him coming. He saw the white of her wrapper when she stepped away from the door and came toward him, walking slowly.

"Marshal? Mr. Shanaghy? Is it him?"

"Yes, ma'am. He was murdered, ma'am."

"Marshal, would you bring him in, please?" Then she paused. "What is happening, Marshal?"

"I found his body, but they locked me in the stable and set it afire."

She indicated a bed and he placed the body there, gently. "Ma'am? They'd left him in the manger, covered with hay, but the worst of this is from bringing him through the roof."

"Even then, with the fire, you took time to bring him out? Marshal, I—"

"Ma'am, forget it. And don't worry. I'll find who did it. I'll find them if it's the last thing I ever do."

Men had crowded around the fire, watching to keep it from spreading, although the building was isolated. Shanaghy glanced toward them and went on to the street again, pausing there a moment to brush the dust from his derby.

There were still a few horses along the street and there was one rig . . . A man was untying the horses and he turned at Shanaghy's footsteps. It was Pendleton.

Shanaghy paused. "Leaving town, Mr. Pendleton? You aren't staying for the fire?"

"I have seen a fire, Marshal." The Englishman turned toward him. "What has happened?"

"Carpenter has been murdered. I had just found the body when somebody set fire to the barn. An attempt, I presume, to destroy both me and the evidence."

"But you got out? And the body?"

"I brought it with me. Is Jan with you?"

"At this hour?"

"I was hoping she was. Somebody . . . a woman, I think, should be with Mrs. Carpenter. I could think of no one better than Jan."

"I'll bring her in. But there's Mrs. Murphy, too, over at the boardinghouse."

Puzzled, Shanaghy watched Pendleton drive away. It was late, almost midnight, in fact, and not a likely hour for anybody to be out. Western towns were not like New York. Here, people arose at daybreak or before and worked the day through. By night they were ready for bed, and sleep.

Shanaghy watched the receding back of the buckboard and then walked across to the hotel.

Carpenter was dead and an attempt had been made to kill him, so it was no longer fun- and party-time. Also, somebody had either been watching the barn or trailing him. More likely the latter.

From his room in the hotel, Shanaghy looked down into the street. He had no light burning and offered no target, yet he himself could see into the street. He was puzzled.

He had always been wary of being followed. This caution had developed from his days around the Five Points, for the area had been a hangout for thugs. Even the children would rob a man, setting on him in gangs and tripping him up or pulling him down. Shanaghy was as sure as a man could be that he had not been followed. Yet he had been observed.

Somebody, or several somebodies, was taking time out from whatever else they were doing to watch him . . . which meant they were worried.

First they had tried to have him killed in Greenwood's, and second, in the burning barn. What next? That there would be another attempt, and that it would be soon, he knew.

He put his derby on the dressing table, took off his boots, and sat down on the edge of the bed.

What actually did he have? He believed an attempt was to

be made to steal the money, which was due in the day after tomorrow by the latest reports.

He believed the mysterious young woman was involved. He believed the supposed railroad detective who had put him off the train was also involved.

Whoever was in on the action had a local base, and sources of local information.

That person, or persons, had hidden the horses, had attempted to kill him.

He thought of the men down there in the street. He had taken food to them, and water. What disturbed him was that they seemed less worried by their captivity than expected.

Escape would not be easy. The posts were deeply sunk and the railing was thick, strong, well-seasoned wood. The sound of a saw or an ax would be heard all over town. Digging the posts out of the ground would be a formidable job.

Had they received some promise they would be taken care of?

Irritably, he got up and paced the floor. In just a matter of hours, the money would be arriving. If Vince Patterson did not come in with his cattle and his riders, the robbers would have planned some other diversion. As quietly as possible, he moved his bed closer to the window, put two pillows behind him and sat up, looking out at the street. From where he sat he could see the two men chained to the hitching-rail. Both seemed to be asleep, and the street was empty.

By now the plotters might have discovered that Patterson was not to make his move. In any event, he must think that way and not blind himself to whatever else might happen.

Suddenly, he sat up. One of the men at the hitching-rail had lifted his head and was peering intently across the street toward a place hidden from Shanaghy's view.

Shanaghy got up, pulled on his boots and slipped into his coat. After donning his derby, he went quietly down the stairs into the deserted lobby. A faint light glowed over the desk but all else was dark. He moved to the wide window where, standing near the pillar, he had a good view up and down the street.

Suddenly he saw the hand of one of the chained men shoot up as if to catch something, then saw him clawing in the dust to get hold of it.

Shanaghy wheeled. Moving swiftly, he went down the hall.

At the back door he paused, then eased the door open, and slipped out into the darkness. As he did so a figure emerged from between the buildings and moved away from him.

There was no chance for identification, not even a glimpse of more than the shadowy figure. Shanaghy started after him, running as softly as possible on the sandy earth.

Some sound must have reached the figure ahead, for Shanaghy caught a glimpse of a startled white face. Then the figure broke into a run, disappearing around a corner. Shanaghy pulled up at the corner, expecting a trap. Then he heard a pound of hoofs and he rushed from between the buildings to catch the merest suggestion of movement and the sound of retreating hoofbeats.

He swore, then spat. The luck of him! Another step or two faster and he might have caught at least a glimpse.

Wearily, he walked back to the hotel and went to bed. He was not especially interested in what had been thrown. He was pretty certain what it had been . . . a lock pick, he was sure. At this point he didn't care, for if the three escaped it would be all the less to watch out for when the showdown came.

He awakened in the cold light of dawn unrested, worried and sure that things were completely out of control.

All hell was about to break loose, and he did not know where or from whom or just how.

After he had eaten breakfast he went from place to place, trying to complete setting up the organization he had told Patterson was already in existence. There was some grumbling, but there was also some eagerness. Things had been quiet in town and some of the townsfolk were ready for action, any kind of action.

Work had piled up at the blacksmith shop. After taking off his coat and shirt he put on a leather apron and went to work. He always thought better when his hands were busy, anyway. Physical labor seemed to open all the channels of his mind.

He completed an order for andirons, made two sets of hinges and put shoes on two horses. It was when he was paring down a hoof for shoeing that the thought came to him. He finished the job, tied the horse at the hitching-rail outside the shop, and stood for a moment, looking up the street.

There were a few places in town from which almost everything could be seen. One of them was Greenwood's.

He hung up his apron, put on his coat and hat and started up the street.

FOURTEEN

H e paused in front of Holstrum's store, then walked over to where the would-be gunmen were shackled to the hitching-rail. He checked their shackles, then commented, "You boys should get wise to yourselves. If they ever brought off this job, how much would you get? The fewer there are around to split with, the bigger the shares for the others."

He pushed his derby back on his head. "Was I running this job I'd see you boys got turned loose just as the shooting starts. You'd help to create a diversion, and you'd get killed in the process."

Shanaghy knew too much about crooks not to know there was always mutual doubt and suspicion. "How well do you know the people you're working with?" he asked mildly. "I'd say you boys better be looking at your hole card."

"I don't know what he's talkin' about, do you, Turkey?" said one.

The thin, scrawny man shrugged. "Surely don't. We just come into town for a peaceful drink."

Shanaghy chuckled. "This here's a right deceiving town," he said. "For instance, I'd bet you boys don't know I've got men staked out all over town? And that when the shooting starts they'll be using shotguns and buffalo guns at close range?" He waved a hand around. "Boys, there ain't an inch of this street that isn't covered at less'n fifty yards, and mostly twenty yards, by shotguns and rifles. You boys are going to be right in the middle of a bloodbath."

Turkey shifted irritably. "What you gettin' at?"

"Only this . . . If you boys should be lucky enough to get loose or get turned loose before the shootin' starts, I'd suggest you just leave out of here as fast as you can go."

"You make it sound like you got everything all figured out . . . whatever it is."

Shanaghy nodded. "That's just it. I have. And do you know why I'm tellin' you? Because you boys are just out to make a fast dollar. I don't figure you're so bad. And we don't want a lot of dead bodies when this is over . . . It's bad for business. What we'll do, of course, is scoop out a big ditch and just dump the lot of you in it, smooth her over and forget it."

Holstrum was coming down the street to open his store. Shanaghy nodded to him, "Mornin', Mr. Holstrum. Looks like a nice day. I was just fixin' to feed these boys."

Holstrum peered at them over his spectacles. "They look to be a rough lot," he said. "If you need any help—"

"They aren't that bad, Mr. Holstrum. Just some poor, misguided lads who won't be with us very long. I'll feed them well, Mr. Holstrum. They should at least have the pleasure of a last meal. It's a poor lot they are, but too young to pass on."

"You are going to *hang* them?" Holstrum asked.

"Oh, no!" Shanaghy looked terribly sad. "That won't be necessary. But when someone isn't needed any more . . . You know how that is, Mr. Holstrum? When people have outworn their usefulness . . . ?"

Holstrum peered at him over the glasses again. "Ah, Mr. Shanaghy! You have a good heart. Well, feed them well, then. If anything is said of the bill when it comes to the council, I will justify it."

"You, Turkey," Shanaghy said. "You first."

The stocky, dark-bearded one sat up. "You ain't feedin' us together?"

Shanaghy smiled. "That would be risky, wouldn't it? Ah, no, lads. One at a time. You know the old saying . . . 'two's company'? Just two of us alone, you know, it makes for better conversation."

"I ain't hungry," Turkey said.

"Too bad, because you're coming along anyway."

Shanaghy unshackled him, then put both cuffs on his wrists, "Come along, Turkey. You . . ." —he looked back over his shoulder at the other— "just rest easy. Turkey an' me will have a nice talk. Then I'll come back for you."

When they were seated and had ordered, Shanaghy filled both their cups. "Feel sorry for you boys," he said. "After all, you're just trying for that fast dollar. You'd no way of knowing what you were gettin' into."

Turkey had a narrow face with snaky black eyes. He looked around, irritably. "Why don't you just shut up?"

Shanaghy smiled. "Ah, lad, don't be so short with a man who wishes you no ill. But that's the way of it. A man never knows who he can trust.

"It's a trap, you know," he said conversationally. "How do you suppose I know so much? I was tipped off," he said quietly, "by somebody who has got a scheme working within a scheme. This party has got it figured so they'll wind up with all the money. Actually," he commented, "it's a three-way cross. Some of those who think they are double-crossing you are actually being crossed themselves."

Shanaghy was just talking. He was trying to undermine Turkey's confidence, to weaken his resolution, to perhaps extract some clue. But as he talked he began to wonder if he hadn't stumbled upon the truth.

These men, probably like some others, were pawns in the game. But who were the principles? And how did they hope to bring it off?

Turkey ate sullenly. All of a sudden he slammed down his fork and swore. "Take me back, damn it!"

Shanaghy got to his feet. "Anybody can get himself into a hole," he commented. "But it takes a wise man to get out while the getting's good."

He took Turkey back and shackled him to the rail and led the stocky one to breakfast. When they were seated in the restaurant he let the man order, which he did, sullenly enough.

"What did Turkey tell you?" the man demanded, his eyes alight with suspicion.

"Turkey? Nothing at all. I didn't figure you boys knew much. After all, you're just here to create a disturbance and take a fall." Shanaghy smiled. "You boys stir up a dust while they ride out with the money."

"What money? I got no idea what you're talking about."

"Just eat," Shanaghy said. "I know all I need to know."

He asked no questions, made no overtures and obviously that worried the man even more than questions. Finally, Shanaghy did say, "You don't look much like a cowhand,"— although the man obviously did—"what did you do? Work on the railroad?"

"Hell," the man was disgusted, "what would you know about cowhands? I've ridden for some of the biggest outfits in Texas. Why, you just ask them and they'll tell you Cowan is—"

"All right, Cowan, you say you're a puncher, but I would think a cowhand would realize that people would see what horse he was riding and remember the brand. Yet you boys left your horses right in the street where anybody could see them."

"What d' you know about brands? Anyway, anybody can borry a horse."

"Of course." Shanaghy was remembering that he still had not discovered the missing horses. In the confusion of finding Carpenter's body and getting trapped in the burning barn, he had forgotten them. Yet where could they be? There were only two or three places left to look.

"How's he comin'? How's Sl—" he caught himself, then said, "You know? That gent you shot? The slim one?"

"Still alive. He's not conscious yet, however. I hope he stays unconscious until he's through talking."

Cowan glared at him from under thick brows. "Hell, you got somethin' on your mind about talkin'! You keep right on fishin', mister. You're going to come up with just nothing at all."

Cowan finished the coffee in his cup and wiped his mouth with the back of his hand. "How long you keepin' us out there?"

Shanaghy shrugged. "Until your boss turns you loose to get killed. Why go to the expense of trying you fellows when you will get yourselves killed by yourselves? When he turns you loose and the shooting's started, they'll take care of you."

"Who's 'they'?"

"Why, your friends, of course. The ones who roped you into

this and now don't want to pay off. Everybody knows that when the shooting starts the action begins."

Shanaghy got up. "Come on . . . back you go. You've offered me nothing, so if you come out of this alive you'll be the one I hang it on." He grinned cheerfully. "Mr. Cowan, I'm going to need somebody, and if you survive I'll have you. Somebody will surely get killed and that will make it a hanging offense. Besides, the local boys haven't had a necktie party lately."

Shackling Cowan to the hitching-rail not far from Turkey, Shanaghy wandered back up the street. If he could get them to worrying enough, one of them might talk. At least when freed they might run. Yet he had accomplished nothing but to implant, he hoped, some element of doubt.

It was a warm, pleasant morning. A few scattered white tufts of cloud wandered across the blue of the sky. Shanaghy paused on the street and thought about New York.

Such a few days had passed since he'd been there, and yet the city was already vague and unreal in his thoughts. He wished suddenly he had the services of that old-timer who had taught him to shoot, wished he had him here to talk to. That was a shrewd old man. Or Morrissey or Lochlin . . . How was Lochlin?

And Childers? What had happened after he left? Childers, as he recalled, had some ties to the West, somewhere. They had supplied the muscle to put through some kind of land-fraud deal along the railroad.

He crossed the street when he saw Mrs. Carpenter. "Ma'am?" She paused. "I did some work at the shop, some stuff your husband had planned. If it's all right with you, ma'am, when this is over I'll either buy the shop from you or I'll buy half of it. And the horses, too," he added.

"He would have liked that, Mr. Shanaghy. He always said you were an excellent smith, that you'd missed your calling."

Shanaghy flushed. "Ma'am, I don't have no calling. I don't have a thing to speak of but a wish that keeps growing in me."

"A wish?"

"Yes, ma'am. A wish to be something more than I am, which isn't much. Maybe if I started with the shop—"

"When this is over, Mr. Shanaghy, we will talk." She paused. "Mr. Shanaghy, I always thought I was a Christian woman, but now all I want is to see the murderer of my husband caught and punished."

"So he shall be. Only don't speak of it now. Ma'am, there's somebody in town who's working with them, somebody . . . I don't know who."

He watched her walk away. Carpenter had been a good man, too good a man to die that way. Shanaghy started for the railroad station, then stopped. Josh Lundy was riding up the street.

"I reckoned you could use me. I got some work caught up so I come on in."

"You come alone?"

Josh looked down from his seat in the saddle. Wrinkles formed at the corners of his eyes. "Well, I set out mighty early . . . It's a fur piece from here to yonder."

"Did you come alone?" Shanaghy insisted.

"Pendleton was right busy, you might say. He did say he might come around later. His son was out on the range roundin' up some horses that done strayed off."

Tom Shanaghy waited, and when Josh said no more, he said, "Can you track?"

"A mite. I lived with the Pawnee one time. Picked up a little here an' yonder. What was it you wanted tracked?"

"A horse or two." Shanaghy explained about the three men who rode in, one of them on a Vince Patterson horse.

"Don't let that fret you. He left a couple of horses up here . . . at least, his brother did. I mean that time he got hisself killed. Somebody was holdin' those horses."

Shanaghy nodded. "All right, tie your horse and come along to the restaurant. I've got some things to talk over with you."

Josh nodded. "All right. You go right on in. I'll be along pretty soon. I'll take my horse down to the shop, an'—"

"Carpenter's dead. He was murdered."

"You don't say? Well, I ain't surprised. He was a good man, too good a man."

Shanaghy walked into the restaurant, removing his derby as he entered. He was halfway across the room when he saw her.

Jan Pendleton was sitting there facing him, and she was smiling. "Good morning. You look surprised."

"Josh didn't tell me—"

"He wouldn't." She looked up at him as he drew his chair back. "I rode in to see you."

"Me?" He was flustered. He drew back a chair and sat down.

"I heard you were having trouble," she said.

"Yes, ma'am. A mite. Here and yonder, as Josh would say. First I was wishing you were here to be with Mrs. Carpenter after he was killed. You know, to have a woman about."

"I imagine her brother was with her. She wouldn't have needed me."

"Her brother?"

"Yes, didn't you know? He's the station agent. The telegrapher."

FIFTEEN

It was quiet in the little café. A few people came and went, but he scarcely noticed. Suddenly he was talking about his boyhood in Ireland, the things he remembered, the stories his father told him, about horses he had known . . . about the Maid o' Killarney.

"Are you returning to New York?" Jan asked.

He waited, thinking. "I don't know," he said at last. "Maybe I'll stay here. With Carp gone there's no smith. It is a good business but not exactly what I wanted."

"What do you want?"

There was that question again. He shifted uncomfortably. "I don't know, ma'am, I—"

"Call me Jan."

He looked up at her and for a moment their eyes met. He was embarrassed. "I'm Tom," he said.

"I know your name. I know more about you than you think."

"You don't. If you did you wouldn't even be talking to me."

Josh Lundy came in and crossed to their table. "Sorry to butt in, folks, but I have to talk to the marshal, here."

"Talk . . . And why didn't you tell me Jan rode in with you?"

Lundy widened his eyes. "Why, Marshal, I hadn't no idea you'd be interested. You figurin' to arrest her?"

"Sit down, Josh. If I could think of a charge, I'd shackle you to the rail along with the others, but I can't."

"Gimme a chance to catch up on my whittlin'," Josh replied. "I found them horses," he added, "at least, I found where they been."

He pointed south. "There's a draw over yonder. Ain't much. Little corral over there and a lean-to. I done checked what tracks was left out behind where they first left their horses . . . I found two tracks like those in that old corral."

"Whose corral is it?"

"Nobody's. Built years back by some passerby with horses or cows to hold. She's only a hundred yards or so from here, but I reckon nobody in town goes there 'lest it's the youngsters. Some of them play Injun over there. One of those horses was a dark gray . . . unusual color. I found some hairs where he'd rubbed hisself on the snubbin' post."

Shanaghy thought about it. Yet he hesitated to ask the question. Finally, he did. "Josh, do you know whose horse that is? The dark gray one?"

"I do." He glanced at Jan, then dropped his eyes. "I guess ever'body does."

"It belongs to my brother," Jan said.

Shanaghy felt the sweat break out on his brow. He hesitated to speak, but Josh interrupted before he could frame any words.

"That doesn't say he rode it. Them horses been runnin' out. Anybody could rope up a horse an' it's often done, often of necessity. Folks don't really consider it stealin' unless somebody tries to ride out of the country or pens up a horse.

"Of course, a man who does that sort of thing better have a good explanation. I've roped up an' ridden other folks' horses many a time when mine played out, or I was in a gosh-awful hurry."

"There were a half dozen of Dick's horses running loose in a little pasture down by the creek," Jan said. "Father was saying the other day that they must be back in the brush, because he hadn't seen them the last few times he rode past."

"Was one of them a little black mare?"

"No." Jan smiled at him. "Was that what she was riding?"

"Holstrum has a black mare with two white stockings . . . pretty little thing."

"It sounds like the mare I saw."

Shanaghy was slowly putting things together. Suppose some strangers came into town and needed horses for a few days? Might they not catch up some they found running loose, use them and then turn them loose?

"Looks to me like I'd better do some riding around the country," he suggested.

"You tell me and I'll ride," Josh suggested. "Nobody would be surprised to see me. I'm always out roundin' up strays or whatever."

"All right . . . but watch yourself. Whoever is doing this doesn't intend to lose. They tried to trap me into a shootout where I'd be killed, and they've already killed Carpenter . . . I guess he got on to something."

"He was a friend of mine," Josh said quietly. "He was a man I liked."

"Josh," Shanaghy said, "maybe the best thing you could do right now would be just to talk about the people here. I don't know much about them. Just whatever you know about where they came from and what connections they have."

"We came from England," Jan said pertly. "We run a few cattle, and my father buys and sells cattle. My brother works with him."

"You know most of it," Josh said. "The town was started by Holstrum, Carpenter and Greenwood. They still own most of what's around here. Pendleton's got him a fine place. Holstrum and Greenwood both have a good bit of land around. They think highly of the town. Some folks don't.

"The three of them worked to get the railroad right-of-way where it is. Now they are working on the state capitol to get the town made the county seat. Judge McBane is with them on that, and so is Pendleton. If it goes through property values will go up."

"Tom," Jan was suddenly serious, "what are you going to do? I hear Uncle Vince is bringing his cattle up tomorrow."

"I've talked to him. He won't make trouble."

"Some of his hands might. When they get here, their job is finished. Some of them will go back to Texas to join another drive, but some will drift. Once they are paid off Uncle Vince no longer controls them."

"I'll have to handle that as it happens." Shanaghy looked up at her from the coffee cup. "I'm thinking about buying the blacksmith shop. Give me a toehold. A sort of place to start."

"Don't pay too much. Mrs. Carpenter is careful when it comes to money. When she sells anything she gets her money's worth. Papa told me that about her. She was angry when Carp first sold land here . . . said he should have leased it, instead."

"Holstrum wanted to buy her place," Lundy said.

"Her home, you mean?"

"She has a section of land south of here. It adjoins Holstrum's place and he wanted it, but she wouldn't sell. They had several long discussions about it but she wouldn't sell at all. I think Holstrum gave up.

"It was taken as grazing land but most of it is good farming land with a good spring and a small creek running through it."

"She proved up on it? What's that mean, exactly?" Shanaghy asked.

"Sink a well, plow some land, build a house, and then live on the land. They don't all do that. She'd go out there, time to time. Sometimes both of them would go but usually it was just her. Carp was busy with the shop."

"Did they build out there?"

Lundy shrugged. "Like they do . . . it was nothing much. Somebody had built a dugout, years ago. She fixed that up a mite and then had the fellow who takes care of Holstrum's place come over and build her a soddy . . . a sod house."

"I've never seen one."

"They just cut squares of sod and use them like bricks, then roof it over with poles. It makes a snug, warm place in winter when snow gets packed around it. But building one is more of an art than you'd figure. Takes some savvy."

"And Holstrum's man? He's good at it?"

"So they say. Name's Moorhouse. He's a good man with stock but damned unfriendly . . . Sullen sort, always packing a grouch. He's big and he's mean. Comes to town about once a month."

All the time Shanaghy sat there, he had the haunting feeling that he was missing something, that events were building in a way he did not suspect, that he was in deeper water than he could handle.

Josh made his excuses and left and they sat silent for a while. Then Jan said, "I wish I could help."

"Just your being here helps," he admitted. He looked at her and shrugged. "I don't know what to do but wait and handle it as it comes."

"There isn't much else you can do." She paused. "Tom? If Uncle Vince's men don't create a diversion of some kind, what will they do?"

"I think the robbers have planned for that. Maybe it will be an attempt to release those men I have shackled to the rail down there. Maybe it will be something else.

"When the train comes in and they unload the gold—"

"What if they don't unload it?"

That idea had passed through his mind before this. "You mean if they leave it on the train?"

"It's been planned so well, so what if they simply take the gold off elsewhere? If they have horses or a wagon waiting for them? What if there is a lot of shooting here in the streets and the train leaves?"

"But they'd have to get it off. Where would they unload?" Shanaghy asked.

"Let's get our horses. I'll show you where. It's only a little way."

They rode swiftly where the long winds blew, over the buffalo grass and the blue grama, here and there prairie flowers blooming. They startled a rabbit, then a small herd of antelope. To their right was the railroad, tracks shining bright in the sun.

They dipped into a hollow, then walked their horses up the far side. She rode well, this girl did, and she knew how to handle horses . . . But, like him, she had grown up with them.

She pulled up atop a small knoll.

"There!" she pointed. "I think that will be it."

A railroad construction shack, a pile of ties, a water tank. "They call it Holstrum. Before they had the water tank in town, they always stopped here for water, and they unloaded track materials there. Pa showed me," Jan added, "and Dick and I used to ride here and water our horses and rest before starting back.

"See?" She pointed. "There's a trail leading off across the country to the south, and another northwest."

"What lies off there?" Shanaghy pointed south.

"Holstrum's place. That's why they called it that. He owns most of this land aside from the right-of-way. He has a nice little cabin over there. Dick and I used to ride by sometimes, when we were younger. But since that mean Mr. Moorhouse has been there, we don't go anymore. Dick made me promise I wouldn't even ride this way."

"He's mean, you say. What's he like?"

"He's awfully big. Hulking. He has a mustache and he's always unshaved. He wears bib overalls, not the western kind, and he's dirty. He's very strong. I saw him pick up a whole barrel of vinegar once and put it on a wagon."

"A barrel of vinegar? Must weigh five hundred pounds!"

"I know. It took two very strong men to lift it off when we got it home. He was helping Mr. Holstrum in town then."

"Do you know Holstrum well?"

"Oh, I suppose so," Jan said. "He's a nice man, but lonely, I think. He still thinks of me as a little girl. I'd be uncomfortable around him if he didn't, I mean, from the way he looks at some girls.

"But . . . I don't know. A few months ago there was a girl came to town . . . Not a very nice one . . . I think she worked in saloons and places like that. She tried to make up to him and he would have nothing to do with her."

Shanaghy chuckled. "He's got his sights set higher. He wants a lady, a real lady. He told me once about one . . . the kind he liked . . . smelling of nice perfume, and very ladylike and . . ."

He stopped abruptly and they looked at each other. "Tom? Do you think—? Could it be? That girl. The one you saw in the restaurant? She looks like a lady, and she does use very good scent. I mean—"

"Jan . . . don't look now, and don't stop. Just keep riding but bear off a little to the north."

"What's wrong?"

"There's somebody there . . . at the water tower. He's watching us!"

SIXTEEN

The water tower was no more than two hundred yards off and the man had a glass. Shanaghy could see the reflected light from it. He was watching them. Fortunately they had not been riding straight toward the tank but a little north of it, planning to turn when they reached the trail.

"Keep right ahead until we reach the trail, then turn north."

"But who could it be?" Jan asked.

"I'd like to know, but I suspect this would not be a good time to go nosing around."

"You'd ride right down there if I weren't here," she protested.

"Maybe . . . But I want them all, not just one man. I want the man who killed Carpenter."

"If it was a man."

"What?" He glanced at her. "What do you mean by that?"

"Women can commit crimes, too. Carpenter was in somebody's way, and I don't think it was only because he was about to find the horses. I think he was in the way anyhow."

Shanaghy glanced out of the corners of his eyes toward the water tower. The man was no longer using the glass but had picked up a rifle.

They rode down a slight bank into the trail and turned north,

133

away from the water tank. Desperately, Shanaghy wished to look back, but he forced himself not to turn his head even the slightest. The trail was one rarely used and showed no recent evidence of travel, so those at the water tank must have come in along the tracks or from the south.

"A little faster," he said. How far were they now? Three hundred yards? No, not quite so much.

They topped a rise and dropped over into a small hollow through which ran a stream. There, at the edge of a clump of willows, a man sat on a boulder.

He was bearded and old, wearing a moth-eaten coonskin cap, fringed buckskin pants and a checked black and white shirt. In his hands he carried a rifle, and over his back a pack in which there was a blanket and poncho.

"Howdy, folks! Nice day!" He noted the badge. "Ha? Marshal, is it? Well, it's about time some of you fellers picked up their sign."

They drew up. "Whose sign?"

"You mean you ain't seen 'em? I mean that triflin' lot who're down yonder by the tank. Lucky this here stream's here or a body couldn't even fetch hisself a drink."

"What d'you know about them?"

"Know? I know all I need to know. They're rough folks. Kill you soon as look at you. They done shot at me."

"When?"

"Three, four days back. Some city feller down yonder by the water tank, he said I was to git away an' not come back.

"I ast if'n he was the railroad, and he said he wasn't but he spoke for them. I ast him if he spoke for Big Mac and he said that made no difference, I was to git. I told him Big Mac said I could have all the water I needed, and he said he was tellin' me I couldn't.

"Well, I could see he didn't know Big Mac, and he surely had nothin' to do with the road, an' I told him so. He ups with a six-shooter and told me to hightail it, and I done so.

"Right then I knowed somethin' was almighty wrong, because Big Mac is division superintendent of this line an' ever'body knows him. Nobody who works for that road would speak slighting of Big Mac . . . He'd skin 'em alive. An' Mac is a friend of mine. Me an' his pa prospected together.

"So I kept nosin' around an' they seen me. I surely wasn't

hidin' . . . No reason to . . . An' one of them waved me off, then this city feller . . . My eyes is still good for distance . . . He ups with his rifle and killed my burro. He killed ol' Buster . . . Buster, he been with me nine, ten year. Killed him . . . creased me.

"Well, Marshal, I ain't about to leave. Not until I get me one of them. Hopeful, it'll be that city feller. I had him true in my sights the other day, an' then that woman come between us. She—"

"What woman?"

"Her who brings 'em grub sometimes. I seen her come over there a time or two, sometimes with a rig an' sometimes a'horseback."

"Young, pretty woman?"

"Sort of. Depends on what a man calls purty an' what he calls young. But attractive, I'd say, mighty attractive."

The old man peered at Shanaghy. "You're that there new feller I've heard talk of. Come right in and come to be marshal right off."

"Nobody else wanted the job."

"I reckon not. Not with Rig hurtin' like he is."

Shanaghy had been about to ride on, but the words pulled him up short. "Rig hurting, you say?" He studied the old man. "You talk like you know where he is."

"I should smile, I do! Nobody knows no better!" The old man chuckled. "Him a'frettin' an' a'sweatin' over all this here, an' me tellin' him not to worry, that you got it under *con*-trol!"

"Where is he?"

The old man cocked his head. "Where? Now wouldn't you like to know? I reckon them fellers down to the tank would give a purty penny to know just where he's at."

He chuckled again, looking very wise. "They *had* him. Had him dead to rights. All lashed up like one o' them Christmas packages, an' I snuck in an' fetched him away!"

He chuckled again. "You should have seen 'em! Like chickens with their heads off, runnin' all over, here an' yonder! An' that woman, she was fit to be tied! Read 'em the riot act, she did!"

Tom Shanaghy held very still. He glanced over at Jan. Her eyes were wide and she was caressing her horse's neck, fooling with the mane. "I'd like to see him," she said. "Is he all right? I mean, wasn't he hurt?"

"*Hurt?* You're darn tootin', he was hurt! They figured they had him killed, but they didn't want him *found*. They figured to have him disappear, like. I reckon so's they'd figure him still around. That way the folks in town wouldn't latch onto somebody to take his place. Like they done you."

He chuckled. "That must've upset 'em! Upset 'em plenty! You comin' in out of nowhere, actin' like you was sent!"

He peered at Shanaghy. "Can't figure out why they ain't kilt you."

"They've tried."

"I should reckon." The old man bobbed his head. "You get through this night . . . you're shot with luck. Up to now they been foolin'. Now they got to git shut of you."

He looked around at Jan. "You're wishful to see Rig Barrett? I'll take you to him."

"Thanks," Shanaghy said, "I was going to ask—"

"Hey, there! Pull up, now! Nobody said nothin' about takin' *you* to him. It was *her*. She done asked an' she's worried about him. I'll take her. Not you."

"But—"

"It's all right, Tom," Jan said. "I'll be all right."

"All right? I should reckon!" The old man peered at Shanaghy. "Jealous, are you? Jealous of old Coonskin, are you? Well, I don't blame you! Here a few year back I used to cut quite a figure amongst the gals! Nobody could dance the fandango like ol' Coonskin Adams! Them gals . . . why, they was all just a'pantin' around after me!

"Looks I ain't got, but I do got *style*! Yes, siree-bob! I got style!"

He turned to Jan. "You come along with me, young lady. I'll take you to Rig. This here marshal, he can do whatever he's of a mind to, but he should watch hisself because tonight's the night! They'll kill him tonight. They don't want nothin' to mess with their big day. An' Rig, he's in no shape to fetch 'em."

"Coonskin," Shanaghy said seriously. "I need to talk to Rig. I need his advice. Look, I don't know what I'm walkin' into."

"You're a'doin' fine. Just you don't trust nobody. *Nobody,* d'you hear?"

They rode away, and Shanaghy watched them go, torn with doubt. That young, beautiful girl, going off with a rough, dirty-looking old man . . . to where?

Turning his horse, he started back to town. As he rode he slowly reviewed what he knew and what he suspected.

The projected robbery had begun either in the mind of someone in town who knew about the money that would be arriving, or someone who had access to the information from other sources. Shanaghy knew enough about crime and criminals to know that no information is really secret. There is always somebody who knows, and there is always somebody who will talk—in the strictest confidence, of course, but talk they will. And if one talks, another will.

A quarter of a million dollars is a lot of money. Vince Patterson's herd would bring him perhaps sixty thousand dollars, but there were other herds not far behind. The money would be needed to cash checks, to pay off hands, and to keep the wheels of trade turning at their proper speed. A large portion of that money would be spent right in town . . . if it wasn't stolen.

How many men were involved? There was at least one man at the water tower, but there had been all those others, too. George, the man on the train, the two men shackled to the hitching-rail . . . and a woman.

There had to be somebody in town. No outsider had smuggled those horses away so quickly.

Turning his horse he cut across the prairie away from the railroad, riding northwest. The prairie was not as flat as it seemed from town, being gently rolling in places with a good many dips and hollows. Here and there was a streambed, most of them dry. Standing in his stirrups and looking back, he could see nothing of Jan or the old man. They had vanished as if they had never been.

He rode into town from the north. As he entered he saw Mrs. Carpenter shading her eyes at him from her door, but when he made as if to ride toward her she went inside and closed the door.

A man whom he recognized as one who worked for the lumberyard was standing in the street as if waiting. Shanaghy pulled up. "Something wrong?" he asked.

"Miz Carpenter wants her horse. That there one you're ridin'."

"Carpenter loaned it to me. He said—"

"Maybe he said. Anyway, Carpenter is dead, as you mighty

well know. That there horse belongs to Miz Carpenter, an' she
wants it back."

There was no friendliness in the man. "She wants it back, an'
she wants it now."

"I'll leave it at the stable."

"Mister, I said she wants it *now*. Right here . . . *now*."

Surprised and irritated, Shanaghy dismounted. "Why, sure.
Although I don't see what she's in such a hurry for."

"You don't? Mister, there's folks around askin' themselves
questions about how Carpenter comes to be dead, and you
with the body, and all.

"You come in here out of nowhere and start workin' with
him. You see he's got him a nice business there. You start ridin'
around on his horse, in a saddle belonging to him, and you
even work there when he's not around, collectin' money for
work and materials and all. Then suddenly Carp, who didn't
have an enemy in the world, is found dead."

The eyes were cold and accusing. "Found dead by you . . .
And you say you escaped from a burning barn that somebody
set afire.

"Now does that make sense? Who would lock you in a barn
and set it afire? Who would kill Carp? Who stood to gain by
it?"

"You're mistaken, my friend," said Shanaghy. "I liked Carp,
and he liked me, we—"

"You say. But who stood to gain? You're the only smith
around. Hear you been cozening up to Miz Carpenter, too.

"Mister, you may think you're some shakes, walkin' around
with that badge and all. Well, let me tell you . . ."

Shanaghy fought down an angry reply. "Take the horse and
saddle to Mrs. Carpenter and thank her for me. I guess I'll just
have to find another horse."

"Not in this town, you won't."

Angrily, Shanaghy strode up the street to the hotel. What in
God's name was happening? Had she gone crazy?

A man standing in front of Holstrum's turned abruptly away
as he approached, and another deliberately walked across the
street, away from him.

Shanaghy pushed open the door and entered the hotel, starting for the stairs. Suddenly he stopped. His gear . . . or,

rather, Rig's gear and his few extra clothes, were bundled up at the bottom of the stairs.

He looked up to find the clerk smiling at him, a malicious smile. That clerk had never liked him, anyway. .

"Sorry, Mr. Marshal-man. We needed your room. You'll have to look somewhere else."

The clerk leaned his elbows on the desk. "We don't want your kind around here, mister. My advice to you is get while the getting is good. They can't prove anything right now, but they will. And when they do, you'll hang. You'll *hang*! D'you hear me?"

SEVENTEEN

Shanaghy emerged upon the street, shaken by the sudden twist events had taken. He stood for a minute or two, his gear beside him, trying to adjust to the situation.

He had been warned they would try to kill him, and they still might. But what they were doing now was many times more effective, or so it seemed to him. The townspeople he was trying to aid and protect had turned against him.

They believed him a murderer, and he had to admit that looking at things the way they were, such a theory was plausible.

Now he had no horse, no place to sleep, and he doubted if he could even buy a meal. Who had started the story? By the time he figured that out, it would be already too late. Whatever was going to happen here would happen within the next few hours.

Taking up his gear he went down the street to Holstrum's store. The store was empty when he entered except for Holstrum himself, who peered at him from over his glasses.

"I need a place to stay," Shanaghy said. "They put me out at the hotel."

The storekeeper shrugged. "I have nothing for you." His

manner was cool. "My advice is to leave . . . while it is still possible. You are not liked here. Since you have come much has happened, and there are many who believe you yourself killed poor Mr. Carpenter. My advice is to go . . . before enough men get together to hang you."

A moment Shanaghy hesitated, but Holstrum had turned away. Taking up his gear he walked out to the street again.

It was impossible, and yet . . . it had happened. Who had started the rumor? And why?

Maybe it was only an idea that started in the mind of an overwrought and grief-stricken woman. And maybe it was an idea put there by somebody who saw a chance to destroy him . . . or at least to get him out of town.

Shanaghy thought suddenly of his prisoners. He must have walked right by them, unthinking. He looked again.

They were gone.

Greenwood . . . He would go to Greenwood.

One man was finishing a beer as he entered. The man glanced at him, put a coin on the bar and walked out.

Shanaghy stepped up to the bar. "How about it? Are you shutting me out, too?"

Greenwood's features were expressionless. "What'll you have?"

"Beer."

Greenwood drew the beer and placed it before him. "It's a small community, and stories get around. Carpenter's been murdered. Folks start asking who stood to gain by it, and your name came up first. Carp was a well liked man. He'd had no trouble before. You come to town, you work at his shop and suddenly he's dead . . . You find his body, but the barn where he was killed burned, and with it all the evidence."

Greenwood glanced at Shanaghy. "You had anything to eat?"

"No . . . and I'm hungry."

"Don't have much here, but I can give you a bowl of chili and some crackers." He dished it up. "Lived in Tucson a good many years back. All you could get in a restaurant there in those days was chili, chili and beans or beef. You'd think I'd be sick of it, but I'm not."

Greenwood put the bowl of steaming chili and another bowl filled with oyster crackers on the bar. "You want to know what I think? I don't believe you murdered Carp. I do know he liked you, and I think you did him . . . well as you knew him."

"We talked a little. I did like him."

Greenwood lit a cigar. "You've got enemies, and if I feed you they'll be my enemies."

"I'll stay away."

"You needn't." Greenwood puffed thoughtfully at the cigar. "In this case your enemies have to be my enemies. I mean those who aren't just misguided but real enemies."

Greenwood took Shanaghy's beer from the bar and put a head on it. "That's partly my money coming in on the train."

"How much of it is yours?"

"The big part. I've got a hundred and fifty thousand coming in. Other businessmen around town have maybe another fifty. Carp has some and so does Holstrum."

"I don't comprehend. Why is so much of it yours?"

"We wanted the cattle business and I had access to more cash than the others. Good credit. So I agreed to carry the weight of it."

Shanaghy looked at Greenwood thoughtfully, then went on with his eating. He was hungry and the chili tasted good . . . very good. Yet there was a feeling that he was missing something, and a feeling of impending doom.

"Greenwood," Shanaghy said suddenly, "if I were you I'd close up shop and keep out of sight. I think your number is up, too."

"Mine?"

"You just said most of that money was yours. By coming into the picture I've messed up their plans. I don't think they intended to kill anyone . . . Maybe they didn't . . . except for Rig. Then when I came into the picture they had to kill me. Well, they haven't done it so far but they'll keep trying.

"Now, they're trying to run me out of town. They've taken my room from me. I've no place to eat, and they've taken my horse. I'd lay a bet I can't even get a ticket out of town, although maybe they'd be glad to see me go."

"What's happening, then?"

"It's somebody right here in town who is mixed up in all this. I tell you, man, they had it all worked out, until Rig Barrett smelled something rotten." Shanaghy paused, then asked, "Whose idea was it to hire Rig?"

"Mine. Judge McBane agreed. So did Carpenter. Holstrum

did, then he worried about it, afraid we'd get a worse lawman than we had. He voted against it finally."

"Carp was for it."

"He was."

Shanaghy finished the chili and drank the last of the beer. "You'd better hole up. I can't promise you where I'll be, but they shan't drive me out. I'll find a horse somewhere—"

"I have several. Take your pick. And there's all the gear you'll need, right out back." Greenwood reached under the bar and pulled out a shotgun. "I have this, and if you need me—"

"You just stay here. I may need a place to come to."

He paused, looking up the empty street. It was too empty . . . and that worried him. "Greenwood, how well do you know Mrs. Carpenter?"

The saloonkeeper looked up the sunlit street where the dust stirred briefly. "Not much." He spoke reluctantly, as one who did not talk about women, at least about decent women. "She kept pretty much to herself . . . Didn't socialize a lot. Folks seemed to like her, but . . . well, she was standoffish.

"Carp was different. He liked folks, enjoyed sitting around talking. He was a serious man, though, and knew what he was about. Sometimes . . ." —he hesitated— "sometimes I figure she thought she was a mite too good for all of us, Carp included."

"And her brother?"

"They were close. Saw a lot of one another, but he wasn't a mixer, either. He'd come in here, time to time, and buy a bottle." He scowled. "Come to think of it, here lately he's been buying more. Sometimes two or three bottles at a time."

"Becoming a drunk?"

"I never saw him drunk. No . . . I don't think so."

"How about other stuff? Groceries?"

Greenwood shrugged. "No . . . Holstrum would be the only one who would know about that."

"I was wondering . . . Maybe he was buying that whiskey for somebody else? Somebody who didn't want to show up around town?"

Shanaghy got up. Greenwood rinsed out the bowls and his beer mug, then dried his hands on his apron. It was cool and pleasant in the small saloon. Shanaghy looked up the street. Already the buildings looked weather-beaten and old. Sun, wind and blown sand would do that. In the prairie country, towns had a way of aging very fast.

The wind picked up a little dust and carried it along, then dropped it. A horse tied at the hitching-rail stamped his feet and blew through his nostrils. Shanaghy missed the clang of the hammer from the smithy.

Carp had been a good man, a solid man. And now he was dead . . . just when he had been trying to help, too.

Was that the reason? Was it just that he was in the way?

Tom Shanaghy stirred restlessly, irritably. He was out of his depth. What *was* going on here, anyway? His thoughts strayed to New York and Morrissey. At least he knew there who his enemies were. Yet now it all seemed so far, far away.

He had wanted no trouble when he came here. He wanted only to board the train and leave. He had even bought his ticket . . . and he could still do that, he could do it tomorrow— if somebody would sell him one . . .

Suddenly his eye caught a flicker of movement up the street. There was a man standing in the deepest shade of the awning in front of the express office. The man had a rifle.

Shanaghy watched for a minute or two, his eyes slowly sweeping the scene before him, his mind racing. They were ready for him. They were all set to kill him, and now they had undoubtedly enlisted some of the good men of the town as well, convincing them that he had killed Carpenter.

Walking into a cold deck like that was not to his liking. He glanced around at Greenwood. "Close up and hole up, and don't let anybody in unless it's me." He paused a minute. "Greenwood, I'm beginning to get the pattern. You were to be the patsy all along. I mean, maybe they started out with other ideas but it was your money they wanted. I'm going to take one of your horses and slip out of town. I'm going to ride to Patterson's outfit for help."

Greenwood shifted the shotgun from one hand to the other, nodding slowly. "All right, Shanaghy, I'll stand pat. But for God's sake get back here."

Greenwood put the shotgun on the bar and mopped his brow. "They won't let you get out of town, Shanaghy. By now they are watching my horses. They might think you'd run but they dasn't take the chance."

Tom Shanaghy was of the same notion. He stared up the

street, trying to fit all the pieces together. There had to be somebody in town . . . Who?

The idea that kept nagging at him made no sense, yet it could fit . . . it did fit. In part at least. If he just knew who his enemies were, he would know better how to proceed.

"What about Holstrum?" he asked suddenly.

Greenwood shrugged. "He stands to lose, too. Anyway, I can't see him figuring this out."

"Some of those big, slow men are damn smart," Shanaghy said. "It doesn't pay to underrate them." He was looking up the street and thinking. They didn't have much time.

He swore bitterly. "Hell of it is, there's some good but mistaken men out there. I don't want to kill anybody who doesn't have it coming."

He looked around. "Greenwood, that girl's in it, I know, and so's that George whatever-his-name-is. But who was it turned the town against me? It surely wasn't one of them. It had to be a local. It had to be somebody folks would listen to."

"Who, then?"

Shanaghy turned his head and stared at him. "They would listen to you, Greenie."

Greenwood shrugged. "It wasn't me. Like you've said, most of that money will be mine. I stand to lose it all. I stretched my credit, Shanaghy. I'll be broke if we lose that money . . . wiped out."

"The judge?"

"Him? Not on your life! He's a solid man, an honest man. If there was one man in town . . ."

Greenwood paused. "Shanaghy, that young woman you spoke of? The one who met the gambler? You said she seemed to come from the south?"

"Aye . . . and that was a thing I wished to speak to him about . . . Carpenter knew her horse, I am sure of it."

Greenwood poured them each a beer. He rested his hands on the bar and wet his lips with his tongue. Then reluctantly he said, "Holstrum has a place down thataway."

"I know. I've been thinking of that. And Holstrum voted against Rig Barrett being brought in."

Shanaghy watched up the empty street. There were two riflemen in sight now, watching the saloon. He had a hunch the back was no better. He glanced at the clock. Almost an hour

. . . but what could he do? To venture out was to get shot. They were going to win. They were going to defeat him, after all. How had he ever been such a fool as to believe he could bring this off? What experience did he have that qualified him to step into Rig Barrett's shoes? But who else had there been?

He thought of Jan. She had ridden off with that strange old man, supposedly to see Rig . . . Where? Did her father and brother know where she was? Her brother? What kind of a bungling fool was he, anyway?

Where was Josh Lundy? And where did he stand now? Restlessly, he paced the floor, watching every window, every door. Nobody was on the street. As if on signal all shopping seemed to have ceased. No rigs were tied along the street.

Nothing could be better for the thieves. Now they had it all their own way, better even than planned. There would be no fight between the town and Vince Patterson, but Shanaghy, the only officer, was pinned down in the saloon and without allies. Fearful of shooting that might develop, the townsfolk had deserted the streets. So the train would come in with its shipment, it would be unloaded at the platform and the train would depart. The gold would be in the hands of the thieves without a chance of interference.

Greenwood, who was to receive the shipment, was also pinned down. Instead of a few fast minutes of work, now they could take their time. The thought irritated Shanaghy. They were so sure now that he was whipped.

Was he?

He swore again, suddenly, bitterly, and Shanaghy was not a man who was inclined to swear. He looked down the empty street. The train would be coming, the gold would be taken from it, the train would go on. Yet what would they do with the gold? Where would it be taken?

"I think Holstrum is in it," he said, suddenly. "I think he has been a part of it from the first. It may even have been his idea."

Greenwood said nothing. He looked into his beer, then swallowed some of it.

"It's the woman," Shanaghy said. "It is because of her. Or maybe Holstrum is tired of this," he said, waving a hand around. "He may want to leave."

"He was unhappy here at first," Greenwood admitted. "He got into it, but things did not move swiftly enough. I believe he expected the town to grow faster, the values to increase. And then," he shrugged, "there was something the town did not give him, something he wanted."

Shanaghy glanced again at the clock. Only a few minutes had passed. He walked back to the bar and finished his own beer.

What would Morrissey have done? Shanaghy didn't know but he had an idea Morrissey would have walked out there and dominated the situation by sheer personality. So would Rig Barrett.

He looked into his empty glass, thinking. Suddenly, his thoughts turned to the water tower. Why were those men so anxious to keep people away? What did the water tower have to do with their plans?

Suppose they had never intended to bring the gold into town? Suppose it was to have been unloaded there, at the water tower, and spirited away from there while confusion existed in town? Jan had suggested it.

If Holstrum was involved, that would make sense. His place was not far off and he had horses, and probably a buckboard or wagon.

"I don't like any of this." He turned on Greenwood. "There's something going on here . . . I don't know what it is. There are too many of the wrong people involved, and I can't believe they are the kind to share. They all seem greedy to me."

He shook his head irritably. "Oh, I know it is all imagination! I don't *know* anything! But I do know what I feel and I've mixed with that kind for half my life! They have a plan . . . But it doesn't feel right to me, so I am thinking somebody else has a separate plan."

"Tom?" Greenwood pointed. "Look!"

Shanaghy turned sharply. A young man in a white buckskin vest was dismounting up the street.

Win Drako!

Bass was with him, tying his horse close by. Bass looked over his shoulder toward the saloon and said something to Win Drako.

A door opened up the street and Drako himself appeared. "It will be a day to remember," Tom Shanaghy said softly, "if a man lives past it!"

"They're coming for you," Greenwood said.

"Who else?"

"There's three of them."

"Aye! 'Tis a thing to think on, Greenwood. Three!"

"They're coyotes," Greenwood said contemptuously. "They kept from sight until they knew the whole town was against you, and then they come!"

"Ah, but the advantage is mine," Shanaghy said. "They are fools."

"The advantage is yours? Are you crazy?"

"No, Greenie," Shanaghy said. "A man who stands alone is the stronger because he knows he has no one on whom to lean. He must do it all himself. When there are more than one, each is expecting the other to get it done. Each holds back a little, hoping not to get hurt."

He smiled. "It is a favor they have done me, Greenie, a favor indeed. For it is my means to get out of here in one piece. Those others, you see, they will stand back to watch. They will watch to see the Drakos kill me."

"Do you want the shotgun?"

"Keep it. You may need it, man, and I shall do what must be done with a six-shooter. However, I could use another if you have it."

"You're really going out there?"

"Aye." He took the gun Greenwood handed him, glanced to see if it was loaded. "Aye, I am going out, and I shall keep going, me lad! I shall go until this is done with and then I'll be going back to New York."

He paused a moment, his hand on the latch. The three men up the street stood together, talking, glancing from time to time at the saloon.

"They will be expecting me there, for I wrote a note to Morrissey. I wished him to know that I had not run out on him, and I told him I'd be back when this was over. Have a care for yourself, Greenie." He lifted the latch.

Up the street the three men had spread out and were walking toward the saloon.

EIGHTEEN

He should feel fear, but he did not. He should be wary, but he was not. The three men walking toward him were coming to kill. Their one intent was to kill him, to shoot him down.

He was disturbed that he was not afraid, for all good sense told him he should be. Three to one . . . the odds were long.

Suddenly he remembered something. There were two other Drakos . . . Dandy and Wilson. He had not seen them but he had heard of them. The moment he thought of them he knew he was in trouble—far deeper trouble than came from just the three men headed toward him.

They were the window dressing, they were the ones to draw his attention. The others would be nearby . . . ambushed, waiting.

Five . . . It was too many. Sweat beaded his forehead but still, he told himself, he was not afraid. He felt a strange sort of triumph. This was something with which he could deal. He was not by nature a plotter or planner. He liked straightforward enemies with whom he could deal in a straightforward way.

Holstrum's store . . . One or more of them would be there,

149

waiting. From the tail of his eye he caught the slightest of movements. He had taken only three steps out from the store, ahead and to the side. Now the awning posts were on his left, slim trunks of cottonwood holding up the awning. He was a little in the shadow, the three men before him in the bright sun. Then he saw the other man, standing on the steps of the hotel. He had a rifle in his hands and he was lifting it.

The man in Holstrum's store suddenly stepped out. Shanaghy caught a fleeting glimpse of the man, wearing a black vest and a red handkerchief about his neck, and then he went for his gun.

As he did so he heard a sharp cry from his right and up the street. *"Win!"* It was Josh Lundy's voice.

And then Shanaghy was firing. He shot over Drako's head at the man on the hotel steps with the rifle. And without glancing to see what effect his shot had, he turned right and shot at the man on the store steps.

His action was swift and totally unexpected, in that both men believed all his attention was on the men before him. At the same moment he heard a burst of gunfire from right and left, and he saw Win Drako down in the dust and Bass running, hands in the air.

Drako was looking at him, lifting his gun. But there was something wrong with Drako, the gun was coming up too slowly. Another shot from the left and Drako turned half around and fell.

In the distance, a train whistled.

Shanaghy saw Josh Lundy come into the street, rifle in hand, and Josh was walking toward the two men down in the street, walking cautiously.

From the other side came a tall young man in a black hat and coat, a man he did not know.

He walked toward Shanaghy, shifting his rifle to his left hand. He held out the right. "Am I always to be getting you out of trouble?" he asked.

Shanaghy stared. There was something familiar, yet . . .

"On the pier, in New York," the man said. "We were boys then and John Morrissey saved our bacon."

"Well, I'll be damned! I—!"

"I am Dick Pendleton . . . Jan's brother. It's been a long time."

The train whistled again, nearer.

Shanaghy grabbed Pendleton's hand, then suddenly everything started to fall into place.

"Dick! Another time!" He ran for Drako's horse, jerked loose the slip knot and sprang to the saddle.

The water tank! Of course, they'd be doing it there and never coming into the station at all. It was only after he cleared the town that he began to realize what he was letting himself in for.

There would be several of them. The women . . . women? Why had he thought that? Then he knew—because there had to be two women. He couldn't make it out otherwise.

Two women who might or might not be present. There'd be George, and George, he thought, would be good with a gun. Used to using one, at least. There'd be the man who had posed as the brakeman . . . and how Shanaghy wanted to see *him*. He'd made him jump off a freight into darkness. Shanaghy had never wanted to kill a man, and he didn't want to kill that brakeman, but he would like to give him a taste of what he'd had.

He slowed his pace. He would be within sight of the train in a minute.

He had forgotten to ask Dick Pendleton about Jan. Was she home? Was she safe? The thought that he had forgotten left him feeling guilty. And that old man . . . Coonskin . . . who wanted a shot at the eastern dude. Where was he?

When he topped the hill he saw the train. It was pulled up at the water tank and was taking on water. There was nobody around.

Had he guessed wrong? Would he have to turn and race back into town again?

He rode down the hill and pulled up, looking at the train. It was longer than usual, at least eight cars. An express car, a baggage car, a passenger car and five freight cars, as well as a caboose.

He checked his guns and flushed with embarrassment. He had forgotten to reload.

He did so now. There was a rifle in the saddle-scabbard, too. What had Win been shooting with? He could not recall. It had happened so fast, there'd been no time to consider anything, even to notice.

Those two men he'd shot. Both had gone down and they must have been the other sons of Drako.

There was some activity on the other side of the train. He heard somebody swear and heard the rattle of trace chains. His heart was pounding. When that train started to move . . .

How many would there be? Too many.

Suddenly a brakeman appeared and gave a signal. The train whistled, then started taking up slack. Then slowly it chugged forward. On the far side of the train the wagon was also moving.

He drew his gun.

The rifle was probably loaded and ready but he felt more at ease with a six-gun. The train started forward and he walked his horse. He was ready, poised. Suddenly the train started to back up. It backed a dozen yards, then stopped, the locomotive puffing contentedly.

Swearing, he rode toward the rear, planning to ride behind the train. It started backing up again. He wheeled his horse, rode alongside the train and leaped for the ladder. He scrambled up the ladder as the train suddenly jerked to a stop, before spinning its wheels and starting forward again. He ran forward along the car tops. Suddenly a bullet clipped near his feet. It had been fired from the engine. Shanaghy fired back and heard the clang of the bullet as it struck, somewhere in the cab.

Another bullet whipped by him and he dropped to the top of the car, clinging tightly with his one free hand. He fired again and then leaped up, ran forward and sprang down to the tender atop the coal pile.

The engineer held a gun in his hand, one hand on the throttle.

"Drop it!" Shanaghy said. An instant the engineer hesitated, then let go of the pistol.

Shanaghy scooped it up, then said, "Now back up, carefully . . . slowly."

"What is this? A holdup?"

"You know damn well what it is," Shanaghy said.

He glanced toward the road that led south. The road was empty as far as he could see. Win Drako's horse was grazing beside the road.

"You," he said to the engineer. "When you get to town, you

go to Greenwood's and report to him and tell him what has happened and what you've done."

The engineer stared at him unbelieving. "You think I'll do that?"

"I do." Shanaghy smiled at him, and it was not a pleasant smile. "You do it. If you don't, or if you try to get away, I'll come after you."

The engineer shrugged. "You ain't done so well so far. Maybe I ain't scared."

"You ask them in town how well I have done. But look, mister, I'm not persuading you. I really don't give a damn what you do, but if I have to come after you you'll wish you'd shot yourself first."

He swung down and walked toward the horse. It looked up at him and started to walk off. Shanaghy spoke gently. The horse stopped, looking at him again, and he caught up the reins and stepped into the saddle.

The tracks of a wagon were in the road, if one could call it that. For it was merely two wheel tracks leading off to the south. Such a wagon could not be far ahead, but he still had no idea how many men were with it. Yet when he crossed the next rise there was no sign of the wagon at all.

The wagon and its cargo had vanished!

Ahead of him lay open road, visible for over a mile, with only a few dips. And there was nothing in sight. The road itself and the plains around it were empty. He rode on, more swiftly, dipping into a dry wash where the banks were caving badly, then up the opposite side.

Nothing . . .

The gently rolling plains stretched far away, and there was nothing in sight but a few cattle, feeding on the drying grass.

He slowed down. Something was wrong, radically wrong.

There had been a wagon. He had seen its tracks. He *knew* he had.

But now there were no tracks!

For a moment he sat very still, simply staring. It was no illusion. There simply were no wagon tracks in the road. Not fresh ones, at least.

He rode right and left on the prairie but found nothing. He swung wide in a big circle . . . Still nothing.

Irritably, he rode on, searching for some sign of a wagon

passing, but he found nothing. So, he thought, the wagon had turned off. Swinging his horse around, he rode back.

He found the tracks again, then lost them in the wash with the caving banks. A moment of digging and he found the wagon, wheels pulled off, the wagon bed lying flat . . . and empty.

There were horse tracks some fifty yards from where he found the wagon, a place where several horses had been tied. He found tracks, but nothing else distinguishable.

He was no tracker and he made no attempt at it now. He rode straight for the cabin that Holstrum had on his claim, where the man named Moorhouse was the caretaker.

There was a small cabin, a stable, and a corral. In the corral were several horses, none of them showing signs of having been recently ridden. As he pulled up in the yard the cabin door opened and a big man came out. And he was very big.

He came out of the door slipping a suspender over his shoulder. "You lookin' for somethin'?"

Shanaghy touched the badge on his chest. "I have to search the place."

The big man came into the middle of the yard. "You'll play hell. If you know what's good for you, you'll git!"

"Sorry, I have to search the place, Mr. Moorhouse."

"Know my name, huh?"

"Of course. The law knows such things."

"Then you should damn well know that tin badge ain't worth nothin' outside of town. And not very much in it."

Shanaghy smiled. "I'd hate to have to put you in jail for obstructing the law."

Moorhouse laughed harshly. "You arrest *me*?"

"That's right." Shanaghy was smiling. "But I'll have a look at the stable first."

"Mister," Moorhouse said, "I given you a chance. You git out of here *now* or they won't be enough left of you to pick up with a sponge."

Shanaghy smiled. "You know, Mr. Moorhouse, I like you. Now I'm going to search the premises, and if you obstruct me I'm going to throw you in jail. We haven't any courthouse and we haven't any city hall and we haven't any jail, but I can shackle you hand and foot, and I'll do it. Maybe next week I'd come out to see how you're getting along, but I might forget."

Moorhouse started toward him. Shanaghy kicked his feet out of the stirrups and dropped to the ground. He moved so quickly, Moorhouse was surprised. The big man stopped abruptly, half turned and Tom Shanaghy hit him.

The punch was a good one and Shanaghy could hit, but Moorhouse didn't even stagger. He swung a wicked round-house blow that Shanaghy went under, smashing both hands to the ribs.

Moorhouse grabbed him by the shirt and vest and swung him around, throwing him to the ground a half dozen feet away. Tom lit on hands and knees and drove at Moorhouse with a driving tackle that brought the big man crashing down.

Shanaghy was up first. "Get up, Mr. Moorhouse. They tell me you're a tough man. You can let me search the place or continue with this nonsense and take a beating."

"Nobody ever beat me," Moorhouse said, and he started at Shanaghy.

Tom feinted and smashed a right to the ribs. He stepped around, feinted again and started to the right. Moorhouse rushed, swinging with both fists. He caught Tom with a round-house left that knocked him staggering, and followed it up with a clubbing right that drove him to his knees. Tom came up fast, hooking to the body again, and Moorhouse grabbed him in his huge hands, throwing him over his knee. "Now I break your back," he said calmly.

Shanaghy turned, twisted and tried to break free, but the big hands drove him back. Excruciating pain shot through Tom's back. He jerked a hand free and smashed a right to the big man's face. He seemed impervious to blows, as Tom hammered him again and again, and then he hunched himself higher and began to press Shanaghy down harder and harder.

Shanaghy threw his legs high, trying to break free, then higher. He managed to lock one leg under Moorhouse's chin and against his throat.

He smashed his knee toward the man's Adam's apple. Although he did not reach it, the big man let go with one hand to tear the leg from his throat. Shanaghy gave a terrific lunge and broke free.

He staggered to his feet and Moorhouse came up, diving at him. Shanaghy clubbed him behind the head, driving him to the earth. Moorhouse came up again, caught him with a wild swing, and Shanaghy stepped inside, ripping wicked uppercuts to the bigger man's unprotected body. Moorhouse staggered and went back, and Tom threw a high overhand right to the chin.

It caught Moorhouse squarely and he went to his knees.

Tom Shanaghy backed off a step. "Get up," he said. "You wanted to fight. Now let's get started."

Moorhouse looked at his bruised knuckles. "There has been enough fighting for today," he said sourly.

"Then I shall search the house."

"Search and be damned. There is nothing there." Moorhouse turned and stared at him from bloody, battered features. "They have beaten you," he said. "You are whipped."

He smiled, revealing a broken tooth and bloody lips. "And now they will kill you. I heard them say it. If it is the last thing they do, they will kill you."

NINETEEN

A quick survey of the house revealed nothing beyond the fact that a woman had been living there. A few odds and ends remained, a broken comb for her hair, some strands of ash-blonde hair, and a faint lingering perfume, almost intangible.

Moorhouse was sitting on the steps, his head in his hands, when Shanaghy emerged. He looked up, a bloody handkerchief in his hands. "You hit hard," he said grudgingly.

"You asked for it."

"That I did. Never figgered anybody could do it."

"No need to feel ashamed. I've done some bare-knuckle fighting."

"Figgered it. Why I quit. There's no use bucking a stacked deck."

Shanaghy sat down beside him. "These folks friends of yours?"

"Not by a damn sight. That woman . . . She's too high an' mighty. Ordered me around like I was a slave. Only one she'd talk to was him."

"Holstrum?"

"Aye. Seems like she'd set her cap for him—only I don't think she liked him, either. They was up to something, all of them together."

157

"They stole a gold shipment that was to pay off cowhands in town. Most of it belonged to Greenwood."

The big man was silent, dabbing at his broken mouth. "Well, I done killed a man or two but I'm no thief. I'd no part in it."

"Didn't think you had. How many of them are there?"

"There's him . . . Holstrum, I mean, and there's that young woman who lived here. Then there was George Alcott, Pin Brodie, an' there was two others whose names I never did get. They didn't come here but once or twice."

"They are all together now?"

"They are."

"Any idea where they are headed?"

"You think they'd talk to me? Scarce give me the time of day. Was I you I'd guess they was going east. Two or three of them are easterners, and her who was running the shebang, she wanted to go east."

"The woman who lived here? She was running the show?"

"Not her. The other woman. I never seen her. She come here a couple of times but at night. Seems like she met them out on the grass somewheres. Now and again I heard talk. Led me to thinkin' she was the bull o' the woods . . . the boss, I mean. She was somewheres over west, I reckon. She come and went from that direction, and from a thing or two she said I figgered she had her a place over yonder."

Shanaghy took his time thinking about it. They were on horseback now, and they were headed south, but he had a hunch that Moorhouse's comment was probably the right one, and that they were headed east.

Holstrum had been looking for a "lady," an eastern woman who had what he considered class. Now he had her, and he would have money and he would be heading east. At least, that was the way he had it planned.

"You liked Holstrum?"

Moorhouse shrugged. "He paid me on time. He never complained none. He just wanted folks kept off and away, especially after that woman come. He didn't want anybody around . . . Not that anybody ever did come."

"I think they mean to kill him."

"What?" Moorhouse passed a hand over his brow. "Well, I feared for it. It was plain to see he figgered he was in charge, but he wasn't. Not a'tall. It was that woman, and after her it was George. Holstrum, he give orders an' ever'body was almighty respectful of him, but behind his back they made their own plans. I heared 'em.''

The whole gang was riding now and they had a good start. Shanaghy had taken time looking for wagon tracks, and he had lost time in his fight with Moorhouse, but from the information he might save time. Never one to arrive at decisions too quickly, he thought the situation over carefully.

"Mr. Moorhouse? What's off to the south?''

"Ain't nothing. Not for miles 'n miles. Nothing but prairie grass an' antelope. 'Casional buffalo. That's why I figgered east. West there's nothing, either, 'cept maybe that other woman's place, an' it don't seem likely she'd take 'em there, her bein' so careful not to be seen, and all.''

East, then. Shanaghy thought of it carefully. Holstrum was known in Kansas City, at least to a few people. If Shanaghy rode after them, he would have to almost kill his horse in catching up, and they might have fresh horses waiting, which would leave him stranded on the prairie and out of action.

He got up. "Sit tight, Mr. Moorhouse. I'll be calling on you.''

"I ain't arrested?''

Shanaghy grinned and held out his hand. "You're too good a man to lie in jail. Besides, you've already been helpful.''

"Well . . . Like I say, I killed a man or two but I'm no thief. My ma raised me better.''

Tom Shanaghy stepped into the saddle. His knuckles were battered and sore and his shirt was torn. He turned his horse and rode back to town.

All was quiet when he rode in. He stepped down at the livery stable and saw Greenwood come out of his saloon and lean on the rail. Judge McBane joined him there.

Leaving the horse, Shanaghy walked slowly down the street. Greenwood glanced at his torn shirt. "Looks like you've had some trouble.''

"I could use a beer.''·

"What happened?''

"Moorhouse didn't want to talk. We went around and around a bit. Then he talked. He's not a bad man.''

"They got the gold,'' Greenwood said. "They said it was picked up outside of town by somebody with an order for it. The order was signed by Holstrum and by Carpenter.''

"Carpenter? He's dead."

"So he is, but how could the express messenger know that?"

Shanaghy accepted the beer and took off his derby and placed it on the bar beside him. Greenwood's news was no more than what he had expected.

"Did the engineer come in here?"

"Him? Why should he? That train stopped only a few minutes and then pulled out. Seemed like they were glad to get away from here."

Nobody said anything for a minute or two. Shanaghy tasted the beer. He was very dry. The beer was cold and it tasted good.

"Drako's dead, and so are his boys," McBane said. "You shoot almighty straight, son."

"I had to. I wasn't going to get any second chance." Shanaghy drank from his glass. "But I had some help, and I've had no chance to thank them."

"Josh had his own score to settle."

"That's right. Win Drako was about to hang him, one time." Tom straightened up. "Is Dick Pendleton still in town?"

"Matter of fact, he isn't. Josh told him you were in trouble and he came in to help. He rode back to the ranch, in something of a hurry, I guess."

"And Josh? I could use him." He finished his beer. "Thanks, Greenie. I needed that."

"Well, you tried." Greenwood rested his hands on the bar. "Have another beer if you like. Might as well enjoy it. I'm cleaned out."

"I don't think so," Shanaghy said quietly. "I don't think so at all."

Startled, Greenwood stared at him.

Shanaghy was smiling. "I may be guessing all wrong, but I don't think I am. If I am, you may have lost all you say, but if I'm right—"

"If you're right . . . then what?"

"We'll get it all back." Shanaghy hitched his gunbelt into an easier position on his hips. "Is Holstrum around?"

"He closed up when the shooting started. Holstrum never did like gunfire. He'll be around when things look quiet again. Believe me, this isn't the first time Holstrum closed up. At the first sign of trouble he hunts cover."

Tom Shanaghy was thinking about Jan. Dick had ridden out of town in a hurry . . . Why? He had not seen Jan since he left her with Coonskin.

He turned to Judge McBane. "Do you know a man named Coonskin Adams?"

McBane smiled, his eyes twinkling. "Don't tell me you've run into him!"

"Met him."

"Didn't know ol' Coonskin was still around. He's a wolf-hunter. Used to trap the Rockies for fur, then worked for a couple of cow outfits cleaning up the predators."

"Where's he live?"

McBane chuckled. "Now *that's* a question! To tell you the truth, I doubt if anybody has ever asked that question. Coonskin is one of those people you see around. He comes and he goes. He's here one day, gone the next. He's not a man who talks of himself even when he is around."

"Somebody killed his burro," Shanaghy said.

McBane's expression changed. "God help them then."

"I need to talk to him."

"Go where you last saw him and build yourself a fire. Send up a smoke. Coonskin is as curious as any wild animal, and my bet is he will come to you. McAuliffe, who is division superintendent, knows him well and he might give you a lead. Send him a wire."

McAuliffe . . . Big Mac? Maybe.

"Judge? Do the folks here still think I killed Carpenter?"

"I am afraid they do. I'd heard the story before ever I got down to breakfast, told me as the gospel. I must say I never believed it for a moment."

The door opened and Josh Lundy came in. His rifle was cradled on his arm. "Heard you was back. They got away?"

"Not yet."

Lundy looked at him carefully. "You got some idea? If I can help, count me in."

"You have helped, but I do need you. I'm going to need some more help."

"I'll come," Greenwood said.

"And I," Judge McBane added. "What have you got in mind?"

Briefly, Shanaghy explained how the train had been deliberately backed in front of him to block pursuit, then described his arrival at Holstrum's place, and what he had learned from Moorhouse.

"Judge, I want authority from you to search Holstrum's store and his living quarters. If he is there, then at least part of my conclusions are wrong, but I am betting that he's gone. And then," he added, "I want us all at the depot to take the evening train east."

McBane shook his head. "Shanaghy, I can't permit you to enter a man's private premises on nothing but suspicion."

"Suppose we go knock on his door? If he answers the door I shall go no further with it. If he doesn't, I want to search the area . . . if I have to," he added. "I shall do it on my own authority." He smiled. "If I am wrong you can please the town by firing me."

"I can't believe Holstrum is involved," McBane said.

"Judge, he is a man with a dream. He's a great, hulking, somewhat nearsighted man, but all his life he has dreamed of young, sophisticated women. Suddenly such a woman is here, and he believes she is going to be his. He believes the money is the key to it."

"Do you mean he planned it all?" asked the judge.

Shanaghy shrugged. "I doubt it. He may have started it or somebody may sort of suggested it . . . Not right out, maybe. I don't know how it all happened. I don't even know if I am right, but we're going to find out."

He turned to the door. "Judge? If you'd like to come? And Josh?"

Tom Shanaghy went up the few steps to the store's walk. His footsteps echoed hollowly as he walked along, followed by McBane and Josh. He paused at the store's door. There was a sign: CLOSED UNTIL FURTHER NOTICE.

"Same sign he always uses," Josh commented.

Tom rapped on the door, and the sound echoed hollowly. He waited, listening. When there was no sound, he rapped again.

"His living quarters are in the back. There's a door around to the side."

Again Shanaghy led the way. There was a sinking inside him. Secretly he had been hoping he would find Holstrum within. He wanted to find no man guilty, and even though all pointed to Holstrum, he could be wrong. He hoped he was wrong. He knew how a dream could die, and how futile had been the dreams of this man. How much worse it would have been for him had he realized the dream in fact, for what could two such people have said to each other? What could they have done together? Sometimes it was better to keep the dream and forget the realization.

Shanaghy rapped on the back door, and there was no response. Josh walked back to the stable. "His horse is gone," he called.

Shanaghy took hold of the doorknob, hesitated. For he shrank at entering the home of another, uninvited. Yet he put his shoulder to the door and the foolish lock burst.

There was a bare, simple room. A rag rug on the floor, plus two chairs and an old leather settee. There were two paintings on the wall, mystic, ethereal things . . . obviously originals, like something Poe might have visioned.

There were a few books, several of poetry, but only the first few leaves had been cut as if the reader had gone that far and stopped. There were a bottle of whiskey and a glass, the bottle half empty. There was a bottle of Chateau LaFite with one drink gone.

The bed was made, neatly tucked in. The few clothes in the closet were nicely hung. The drawers were half closed as if Holstrum had packed in a hurry.

The drawers were empty except for one. There was a dainty handkerchief edged with lace . . . perhaps a memento of the girl Holstrum had seen but once and then never again. Shanaghy picked it up, glanced at it and dropped it back into the drawer. He remembered something Holstrum had said, or that had been said about him, about looking in a window and seeing some elegantly clad people dancing. Well, Holstrum was still looking in windows, and he was still standing outside.

Shanaghy swore softly, and McBane glanced at him. "He's missed the boat again," Tom said, "I wish he could have made it, just once."

"You have compassion, my friend. One does not often find it in an officer."

"More often than you think," Shanaghy said.

"And maybe Holstrum will make it this time."

"No . . ." Shanaghy shook his head slowly. "I know the kind of people he is dealing with and he does not. He is thinking of her, and of what they can do in some great city. She is thinking of that money, and what she can do. And George is thinking of the money and wondering how he can wind up with all or most of it. And I think that other man, I think he is the one named McBride. I think he intends to have it all and knows how he will . . . And they are all wrong unless I can stop something here."

"Here?"

"We must get our tickets."

Shanaghy closed the door behind him, fastening it as securely as possible. They walked back up the alley together. A few people were in the streets now, and some were talking, pointing out where the men had stood when the gunfight took place.

Shanaghy paused. "You said . . . I killed them?"

"Both," Josh said, "dead center. I never did see better shootin'. Wilson Drako was here on the steps. He went down right there, and Dandy, who was clerkin' at the ho-tel . . ."

"The clerk was a Drako? The one with the rifle?"

"Didn't you know? Sure, he was a Drako, and he hated your guts."

They had paused on the boardwalk in front of Greenwood's saloon. "Judge, Josh . . . where we're going isn't far, I'm thinking. But at the end of it there will be shooting, and when there's that much money at stake they won't care who they kill, or how many."

"I cut my teeth on a shootin' iron," the judge said dryly. "I fit Injuns before I was dry behind the ears, and I served four years in the War Between the States. I can stand beside any man when it comes to gunfire."

"All right." Shanaghy paused. "Judge, we're going to take that evening train out. Josh, you go down and get the tickets for us. Don't mention where we're going, just buy tickets for Kansas City."

Shanaghy took the money from his pocket. "And above all, don't tell that agent or anybody else who's going along. If you want, tell them it's for the Pendletons."

"Do you think he's in on this?" McBane asked.

"I do."

"And that engineer? And the brakeman?"

"I think they were slipped a few dollars just to act stupid with the train. And, if anybody came along, to block the road.

"They had it all timed nicely. I think they had practiced taking that wagon down, and I believe they had horses waiting. And I think they ran them hard to the Holstrum place and then took off on fresh stock.

"By now they are swinging back around to meet the railroad line—"

"What if they don't?"

"Then I'll have my work cut out for me. But look at it this way. Some of these people are easterners. The railroad is something they know. They'd have to ride a long, long way to get anywhere a'horseback. They won't have any idea we have this figured out, and they'll think we're running in circles back here. When that train pulls in and they want to board it, we'll be waiting for them. With luck we can do it without shooting . . . but don't bank on it."

It was a long shot, and he knew it. Shanaghy checked his guns, then reholstered them.

"Judge"—he saw Josh coming back up the street with the tickets—"there's one more thing. Maybe I've read this right and maybe I haven't. Somebody said once, 'Set a crook to catch a crook.' Well, I'm no thief but I've known a'plenty of them back in New York town. I think what we've got here is one of the nastiest triple-crosses I've ever seen."

"We'd better get on down to the station," Greenwood suggested.

"Wait . . . we'll hear the whistle and we can start then. It's less than a hundred yards.

"What's happening must have started just about the time you people got together and planned to bring money in here to pay off the cattle drivers, and I don't know whose idea it was . . . Maybe it started in two or three places, but I do know there's one person who not only wanted *all* the money, but was a bitter, vengeful person along with it.

"They think they've won. They have the money, or think they do, and only one thing remains. That's to kill the man who caused them so much trouble, and somebody has figured out a way of doing it without risk."

"Without risk? *You?*" Josh exclaimed. "That's crazy! Why, I've seen you in action and there isn't a man—"

"That's right," Shanaghy said quietly, "so . . ."

Mrs. Carpenter was walking up the street toward them.

TWENTY

S he was neatly dressed in a fashionable black traveling dress, with a small bonnet perched on her head. In her hand she carried a handbag.

"You've got to be crazy!" Greenwood said. "Why—!"

"The story is around that I killed her husband. She is a bereaved wife. Who else could kill a man, in this country, and get away with it? Even have the blessing of most of the townspeople?"

"You mean she was in on it?"

"Maybe not from the beginning, but you can just bet most of the planning was hers. And right now, if she kills me, she can board that train and ride off a wealthy woman, sharing with no one but her brother."

"But they have the gold!"

"Maybe, but I doubt it. I don't believe the gold ever left the train."

She was walking up to them now and she had slipped her hand inside her bag. She stopped. Her thin, rather pretty face was drawn in suddenly hard lines.

"Marshal, you are an evil man! You murdered my husband! You killed him and then tried to burn the—"

"Mrs. Carpenter," Shanaghy said. "Sure, ma'am, and you're too late. It's all over. We know what was done and how it was done, and we know that you yourself killed your husband, and that it was you who closed the doors and set the barn afire.

"It was you, with your brother, who planned to steal all that gold."

Her eyes tightened at the corners, as did her mouth. "I have no idea what you are talking about, and—"

"Mrs. Carpenter, I have no desire to be rough with a woman—even one who has murdered her husband and probably others as well. So please . . . Do not try to take that gun from your purse, because I—"

Her hand started to come out from the handbag, but almost casually Shanaghy slapped the purse from her hand with his left and then brought his right hand up under the barrel, twisting it up and away. It was let go or have a broken finger, and Mrs. Carpenter let go. Shanaghy passed the gun to Judge McBane.

"It is all over, Mrs. Carpenter, all over. None of it worked."

She was very cool. The hardness became only a shadow in her eyes, covered by amused contempt. "You're such a *little* man, Marshal, so pleased with yourself, taking a gun away from a woman. Mr. Holstrum will testify—"

"Holstrum is dead," Shanaghy said.

McBane turned his head sharply and Josh was staring.

"Or if he is not, I shall be very surprised. You see, Mrs. Carpenter, some of the others were thinking just as you were. Once outside of town Holstrum was no longer needed, so why share with him? I am betting they killed him somewhere between his ranch and that little station thirty miles east where they planned to rejoin the train." He smiled. "Rejoin it with what they thought was the gold."

"You mean they don't have it?" Greenwood exclaimed.

"As I said, it never left the train. What they took off at the water tank were some boxes prepared for the purpose. Mrs. Carpenter's brother, as station agent, had connived to get the manifest changed. The boxes that actually contained the money were being shipped right back to Kansas City . . . where Mrs. Carpenter would pick them up."

"You mean they have already been shipped back?"

"My guess is that they went west last night, and that they will be on the evening train when we board it."

Mrs. Carpenter stood stock-still, her hands clasping her purse, staring off into space. Yet, while there might be some shock at being frustrated, at having all her carefully laid plans go sky-high, Shanaghy had an idea her mind was working swiftly toward some sort of a solution.

"I'd like to go home now," she said suddenly.

Shanaghy shook his head. "You're not thinking clearly, Mrs. Carpenter. You are under arrest. But something which you should be thinking of now is your friends, if you can call them that."

She merely looked at him.

"If they have not already discovered that they do not have the gold, they will discover it very soon. They will also suspect what has happened, and when they do I would imagine they would be looking for you.

"Of course, your plans were to be on the train going east by now, and so safely away. But you are not going east, and neither are they."

He paused. "So I shall lock you up until we return."

She looked her contempt. "Will you shackle me to the hitching-rail as you did those others?"

He shook his head. "No, Mrs. Carpenter. Holstrum has a storeroom where we can leave you until we return, which will not be long."

In the distance, a train whistled. "Greenwood, would you lock her up? And stay here, if you will. Vince Patterson and his boys should be riding in today and they will want some drinks. Get hold of Vince and tell him what has happened. Tell him everything."

They walked to the station. The train whistled again, still far off. Josh reached into his pocket. "By the way, this letter was in your box at the ho-tel. I seen it there after we checked the clerk's body . . . You know, Dandy Drako? I figured you'd be wantin' it."

Shanaghy glanced at it. He recognized the handwriting. The letter was from John Morrissey. But there was no time to read it now. That could wait for a more leisurely time. He put the letter in his shirt pocket.

For the first time he took a look at himself. His shirt was

badly torn. His face felt stiff and sore from several punches he had taken. He did not even remember them. You never did, at times like that, except maybe the very hard ones.

The train was coming down the track and the agent came out to the platform. He looked at them, stopped and started to go back inside.

"Don't do it," Shanaghy said in a conversational tone of voice.

The agent looked at him. His tongue touched his lips. He was trying to make up his mind, and Tom Shanaghy was remembering that the man had a gun . . . probably back inside.

"He means it, Burt," Josh Lundy said. "If I were you I wouldn't try."

"What's wrong? I don't know what's going on."

"You just come with us. You'll learn."

"Come with you? Leave my post, here? I can't do that, and you can't make me. I—"

"You won't be gone long, not this time." Shanaghy smiled. "Someday we will have to sit down and you can tell me about your sister. She's an interesting lady."

"Helen? You mean Mrs. Carpenter?"

"I do."

"I've no idea what you're talking about, Marshal. Look, I've got to go in there and clear some messages and also let them know this train's gone through."

"Later. Right now we're just going down the track a little ways to meet some of your friends. If they haven't discovered the double-cross you two have pulled off, they'll be wanting to load those boxes off the pack animals they have. If they have discovered the cross, they'll be hunting you and your sister."

Burt's face had taken on a sickly expression. "Marshal, I don't know what you're talking about."

"You do know." Shanaghy watched the train pull in. "Search him and take him aboard," he told Josh. "I'll just walk along and check the engineer."

The engineer was a different man from before, a burly fellow with white hair and a florid face.

"My name is Shanaghy," Tom said, "and I'm marshal here. There's been a little trouble and some of us are going to ride down the track with you. About thirty miles down the track, there will be some men waiting at that little way station, some men and probably one woman. Stop the train and then get down on the floor. There may be a little lead flying."

Once seated on the train, Shanaghy looked over at Josh. "Tell me what you see as we come up to the station," he suggested. "I want to have a little talk with Burt, here." Tom glanced over at Judge McBane. "Judge? Would you like to join me? Maybe if we can ask this man the right questions we can keep him alive."

"Keep me alive?" Burt started up and Shanaghy pushed him back down into his seat. "What do you mean?"

Shanaghy smiled. "Now, see here! You and your sister double-crossed your partners. You don't expect them to like it, do you? You've been playing with some pretty rough company, Burt, and now that the bottom has fallen out of your plans, they are going to think it was you . . . they will know it was you.

"They will be waiting at the station right ahead of us, but if you talk fast and give us everything you know we may be able to save you."

"I don't need to be saved!" Burt protested. "I've nothing to—"

"Then you won't mind getting off at the next station to meet George and Pin? They'll be there, you know."

"The train's not stopping," Burt protested. "You can't pull that on me. I sent the orders."

"Of course, you did. I just changed them. I know that you and your sister expected to be on this train, and you expected it to fly right by, leaving your old friends standing on the platform. That was the idea, wasn't it? You'd have the gold and they would just have several small but heavy boxes.

"Well, that isn't the way it's going to happen. We are going to stop there, but just long enough to put you off."

Burt was sweating, his brow was beaded with it. His face had taken on an even more sickly look, and his eyes seemed unusually large. "Marshal, you can't do that! You can't put me off! Why, that would be murder!"

"Like what your sister Helen did to her husband, you mean? Like what your associates have done with Holstrum?"

"Holstrum? He's dead?"

"Well, we don't know, but he left with them and with that woman he was sweet on, but I'm betting they decided once they had the loot that they didn't need him anymore. I hope I'm wrong. But you know how it is. They'll be thinking just like your sister and you . . . who wanted it all."

"Where is she?"

"We have her . . ." Shanaghy took out his big silver watch. "Well, it won't be long now. Josh, you see anything yet?"

"Too soon."

Shanaghy got up. "Judge, talk to this man, will you? We've got maybe twenty miles to go, and if he doesn't tell us anything by the time we get there I'm going to just drop him off at the next station. You talk some sense into him if you can while I go along up to the baggage car."

Only three passengers rode in the only other passenger car and Shanaghy walked through, opening the door into the baggage car.

The expressman looked startled when Shanaghy walked in, then relieved when he glimpsed the badge. "Something I can do for you, Officer?"

Shanaghy glanced around, unsure of what to look for beyond an approximate capacity. "Your heaviest shipment," he said, "I'd like to see that."

"Heaviest?" the expressman looked thoughtful. "We have several heavy ones. Right there"—he indicated several solidly built boxes—"those are the heaviest ones."

"Where were they loaded?"

He shrugged. "They were here when I took over from the other man," he said. He glanced at the labels tied on the boxes. "Kansas City," he said, "to H. R. Carpenter. It's stenciled on the boxes, too."

"It's a stolen shipment," Shanaghy said. "If you check your records you will see that such a shipment was directed to Greenwood, Holstrum & Carpenter yesterday. The weights will be the same."

"You taking this one?"

"We are, in the name of the above parties. I will sign for it. Judge McBane is with me."

"I don't know whether I can do that, Marshal. Maybe we—"

"Leave it to us. And one more thing, when the train stops don't open your doors under any circumstances. If I were you I'd lie down on the floor behind those boxes and stay there until we pull out of the station."

"There'll be shooting?"

"Unless I miss my guess there will be some, but we will be doing our share."

The train was slowing. Swiftly, Shanaghy ran back through the cars.

Josh was at the door with a Winchester. There was another man beside him. "This here's Joel Strong. He was on the train, and when he found out what was happening he wanted a piece of the action."

"I remember him. He was speaking to the judge here on my first morning in town. All right, consider yourself a deputy."

He walked over to McBane. "Well, Burt," he said, "have you anything to say?"

"He's said it," McBane replied. "We have all we need."

The train was slowing down for its stop at the station. Shanaghy took his gun from the holster and checked the chambers once more. Then the other gun.

George . . . George would be good with a gun, he knew that. Pin McBride would, also. McBride was the man who made him jump from the moving train. If it could be done without shooting, well and good . . . But Shanaghy did not believe it could.

McBane stood beside him. "It began with Greenwood and Holstrum when they went to Kansas City to arrange for the shipment of gold. The blonde woman, I do not have her name straight, was at dinner with friends, and she heard of these men who had come into the bank, and of the gold shipment they had arranged. She was a girl who had once been wealthy and wanted to be again, and the idea came to her. She had seen George a time or two, knew he was a gambler and worse, and she got the hostler in a stable to bring him to her.

"She's a very cold, assured young woman," McBane said. "She apparently knew exactly what she was about and believed she could take care of herself. Deliberately, she arranged to meet Holstrum and played up to him. She agreed to come to his town and see it, and when she arrived there she began at once to talk of the pleasant places in Chicago and New York, and what could be done if they only had the money.

"She kept Holstrum at arm's length, and that made him admire her all the more. It seems to have been painfully easy to win him over. He had told her she must not come to town when the money arrived because Vince Patterson and his men might actually try to burn the town.

"It was she who suggested that somebody might take that chance to steal the money . . . and who would know the difference? She had George standing by and he had recruited McBride and the others.

"Mrs. Carpenter had heard of the shipment from her husband. Some of the money, but only a small amount, would be his. By this time she wanted no more of Carpenter or the town.

"She had seen the blonde woman in town, and she had seen George in deep conversation with Holstrum, and she was no fool. She is a woman who trusts no one, who suspects everyone. Knowing about the shipment, she became suspicious. She talked to Burt about the gold, when it would arrive and what would be done with it. How long it would be on the platform, and if it were stolen how the thieves could get away with it.

"Burt was scared. But she kept after him. She kept after him with her questions and asked, finally, why the gold had to leave the train at all? If they were going to steal it, why not just change the delivery directions and reship it? And the more he thought of it, the better it looked.

"Burt swears he wouldn't have gone into it at all but for the fact that he started thinking about the others stealing it, if that was what was planned. Unloading at the water tank at Holstrum had not occurred to him, and he got the idea that if they stole it they would have to kill him."

Tom Shanaghy walked to the door of the car. The station ahead was only a boxcar dismounted from its wheels, with a plank platform in front of it. He could see several horses with saddles and others with packsaddles.

There was only one man in sight, standing alone on the platform. Beside him were several boxes, stacked neatly. Evidently they had not discovered they had been tricked. The man moved forward as the train came to a stop.

"Open up!" he shouted. "We've got some express!"

Nothing happened. Impatiently, he stepped closer. "Hey, in there! Open up!"

Tom Shanaghy glanced at the freight car. Only one man could come out of that door at once, and he saw but one window.

"Josh," he said over his shoulder, "if shooting starts put a bullet through that window."

He stepped down on the platform. "Something I can do for you?" he asked.

Sunlight struck the badge and the man went for his gun. Instantly, another man loomed in the door. It was George Alcott.

Shanaghy drew and fired in the same instant, shooting at George, whom he suspected of being the best shot. He fired, a second time, at the man beside the boxes.

Josh dropped to the platform, shooting into the window. There was a cry from within, and as quickly as it had begun it was over.

George was down in the doorway. The man beside the boxes was clutching a bloody arm, his gun on the platform at his feet.

Tom Shanaghy walked toward the door and said, "All of you inside there, step outside, hands in the air."

There was a moment of hesitation and then Shanaghy said, just loud enough, "If you imagine those walls are shelter, let me tell you this. A forty-four or forty-five bullet will go through six inches of pine . . . You've got about an inch. Come out, hands up, or we are going to shoot that car so full of holes it will look like a sieve."

They came out—another stranger first, then the girl, and lastly, Pin McBride.

"Where's Holstrum?" he asked.

Nobody said anything. The blonde girl's face was drawn and her lips were compressed. She was staring at him, frightened and angry.

As she stepped around George's body, she shrank from him, holding her skirts away. She did not look at the man seated on the boxes. He was holding his wounded arm and cursing in a low, monotonous voice.

Shanaghy walked to McBride and took a pistol from him. McBride glared at him. "Damn you! I should have killed you!"

"You might have," Shanaghy replied, "makin' me jump that way. If it will give you any pleasure, you might as well know that making me jump off that train and then throwing that gear after me was what blew up your show."

"What d'you mean?"

"First, you made me mad. Second, those duds you threw

after me belonged to Rig Barrett. His guns were in the bed-roll." He smiled. "You see? It was your own pigheaded attitude that brought you to this."

The girl's eyes were furious. "Just what do you think you're doing?" she demanded. "I was just waiting for the train—!"

"Good!" He smiled at her. "Because it's right here, waiting for you. Before we put you aboard, we'd better have a look at these nice little boxes you have here.

"Now, these boxes should contain about twelve thousand twenty-dollar gold pieces, and about ten thousand dollars in silver."

From the engineer Shanaghy borrowed a hammer and knocked loose a couple of boards. He lifted the boards and tore loose the sacking inside the boxes.

"All of you . . . have a look."

McBride swung around, angrily. "You don't have to show me . . . !" His voice broke off and he stared, his face slowly turning pale.

The boxes were filled with nuts, bolts and screws.

TWENTY-ONE

At his expression the blonde girl turned her head. When she saw the boxes Shanaghy thought for a moment she was going to cry. Then her face took on a hard, ugly look.

"The trouble with being a crook," Shanaghy said mildly, "is that you have to associate with so many dishonest people."

"Who did that?" McBride demanded. "How the devil—?"

"Looks like you boys have been played for suckers," Shanaghy continued. He turned to Josh. "You an' Joel hogtie this lot, including the lady. If you take my advice you'll watch her most of all."

She kept glancing at the train, and clutching her handbag in her left hand. He reached over and took the handbag from her. She started to pull it away but he took it with a quick jerk. When he opened it he found a .44 Derringer. He showed it to Joel Strong and Josh. "Can't be too careful," he added.

"What happened to that gold?" McBride demanded.

"If it gets into the papers, you can read about it there," Shanaghy said. He turned to Josh. "Take 'em aboard now."

"Where are we going?" Judge McBane asked from the doorway.

"Back to town," he said. "I'll speak to the engineer."

The train started to back up the track. Shanaghy walked forward to the express car. When he opened the door the express messenger shook his head. "Man, they had me running scared there, for a minute, with that shootin' and all."

"Don't let it worry you. I think it's all over."

He glanced at the shipment, then walked back to the car where the prisoners rode. Despite their mild objections, McBane had moved the other passengers into the other coach, so they had the prisoners and themselves in the car alone.

Josh had taken a seat at one end of the car facing the prisoners, and Joel Strong at the other. Two of the prisoners were seated together. McBride sat alone as did the girl.

Shanaghy was tired. He was feeling the letdown from days of thinking and worry. He paused by McBride. "Are you the one who shot an old prospector's burro out by the water tank?"

McBride looked up. "You going to arrest me for that, too?"

"No," Shanaghy said. "I think with trying to steal the gold shipment and the murder of Holstrum, we've got enough on you. Then there's the attack on Rig Barrett, resisting an officer and a good deal more. Take my advice, though. If you get a chance to escape, don't take it."

"What's that mean?"

"That old man whose burro you killed. He'd like nothing better than to get a shot at you. And if you do escape I am not even going to look for you. He'll take care of it."

"That old blister? Hell, I should've shot him as well as his burro."

"Well, you didn't, and that's a mighty hard old man. And he loved that burro. He's taking it mighty bad."

Greenwood was at the station when the train backed in and he watched the prisoners get off. He also watched the body of George taken from the train.

"Holstrum?" he asked.

"I think they killed him. They aren't talking about him, so I'll have to ride out that way and have a look. Anyway, he didn't show up here."

Shanaghy himself helped unload the boxes containing the gold. "There it is, Greenie," he said. "Now you can supply the money to pay off those cowhands."

Greenwood looked at the boxes and shook his head. "Tom,

I'm damned if I know what to say. You've saved the town and our money, too, and mighty poor treatment you've had for it."

"Fix me up with a room at the hotel again, and I'll ask for nothing more."

"No problem. They all know who killed Carp now, and most of them are sorry for the way they acted." He paused. "By the way, you've some friends in town . . . at least they were asking for you."

"Friends? I don't know anybody in this part of the country."

Greenwood lit a cigar. "Don't appear to be from around here. I'd say they were easterners. There's four of them."

Easterners? Who— Suddenly he remembered the letter from John Morrissey. He felt in his pockets for it, then opened it.

> *Dear Tom:*
>
> *No need for you to come back unless you wish to. What you started when you left worked out fine and the Childers people are gone . . . cleaned out. However, if I were in your boots I would keep a sharp eye out. The Childers are still around and you were the one they wanted most of all.*
>
> *Lochlin is well, and sends regards.*
>
> *My advice is stay west. You are too good a man for this, and you could make a place for yourself in that new country like I did when I landed in New York.*

The letter was signed with a flourish, *John Morrissey.*

Greenwood was watching him as he read. "What is it? Bad news?"

Shanaghy folded the letter and put it in his pocket. The Childers family had come from someplace in the west or midwest, and so might know this country. Finding him would not be difficult, especially if they had somebody keeping an eye on Morrissey's mail. This letter was probably written the same day Morrissey received his note. Even without that, there were only two rail lines into the west and this was the logical one.

"It could be trouble," he admitted. "Those men you spoke of could be some old enemies, from New York."

His eyes on the street, he explained, briefly. The thoroughfare was busy now, the people coming and going about their shopping, for this was a Saturday, always a big day in town.

"If it's who I think it is," Shanaghy said, "this is my affair. They are hunting me and nobody else."

"You're our town marshal," Greenwood objected, gently. "And we don't like outsiders meddling in our affairs." He grinned. "Meaning no offense."

"You know," Shanaghy said, "the only one of them I have any sympathy for is Holstrum. He had a dream. Maybe it was foolish, maybe not. Seems that was all he wanted from life."

"We'll miss Carp. He was a good man."

"Aye," Shanaghy was watching the hotel. Where were they? Did they know he was back in town? He looked around, taking his time.

Judge McBane walked over. "We've locked up your prisoners. That young woman wants to talk to you."

"All right." He walked away, following Strong.

She had been locked in another storeroom at Holstrum's, the place where he kept sacks of flour, sugar, and seed. It was a temporary place at best.

She was sitting up when he came into the room, and she got quickly to her feet. "Marshal, you can help me. I've got to get out of this!"

"What do you mean?"

"All this. I never intended . . . I mean I never meant for this to happen! It's impossible! I mean, my family, my friends —"

"You should have thought of that before."

"How could I? I never expected—"

"You never expected to get caught, is that it? You never expected to have to go to prison, to have a trial, to be in court as a person on trial for robbery and murder."

"*Murder?*" she gasped. "You can't believe I had anything to do with *that!*"

"You started it all, ma'am. You were the instigator, and as such you're the most guilty of all. The truth of the matter is, ma'am, that nobody would commit a crime if they expected to get caught. Every criminal believes he is going to get away with it."

"But I never did anything like this before! Marshal, it was my first offense, and believe me it will be my last. Doesn't that count for anything?"

"I will do as much for you as you will for Holstrum."

"But he's *dead!*"

"That's right, ma'am. So is Mr. Carpenter. All because a greedy, selfish girl wanted more than she had. When you can bring them back to life, ma'am, you come and ask me for help. Every man and woman should consider the consequences of his or her actions, and those actions should be considered beforehand, not after. I've no use for crybabies, ma'am, male or female."

The pleading, woebegone look was gone from her eyes. What Shanaghy saw now was pure hatred, but he wasn't talking any more and he wasn't listening any more.

When he closed the door behind him, he didn't feel any better. Suddenly all he wanted was to be finished with it all. He wanted to sit down to a quiet meal and a cup of coffee, and most of all he wanted to see Jan.

They would be taken east somewhere for trial. No doubt he would be called upon to testify, as would Greenwood, Judge McBane and others. And Burt . . . who had turned state's evidence.

When Shanaghy came out of Holstrum's store, Josh Lundy was standing in front of Greenwood's with Joel Strong and Judge McBane. Greenwood came out as Shanaghy appeared.

All were armed. "What is this?" he asked. "Another war?"

"It could be. Those are Childerses up there. They say they are hunting you."

"Thanks, gentlemen, but that's my problem."

"Not if there's four of them and you're our marshal."

Tom Shanaghy had taken no more than half a dozen steps when there was a rustle of movement and the soft pound of hoofs. Several riders brushed by him. Others came through the intervals between the buildings, slowly converging on the hotel.

He caught a glimpse of the Childers men on the hotel porch, and then they were blocked out by at least twenty riders in the street.

Shanaghy paused, and between the horses he glimpsed the Childers men being escorted toward the station by a dozen riders, all with Winchesters.

One of the other riders turned and rode toward him. It was Red, the Vince Patterson rider he had seen at their chuckwagon. "We're just a'showin' those boys some horsepitality," he said, "guidin' 'em to the *dee*pot, like. We surely can't afford to let a man get shot who offered to stand for drinks for the crowd now, can we?"

"This was my fight," Shanaghy objected.

"What fight?" Red asked, innocently. "Come on, Irishman, keep your derby on. Let's just head back down to that drinkin' establishment I see yonder."

Shanaghy turned and walked back to Greenwood's. He had scarcely reached the bar when Vince Patterson strode in. "Everything all right, Marshal?"

"Sure, everything's all right. Have yourself a drink. As Red here reminded me, I'm standing treat."

"With pleasure." Vince Patterson accepted the drink and then said, "A couple of my boys found the body of your storekeeper a few miles south. We brought it in. He'd been shot in the back of the head at close range."

"It's been a trying time," Shanaghy said, "a most trying time."

"My boys are glad to be here," Vince assured him, "and I am sure they will cause no trouble."

"Red," Shanaghy said, "will you boys hang up your guns here until you leave town?"

Red shrugged. "Looks like we got no choice." He grinned. "I wouldn't want to get mowed down by those *fee*rocious townspeople you got here."

Tom Shanaghy finished his drink and walked outside with Vince.

"Why don't we ride out to the Pendletons?" Vince suggested. "I hear there's a young lady out there who is most anxious to see you. And," he added, "she has a gentleman who is recuperating from some serious wounds, a man named Rig Barrett who would like a firsthand report from a deputy he never heard of."

It was long after dark when Tom Shanaghy rode into town, and Josh Lundy met him in the street. "Pin McBride escaped!" he said. "Somebody got the door open and let him out."

Shanaghy dismounted and handed his horse to Josh. "Put him up, will you? We'll go hunting for his body in the morning."

"Body?"

"Rig Barrett was out at the Pendletons. Jan got Coonskin

Adams to help her get him out there to her place, where they could take proper care of him."

"What about Pin?"

"No trouble. I am sure you'll find his body out east of town not far from that water tank. Just look for the carcass of a dead burro. His will be right close by."